Greatly Exaggerated

OTHER BOOKS BY MARC EDGE

Pacific Press: The Unauthorized Story of Vancouver's
Newspaper Monopoly

Red Line, Blue Line, Bottom Line: How Push Came to Shove
Between the National Hockey League and its Players

Asper Nation: Canada's Most Dangerous Media Company

Greatly Exaggerated

The Myth of the Death of Newspapers

Marc Edge

 NEW STAR BOOKS • VANCOUVER • 2014

NEW STAR BOOKS LTD.

107 – 3477 Commercial Street | Vancouver, BC V5N 4E8   CANADA
1574 Gulf Road, #1517 | Point Roberts, WA 98281   USA
www.NewStarBooks.com | info@NewStarBooks.com

The publisher acknowledges the financial support of the Canada Council for the Arts, the Government of Canada through the Canada Book Fund, the British Columbia Arts Council, and the Province of British Columbia through the Book Publishing Tax Credit.

Cataloguing information for this book is available from Library and Archives Canada, www.collectionscanada.gc.ca.

Cover design by Oliver McPartlin
Printed on 100% post-consumer recycled paper
Printed and bound in Canada by Imprimerie Gauvin, Gatineau, QC
First printing, November 2014

*The challenge of the American newspaper is not to stay
in business. It is to stay in journalism.*

HAROLD EVANS, 1998

Contents

To Juliet Thomas, for all her help

Preface

This book has been almost five years in the making. That doesn't mean that I spent the last five years working on it, however. An insane career diversion to Fiji, where I took a position in mid-2011 as Head of Journalism at the University of the South Pacific, caused the project to be shelved for eighteen months. I resumed work on it in earnest after I was run out of the country by the military dictatorship there at the end of 2012 for speaking out against its media repression on my blog, Fiji Media Wars.

The project had originally been proposed by my publisher, Rolf Maurer, who is an old newspaper reporter like myself. At the height of the newspaper crisis in 2009, when several dailies folded and predictions ran rampant of an imminent extinction of the species, he asked me if I believed newspapers were dying. No, I replied. Well, why don't you write a book about it? OK, I said.

It was originally planned for publication in 2011. I spent the summer of 2010 hard at it and went through the annual reports of all sixteen publicly-traded newspaper companies in Canada and the U.S. going back to 2006, before the recession started. I found that despite reduced revenues as a result of the recession brought on by the 2007–09 financial crisis, none had recorded an annual loss on an operating basis. Some may have recorded a quarterly loss, but I wasn't about to multiply my research fourfold by examining all their quarterly reports. All had been able to reduce their expenses, i.e. lay off workers, sufficiently to stay in the black on an annual basis. Most had reported huge extraordinary losses, however, which grabbed the headlines but were mostly "paper" losses that simply accounted for the estimated reduction in the value of their businesses as a result of their falling revenues. Read on for a more detailed explanation.

I had hoped to finish the book in the summer of 2011 (such is the life of a professor), but I had to rush off to Fiji instead, where I got little to no work done on the project, which was shelved for a year, and then for another year. When I got back to work on it in 2013, the story had gotten even better. Not only were newspaper companies all still making money, but their profit levels had largely bounced back to very healthy levels indeed. Their revenues and earnings had undeniably been reduced, by half or more in the U.S. and by about a quarter in Canada, where we have more sensible banking regulations. The ratio of their earnings over their revenues, however, which is how profit margins (return on revenue) are calculated, was 10–15 percent in most cases, with some being over 20 percent. That was a far cry from when most were routinely over 20 percent and some were in the 30–40 percent range.

Plus by this time the secret sauce had been discovered that promised to help newspapers not just survive, but even thrive, although probably not to the extent they had during their salad days in the late twentieth century. With advertising revenues plummeting, most newspapers came to realize that they had to charge their readers more, which they did with higher cover prices and subscription rates. Most also decided to stop giving away their content for free on the Internet, which had caused many people to stop reading the newspaper and to get their news online instead. When newspapers erected paywalls that required online readers to buck up for a subscription, they found that a good proportion were willing to do so. That's because newspapers don't have just readers, they have some very avid readers, even fans. Research had shown that a small percentage of readers accounted for a majority of pageviews on news-paper websites.[1] They would be more than willing to pay. Others, who hated the thought of losing their daily newspaper, would too. But in their quest for online revenues, newspapers had also pro-ceeded down the perilous path of "native" advertising, which was a troubling development, so the story got even better in more ways than one.

The story grew so much that I didn't quite make my deadline. I promised my publisher I would have it finished by the summer of 2014. It was the end of September, however, by the time I submit-ted my manuscript. Publication had been postponed by this time to the spring of 2015. It was too late for inclusion in his spring cata-logue, however, so Rolf told me it would have to go over to the fall of 2015. Then he started reading it. He quickly realized that this was a tale that couldn't wait to be told. Instead of coming out in the fall of 2015 or even the spring of 2015, he decided it had to be published in the fall of 2014 and booked a press time that was only a month away. While I had hoped to take October off to unwind a bit, I found myself with my nose still firmly affixed to the grindstone, writing the Introduction and this Preface, not to mention making corrections and preparing the Bibliography and Index. After Rolf was firebombed for the fifth time since 2012, I figured I'd better do what I could to get this thing into print before the whole shebang went up in flames.[2] Plus the story kept growing with Postmedia's purchase of the Sun Media chain in October 2014, which changed the newspaper landscape in Canada once again. I wrote about that for the online publication The Tyee, to which I often contribute, as well as for the blog Greatly Exaggerated (http://greatlyexagerrated. blogspot.ca/), which I set up for this book.[3] That's OK. My nose was a little bit too big anyway.

Looked at from another perspective, this book has been more than fifteen years in the making. I began researching the newspaper industry in North America in the late 1990s as a doctoral student in the E.W. Scripps School of Journalism at Ohio University. I had the good fortune to study under Professor Patrick Washburn, one of the foremost U.S. journalism historians until his recent retirement. I had hoped to study Media Management and Economics and thus build on my first two degrees in Business, but I found there were no such courses at Scripps despite it being listed as a concentration area. Pat explained that as graduate director he had simply imported the concentration areas from Indiana University, where had done his doctorate. They had planned to hire someone to teach Media Management and Economics but hadn't got around to it by the time I graduated, so I was mostly self-taught. I ended up taking so many Independent Study courses that they had to put a limit on them. I'm glad to see they hired Hugh Martin a few years ago, as he had done some of the research I cite in this book.

My first ever conference presentation was in New Orleans of a term paper I had written on the Pacific Press arrangement where I had worked for fifteen years at the Vancouver *Province*. Pat convinced me this would make a fine dissertation topic, and it did. It won the annual dissertation award of the American Journalism Historians Association and New Star published it as my first book.[4] I also wrote a chapter on the "church–state wall" brouhaha at the *Los Angeles Times* for a book that Professors Joe Bernt and Marilyn Greenwald were working on that was published in 2000 as *The Big Chill: Investigative Reporting in the Current Media Environment*.[5]

I have been researching other bits of the story that would become this book ever since. I examined the takeover by Conrad Black of the Southam newspaper chain that owned Pacific Press and numerous other major Canadian dailies for a 2003 article in the *International Journal on Media Management*.[6] I presented a paper at a 2004 conference in Stockholm that examined the collapse of Black's Hollinger empire, which was published in Robert Picard's book *Corporate Governance of Media Companies*.[7] I wrote a 2007 book titled *Asper Nation: Canada's Most Dangerous Media Company*, which examined mis-management of the Southam dailies by Canwest Global Communications, which bought them from Black in 2000.[8] Coming from the television business, Canwest's owning Asper family had little understanding of now newspapers worked and thought they could impose their ideological agenda on the dailies. That sparked so much outrage among journalists and even ordinary Canadians that it led to a Senate inquiry. It also showed the folly of newspaper-television "convergence" as a business model for news media, which quickly fell apart in Canada. I don't think I can rightly be blamed for Canwest's 2009 bankruptcy, but I like to think that I helped shine a little light on their operations.

I was revising journal articles on the collapse of convergence in Canada and on the French-Canadian multimedia company Quebecor Inc. in 2010 when I had the good fortune to be chosen for the annual Reynolds Fellowship in Business Journalism at Arizona State University. Spending a week learning how to read financial reports, among other things, at ASU's fabulous new journalism campus in Phoenix proved a revelation. I couldn't believe I had written two books on publicly traded media companies and had scarcely cracked one of their annual reports. I quickly set about scrutinizing financial statements for Canadian media companies in revising my articles. This immensely improved the published versions that appeared in *Media, Culture & Society* and in Picard's *Journal of Media Business Studies*.[9] In a media world where myth and misinformation prevail, it is nice to have hard facts to fall back on. Publicly traded companies are required to provide regular audited financial statements on which investors can rely. To fudge the facts there can risk severe regulatory sanctions, and even criminal charges. What I found on their pages was quite different from the dominant narrative surrounding the financial health of media companies, as you will read.

Of course, a number of people helped with this along the way. I am most grateful for feedback on my draft manuscript from Professors Vincent Mosco and Gary Rice. With our rush into print, however, I was not able to follow up on most of their many interesting ideas for improvement. Perhaps they can serve instead as suggestions for further research. I am also grateful for the sage advice, as always, of Professor Robert Hackett of Simon Fraser University, who has been of enormous assistance in sorting out the meaning of it all. I also appreciate David Beers, founding editor of The Tyee, always being ready to publish my work. Kelly Levson of Newspapers Canada helped by providing data on advertising revenues. I wish to acknowledge a research grant from the Faculty of Arts, Law and Education at the University of the South Pacific that enabled me to interview publishers in San Francisco, San Diego, and Seattle in the summer of 2012. Unfortunately they wouldn't talk to me at the *Los Angeles Times*, no doubt due to the ongoing bankruptcy of their parent Tribune Company. I'm sure it had nothing to do with my 2000 chapter on their church-state travails. I am also grateful for the opportunity to teach a special topics course in The Changing Business of Journalism at California State University, Fresno, in the spring semester of 2014, where I was honored to be selected as Roger Tatarian Endowed Faculty Scholar in Journalism. That helped me to develop some of the ideas I had been working on for this book and to bounce them off a class full of students eager to learn about the business side of journalism. Most of the credit has to go to my publisher, however, who not only came up with the idea for this book, but also performed heroically under trying personal circumstances in bringing it to press on an extremely tight timeline. Rolf Maurer is a force of nature that will take more than a Molotov cocktail or five to stop. His assistant Mike Leyne was also of immense assistance in the proofreading and production stage. Of course, any errors or omissions are entirely my own responsibility, and I am sure there will be several given the frantic rush at the end.

Greatly Exaggerated

INTRODUCTION

The Battle of New Orleans

The end had finally come for the venerable daily newspaper, executives of Advance Publications decided. The giant newspaper chain
had taken on mountains of debt in acquiring even more dailies
just before the financial crisis of 2007-09 dropped their advertising revenues sharply. That was on top of steep losses in classified
advertising to the Internet, which proved much better at helping
people find things like homes, jobs, and cars. Advance had already
cut home delivery of several of its newspapers in economically
depressed Michigan from daily to three times a week in 2009. It
had even cut its *Ann Arbor News* to twice weekly print publication
and renamed it *AnnArbor.com* after its newly-emphasized website.
As second-place dailies started dying around the U.S. — in Cincinnati, Albuquerque, Denver, and Seattle — nervous industry watchers wondered which would be the first major American city to lose
its last daily newspaper. Some predicted it might be San Francisco,
Miami, or Minneapolis.[1]

Advance, a privately-owned company based in New Jersey,
decided it would be New Orleans. Times had been tough there
ever since the city was devastated by Hurricane Katrina in 2005,
and its population had dropped almost 30 percent. Journalists
at Advance's long-publishing *New Orleans Times-Picayune* had per-

formed heroically during the crisis, staying in the flooded city even after the authorities had fled. Unable to print an edition for three days, they had kept the world updated with stories posted to the newspaper's website. Now the Internet would prove their newspaper's undoing, as Advance decided that publishing online — not in print — was the way of the future. The *Times-Picayune* and three Advance dailies in Alabama would go "digital first" and post news stories first on their websites, the company announced in mid-2012, and would publish print editions only on Wednesdays, Fridays, and Sundays. About 200 *Times-Picayune* workers, including a quarter of its newsroom staff, would be laid off.

The reaction from New Orleans residents was not unlike Hurricane Katrina itself. Howls of protest accompanied the announcement. Protest rallies were held. Websites and blogs were launched to criticize the change. A Facebook group was formed to co-ordinate support for laid-off workers. A coalition called the Times-Picayune Citizens Group demanded the newspaper continue to publish daily and held a rally that brought out 300 supporters. "I don't know if I'd be in business without *The Times-Picayune*," said John Blancher, owner of the bowling alley where the rally was held. "Back when I opened in 1988, the most games I had on a weekend was 60. In January 1989, the paper did a story — it came out on a Tuesday — and that following weekend, I had 600 games. I keep hearing about all the new New Orleans entrepreneurs coming to town — and there's no daily newspaper for them?"[2] A website called "Ricky Go Home" was set up to vilify *Times-Picayune* publisher Ricky Mathews, who had recently arrived from Advance's operations in Alabama to co-ordinate the move to digital first publication. It featured "wanted" posters with Mathews's face on them. "He has the gall to move to town and dismantle our newspaper," it said. "Even Hurricane Katrina couldn't do that."

> Ricky Mathews doesn't know us. He doesn't know our city. Yet he is attempting to dismantle a lifeline and a common thread. Ricky, please go home. ... And give us our newspaper on your way out of town.[3]

The vitriol surprised even some long-time residents, as it betrayed the depth of affection for the city's daily lifeline. "It was as if a bomb went off," noted Micheline Maynard. "Now, a wide swath of high profile New Orleanians, including the city's archbishop, university presidents, actors and community leaders, are teaming up to demand that the paper remain a seven-day-a-week proposition."[4] The *Times-Picayune* was much loved by New Orleans residents, and at 65 percent market penetration it had one of the most avid readerships of any daily newspaper in the country. "For a city that nearly drowned on television in 2005, only to absorb the BP oil spill's economic impact on fishermen, seafood and restaurants, the Advance decision to end the newspaper as a daily hit like a sledgehammer," observed *The Nation* magazine.[5] Local celebrities such as James Carville and Wynton Marsalis demanded that Advance sell the *Times-Picayune* to someone who would publish it daily because reducing it to three days a week would damage the civic and cultural life of the city. "This makes no sense to me," complained comedian Harry Shearer. "The *Times-Picayune* is not Starbucks or Rite-Aid or Winn-Dixie sitting on the sidelines waiting for the recovery. It is the paper people in New Orleans love, or love to hate."[6] Wags derided it as the *Sometimes-Picayune*.

The Advance of Digital First

Even many advertisers were aghast at the move, and nine of them joined the Times-Picayune Citizens' Group in a bid to block the changes. "Anybody who tells you they know how three days is going to work is only kidding themselves," said furniture store owner Mitchell Mintz, who lamented the loss of the Saturday edition.[7] Car dealer Ray Brandt, who estimated he had spent almost $35 million on *Times-Picayune* ads over the previous three decades, cut back on his advertising by 80–90 percent "to show that we believe it's a mistake."[8] Deep suspicions were harboured by the New Orleans business community about the motives of the secretive Newhouse family, which owned Advance. "The community does not believe that it is that dire," said Greg Rusovich, chair of the economic development group Greater New Orleans Inc. "The word is, they've been doing quite well on both advertising numbers and subscription numbers."[9] To most, the move to thrice-weekly publication of the *Times-Picayune* made little sense from a business perspective. "There's a sense of bafflement," wrote former *Times-Picayune* reporter John McQuaid. "The owners have said the paper is currently profitable."

> Why a radical overhaul that will damage its journalistic foundation, and a push to the web in a city where nearly a third of the population has no Internet connection? New Orleans would seem to be the last place to do this, not one of the first.[10]

The move to digital-first publication was all about the future of news, and the consensus among media theorists was that the future was online. Journalists, who had always been more connected to the real world, weren't so sure. To newspaper companies like Advance, steep declines first in circulation and then in advertising meant they should get out of the printing business and into the brave new world of digital media. One of the largest U.S. newspaper companies even renamed itself Digital First in a much-ballyhooed bid to focus on online journalism with a Manhattan-based "Thunderdome" news hub that fed digital content to its 800 "multi-platform products" across the country. Advance was the first to dump daily print publication, however, in a quest for online success. From New Orleans, it planned to expand its move away from daily publication to its other major dailies in Cleveland and Portland, Oregon. As print advertising revenues fell by more than half at U.S. newspapers from 2005–2010, the future had begun to look decidedly online, where without the need for printing or distribution production costs could be cut by more than half. The only problem was that, after several years of exponential growth, online advertising revenues stubbornly refused to grow for newspapers after the recession ended in 2009, and came nowhere close to making up for their lost print advertising revenues. Oversupply drove down online advertising rates, and studies showed that web surfers, unlike newspaper readers, considered advertising a nuisance. "Advance's Internet strategy has never been about journalism or news," noted McQuaid. "It's about clicks."

> They present news in a rolling blog format, as it is fed to them, without regard to its importance or community interest. In this framework, news is primarily a click-generating engine, featuring movie listings, weather forecasts, or the doings of the Kardashians.[11]

To others, it was all about the money. According to journalism professor John Hartman, the Newhouse family was converting its newspapers to little more than "shoppers," which had long been derided by journalists for carrying little news. "The reason is simple: to restore generous payouts to family members," wrote Hartman in the industry magazine *Editor & Publisher*. "The privately held Newhouse empire provides a comfortable living for dozens of family member owners, and tight times in the newspaper industry apparently have cut their payouts and perhaps their lifestyles." With an estimated worth of $14 billion, the Newhouse family was one of the wealthiest in the country, but its members had multiplied with each generation, which meant that the wealth was being spread ever more thinly. "The only way to push the stipends back in the direction of comfortable is to dramatically cut expenses while maintaining advertising revenue," noted Hartman.[12] Rebecca Theim, a former *Times-Picayune* journalist who helped to organize a "Save the Picayune" page on Facebook and started a blog at dashTHIRTYdash.org to assist laid-off workers, blamed Advance executives for both hatching and botching the hare-brained scheme. In her scathing 2013 book about the brouhaha, *Hell or High Water*, she was especially critical of *Times-Picayune* editor Jim Amoss for having "seemingly swallowed a corporate line with little critical consideration of the true underlying dynamics."[13]

'My Digital O'

Sensing an opportunity to exploit an underserved market and community outrage, the nearby *Baton Rouge Advocate* decided to move into New Orleans with a daily edition in October 2012. Owned by the local Manship family, the *Advocate* already had a bureau in New Orleans, which it beefed up by hiring some of the award-winning reporters and editors who had been laid off by the *Times-Picayune*. The *New Orleans Advocate* quickly attracted more than 20,000 subscribers, with copies printed in Baton Rouge and trucked seventy miles south overnight. The competition obviously rattled Advance, which announced in June 2013 that it was launching a tabloid called *T-P Street* to publish on the days its *Times-Picayune* didn't. "We see this as recognizing that we didn't have all the answers," said Mathews.[14] All of a sudden, New Orleans had more newspapers than before. "It's been a jaw-dropping blunder to watch," observed David Carr in the *New York Times*. "Advance misjudged the marketplace . . . and failed to execute a modern digital strategy. Now it is in full retreat with new competition."[15] In October 2014, Advance also reinstated Monday delivery of the *Times-Picayune*.

When Advance announced its digital-first strategy in Cleveland that spring, it retained seven-day print publication of its *Plain Dealer*, although it cut back on home delivery to three days a week. After complaints from car dealers, however, it restored Saturday delivery.[16] After it eliminated fifty positions from the *Plain Dealer*'s already emaciated newsroom, culling its staff by a third, frustrated journalists paraded in protest.[17] In Portland, more than one hundred *Oregonian* workers were laid off and its remaining reporters were put on an incentive system. "As much as 75 percent of reporters' job performance will be based on measurable web-based metrics, including how often they post to Oregonlive.com," reported the alternative newspaper *Willamette Week*. "Beat reporters will be expected to post at least three times a day, and all reporters are expected to increase their average number of posts by 40 percent over the next year."[18] Some of the changes were ridiculous. "Consistent with Advance's marketing and messaging faux pas, it has also named its daily e-edition, 'My Digital O,' to the guffaws of many," noted media analyst Ken Doctor. "Talk about service journalism."[19]

The irony was that, as with the first Battle of New Orleans, the war had already been won. The combatants just didn't know it yet. When the last battle of the War of 1812 was fought, the war had already ended with the Treaty of Ghent, which had been signed in Belgium two weeks earlier. As the news from Europe had to come via sailing ship back then, the combatants were blissfully ignorant of the fact the war was over. So too, it seemed, with Advance Publications 200 years later. Even in an age of information overload, and probably more so, the problem remained understanding what information meant and connecting the dots. Advance appeared blind to the fact that the *New York Times* and other dailies had already been able to generate hundreds of million of dollars in new revenue by erecting "paywalls" around their digital content. Advance steadfastly refused to charge online readers, instead attempting to entice as many visitors as possible to its websites in a bid to maximize online advertising rates that just kept falling anyway. This perpetuated the "original sin" that newspapers had committed in the early days of the World Wide Web when they decided to give away their online content in pursuit of the empty calories that pageviews turned out to provide.

The extra income provided by paywalls promised to save dailies, which had almost all been able to reduce their expenses well below the plummeting level of their revenues anyway, mostly by laying off workers. In fact, most were still recording double-digit profit margins that would be envied in other industries. The newspapers that had closed in Cincinnati, Albuquerque, Denver, Seattle, and a few other cities had been second-place dailies, which under the peculiar economics of the newspaper business had long been an endangered species. Newspapers weren't dying. Newspaper competition was. It was a trend that had been seen for decades, and the financial crisis and high-speed Internet simply accelerated the trend. But since the *Rocky Mountain News* and the *Seattle Post-Intelligencer* closed in early 2009, no major North American daily has folded, despite dire predictions of a newspaper extinction. This book explains why. It also shows how changes in journalism at many newspapers, brought by pressure to boost profits, could see marketing and propaganda infiltrate the news to an increasing extent.

The Natural Monopoly Theory

As this book went to press, significant changes loomed in ownership of newspaper companies in the U.S. and Canada. The giant Digital First chain in the U.S., which had been bought up by hedge funds, was put on the block after they found the pursuit of increased online advertising revenues fruitless. The equally enormous Tribune Company of Chicago, which owned the Los Angeles Times and numerous other major dailies, similarly put its newspapers up for sale after exiting Chapter 11 bankruptcy in 2013 following four years of legal wrangling. Prospective buyers for the chains included media mogul Rupert Murdoch, who already owned the world's largest newspaper company, News Corp., including the Wall Street Journal. Other chains mulled mergers and acquisitions that would drive up the level of newspaper ownership concentration to unhealthy levels and thus likely require federal approval. Dire economic prospects for newspapers were invariably advanced as justification for the required relaxation of anti-trust laws and increased corporate control of the news media. That is not borne out by this study, which examined newspaper company annual reports going back to 2006 to find they have all continued to publish profitably and should for years to come. After all, there are large newspapers and there are small newspapers. Large newspapers have just been getting a lot smaller lately. Small newspapers, ironically, are often more profitable than large ones.

The effect of high levels of newspaper ownership concentration can be seen in Canada, where the bulk of the country's newspapers came to be controlled by three giant chains. In October 2014, however, two of the chains did a deal that would reduce that number to two and give one of them inordinate dominance in several major markets. The Sun Media chain of mostly tabloids was sold by multimedia giant Quebecor Inc. to the Postmedia chain for $316 million. That would result in Postmedia owning both dailies in Edmonton, Calgary, and the nation's capital of Ottawa, plus two dailies in the ultra-competitive Toronto market, which had enjoyed four daily newspapers with separate owners. The deal, which was subject to approval by the federal Competition Bureau, would create three more local newspaper monopolies similar to what Postmedia already enjoyed in Vancouver, where the dailies had published jointly since 1957. That merger between supposed competitors had been ruled illegal by federal anti-trust regulators, which nonetheless allowed it to stand on the basis of "economic necessity," as I chronicled in my first book, *Pacific Press*. Owners of the *Vancouver Sun* and the *Daily Province* argued that under the prevailing Natural Monopoly Theory of Newspapers one of them would inevitably fold if they weren't allowed to go into business together. Forget that three daily newspapers were then being published in Vancouver — Pacific Press bought the morning *News-Herald* and quickly folded it.[20]

But newspaper competition didn't die in Canada, and therein lies a tale. After second-place dailies closed in Winnipeg and Ottawa in 1980, the nation was so horrified that a Royal Commission was called to investigate. It recommended limits on how much of the nation's press a chain could own, but the proposed measures were never passed into law. In Winnipeg and Ottawa, however, colourful *Sun* tabloids sprang up to fill the void left by deceased dailies, and they proved highly successful by appealing to a younger readership. Modeled after the popular *Toronto Sun*, which had been launched in 1971 from the ashes of the folded *Toronto Telegram*, *Sun* tabloids also prospered in Edmonton and Calgary, effectively repealing the Natural Monopoly Theory of Newspapers. Pacific Press even converted its *Vancouver Province*, where I was a reporter, to a tabloid in 1983, and it also proved highly successful. By 1999, however, five chains owned 93.2 percent of Canada's dailies.[21] Convergence visited the country's media the following year and its largest newspapers were quickly married to television networks in a fruitless quest for "synergies" between the two media. That brought the level of media ownership concentration in Canada, and particularly in Vancouver, to among the highest in the free world. Canwest Global Communications, as I chronicled in my 2007 book *Asper Nation*, came to own not just both Vancouver dailies, but also its dominant television station and most of its community newspapers.[22] Even worse, Canwest's owning Asper family imposed an ideological agenda on its news media outlets before the company mercifully went bankrupt in 2009. Its newspapers were sold to Postmedia separately from its Global Television network, joining a worldwide trend toward de-convergence of media.[23]

The 2014 Postmedia purchase of the Sun Media chain would see it own a third or more of the nation's press, however, and dominate the Edmonton, Calgary, and Ottawa markets as has been seen in Vancouver for decades. The purchase was justified by some journalism educators on the basis that both newspaper chains were hurting financially. "What we're talking about here is one threatened company ... buying properties whose future was in doubt," said Ivor Shapiro, chair of the school of journalism at Ryerson University in Toronto. "That is way better at the end of the day than seeing both of those news organizations close down."[24] On the contrary, a quick glance at the annual reports of Postmedia and Quebecor would show that both were highly profitable. "Worrying that a smaller and smaller number of companies own a larger number of newspapers is kind of beside the point," added Christopher Dornan of Carleton University in Ottawa, "because the newspapers themselves have been eclipsed in their social, political and economic prominence by the new digital concourses of communication."[25] That is also a media myth, one of several this book hopes to explode.

Persistent Media Myths

The advent of the Internet as a new mass medium caused much discombobulation among journalists and even more among journalism educators. Media owners in the U.S. stepped up their calls for removal of the Federal Communications Commission's prohibition against newspaper owners also owning television stations, claiming that the convergence of all media online was inevitable. In Canada, no such prohibition existed. One had been imposed briefly by a Liberal government in the mid-1980s after a warning by the Royal Commission on Newspapers against allowing cross-media ownership. It was quickly removed, however, after government passed to the more business-friendly Progressive Conservative party in 1984.[26] This led to the ugly spectacle of Canada's news giants seeking financial assistance from the country's broadcasting regulator after the 2007–09 financial crisis left the convergence model in ruins. The television networks claimed they were in dire financial straits, but they weren't. The country's converged news media weren't the ones to get to the bottom of that story, however. Instead it fell to a few enterprising media scholars to sift through the financial reports that showed they were still making good profits, just not as good as they had been making.[27] The FCC's cross-ownership ban likely saved U.S. news media from similar convergence perils.

Faculty members in many journalism schools similarly assumed that the future of news was online and began revising their programs to better equip students for a multimedia world. Student newspapers became converged with television newscasts, and news writing and reporting classes became multimedia oriented. Brigham Young University's journalism school was one of the first to embrace the convergence model in 1995, combining its student newspaper and television newsrooms and teaching multimedia journalism. After convergence fizzled, however, faculty members voted to reverse course in 2006. "Convergence took away necessary depth in core writing skills," explained Dean Stephen Adams. "Students knew a whole lot about a whole lot of things, but didn't know very much in depth."[28] Other journalism schools, boosted by funding from foundations and media corporations desperate to discover the future of news, offered programs in computer programming and even Integrated Marketing Communications, which combined journalism with advertising and public relations.[29]

The main complaint of multimedia advocates against newspapers is that they had been too slow to react to the Internet. Newspaper executives had been "stubborn and arrogant" in failing to recognize the disruptive potential of the new medium, according to Keith Herndon in his compendious 2012 book *The Decline of the Daily Newspaper.*[30] As a result, the newspaper industry failed to "exploit the digital era."[31] Exploit it for what? It turned out there wasn't a lot of money to be made in attracting eyeballs online, especially not in advertising. The websites most successful at attracting advertising proved to be search engines and social media, but it is highly unrealistic to expect newspapers to have pioneered those innovations. The newspaper industry had been experimenting with online delivery of news long before the Internet exploded in the late 1990s and had concluded it was not economically viable. Newspapers that weathered the Internet's disruption best turned out to be the ones that ignored it best. "The Internet is not your friend," warned three business professors in their incisive 2009 book *The Curse of the Mogul*, in which they demolish numerous media myths. "Convergence may sound sexy, but . . . it is a classic case of one plus one being substantially less than two."[32]

ONE

Newspapers Are So Over

The death of newspapers has been predicted more than once. When radio appeared in the 1920s, many assumed that this new media miracle would put the daily newspaper out of business. The birth of broadcasting, after all, broke print's long-held monopoly on news and advertising. Radio not only offered instantaneous transmission but it came into people's homes right through the walls, as if by magic, without the need for printing or delivery. It even allowed listeners to hear the voices of newsmakers themselves. Who would ever want to read a newspaper again — or so the reasoning went — when you could listen to the news as it was happening on the radio?

Of course, it didn't quite work out that way. Newspapers survived that scare quite nicely because, while it had some definite strengths, radio news turned out to be limited in many ways. It was best suited to short, regular bulletins containing much less information than the average newspaper article. What radio turned out to be best at, besides playing music, was talk. It allowed politicians to communicate directly with audiences, like U.S. president Franklin Delano Roosevelt did in the 1930s. His ideas about how to get the economy out of the Great Depression by using government spending to create employment were scorned by the country's powerful publishers as too much like socialism. Adding a new medium to the mix, however, allowed FDR to circumvent the newspaper gatekeepers and take his policies right into people's living rooms with his fatherly "fireside chats." All of a sudden newspapers were not the only powerful force shaping public opinion. Newspapers adapted, however, and survived. They even thrived. Instead of focussing on simply what happened, which radio increasingly told people first, newspapers began to offer readers more in-depth analysis of why things happened and what they meant. Newspapers also became stronger businesses, often buying up their competition and forming into great chains that made money at a dizzying rate.

Then along came television. Surely this meant the end of newspapers, the cognoscenti concurred. The printed word, after all, could scarcely compete with the ability of television to put viewers right at the scene of the action. As television news expanded and added satellite transmission, newspapers scrambled to compete by trying to be more like television. They offered more and bigger pictures together with lighter and fluffier "human interest" stories. This trend reached the heights of frivolity in the 1970s with "disco" journalism, so-called because it was said to be aimed at "people who move their hips when they read."[1] Colour television was matched by colour printing. Stories became shorter and more easily digestible, as exemplified by Gannett's 1982 rollout of USA Today, which featured endless colourful "infographics."

Television did largely kill off one species of newspaper — the afternoon daily. People coming home from work wanted to relax and watch the news on TV, not read it in the newspaper. Afternoon newspapers mostly moved to morning publication or went out of business. Morning newspapers, however, continued to thrive, especially if they could outlast their competition and gain a monopoly, which would allow them to set their subscription prices and especially their advertising rates as high as they wanted. They attracted readers with lots of things they couldn't get on television, like comic strips, horoscopes, crossword puzzles, and — most importantly — TV listings. Television was more suited to national brand advertising, so local retail merchants continued to favour the local daily. Even readers could advertise in the newspaper, and the reams of classified advertising they took out proved highly profitable for publishers.

But as the third millennium loomed, yet another new medium appeared in the form of the Internet. This time newspapers were doomed for sure, all agreed. The Internet could do many things much better than newspapers could, and it did many of them for free. People could read the same news — and more — that was in their morning newspaper, and it was transmitted instantly to their computers from around the world at any hour of the day. They could also shop for things like cars, jobs, and homes much easier online through sortable databases, which caused most classified advertising to dry up.

Newspapers desperately tried to get in on the game, launching their own websites in an attempt to compete in this brave new information environment. But no matter how they tried, the geeks kept coming up with new and better ways to attract people's eyeballs. Soon people had less and less time for the newspaper. Circulation began to drop. Worse, advertising started to dry up as businesses began to find better and cheaper ways to reach their customers online. In his 2004 book *The Vanishing Newspaper*, journalism professor Philip Meyer calculated that, due to declining interest, the last newspaper reader would be lost some time in March of 2043.[2] *Advertising Age* columnist Bob Garfield thought that was a bit optimistic, noting in 2007 that readers and advertisers were deserting newspapers so fast that they would soon be left without visible means of support. "We are not witnessing the beginning of the end of old media," insisted Garfield. "We are witnessing the middle of the end of old media."[3]

Then came the financial crisis, which promised finish newspapers off. The recession that began in late 2007 saw advertising revenue fall off a cliff at U.S. newspapers. In the space of five years, it dropped by more than half, and it just kept on dropping. Nothing like it had ever been seen in the newspaper industry, which tended to suffer its ups and downs in lockstep with the economy. Advertising revenue always went down during a recession, but it always went back up again when the economy improved. This was differ-ent. This was freefall. Because of the Internet, advertising would never return in the same volume, warned the pundits. The news-paper as a species was doomed for sure this time by the perfect storm of a tanking economy and technological change.

Soon newspapers began going out of business at an alarming rate. The *Cincinnati Post* folded at the end of 2007, and the *Albuquer-que Tribune* and Madison, Wisconsin, *Capital Times* soon followed, but they were all struggling second-place dailies. In Canada, the relatively youthful *Halifax Daily News*, which had only been in oper-ation for 27 years, announced that it would transform itself into a giveaway commuter tabloid and that most of its staff would be laid off. Then the venerable *Christian Science Monitor*, which had been founded in 1908 and was subsidized by the Church of Christ, Sci-entist, decided to cut back on publication from daily to weekly due to losses that had reached $18.9 million a year.

Stocks of publicly traded newspaper companies, which made up almost half of the industry in the U.S. and about 90 percent in Canada, crashed. An index of newspaper stock prices calculated by *NewsInc.*, an industry newsletter, dropped more than 25 percent in the first week of July 2008 alone.[4] The following week ended with what industry analysts called the worst day ever for news-paper stocks. The largest U.S. newspaper company, Gannett, saw its stock price close at its lowest point since 1990. Its shares, which had traded above $90 in 2004, fell that day to $17.42. Shares in the New York Times Co., which owned the *Boston Globe* in addition to its eponymous flagship, closed at their lowest point since 1996.[5] Then that October the stock market crashed. By year's end, five of the fourteen publicly-traded U.S. newspaper companies were down by more than 90 percent for 2008. Three of them were down by more than 99.5 percent. Several had been kicked off the New York Stock Exchange's "big board" after their share price fell below a dol-lar and they became "penny" stocks. Two of them were trading at 4 to 6 cents by year's end. Journal Register Co., once one of the most profitable newspaper publishers of all, saw its stock fall to one one-thousandth of a cent per share. Even former blue-chip stocks like Gannett (80 percent) and the New York Times Co. (59 percent) were off massively for the year.[6]

Soon fairly major newspapers began going out of business. The *Rocky Mountain News* in Denver threw in the towel in early 2009, putting 215 staff members out of work. Founded in 1859, the *Rocky* had won four Pulitzer Prizes in a decade but had lost $123 million in the 1990s for its owner, the E.W. Scripps chain. As publisher John Temple watched reporters clean out their desks, he issued a warning. "We're going to see the collapse of many newspapers," he said.[7] A few weeks later, the *Seattle Post-Intelligencer* (established 1863) was converted to online-only publication by its owner, Hearst Corporation, the country's largest privately-owned newspaper chain. Of the *P-I*'s 165 employees, only a skeleton crew of twenty was kept on to update its website, while another fifteen sold ads. Then the jointly-operating *Detroit News* and *Detroit Free Press* stopped home delivery Mondays through Wednesdays, offering only scaled-down newsstand versions of their money-losing editions on those days. "We're fighting for our survival," explained *Free Press* publisher Dave Hunke. Canada's *National Post*, which was piling up big losses for owner Canwest Global Communications, announced it would eliminate its money-losing Monday paper for the summer. In May, the 138-year-old *Tucson Citizen* was closed by Gannett, the country's largest newspaper chain. In July, the *Ann Arbor News* ceased daily publication after 174 years, was renamed *AnnArbor.com* after its website, and began to publish twice weekly.

On the same day the *Rocky* folded, the American Society of Newspaper Editors cancelled its annual convention for the first time since World War II and conducted its meetings online instead. ASNE members voted to drop the word "newspaper" from its title, changing the group's name to the American Society of News Editors.[9] The doomsayers suddenly found their full throat. "By the middle of this year, as many as a third of the daily newspapers in America may be under the protection of a bankruptcy judge," warned investment banker John Chachas in a *Dallas Morning News* column. "Dozens more could be shuttered, with thousands of jobs lost."[10] Some who had been in the newspaper business for decades concurred. "In less than five years, newspapers will print for Sunday only," predicted newspaper design expert Alan Jacobson. "In less than 10 years, no newspapers will be printed."[11] *Vanity Fair* columnist Michael Wolff had an even more dire prediction. "About 18 months from now, 80 percent of newspapers will be gone," he told one of the many panels convened to debate the future of news.[12] Others had a slightly more optimistic timeline. Steve Ballmer of Microsoft gave newspapers — and magazines — a decade at most. "There will be no media consumption left in 10 years that is not delivered over an IP network," he predicted in 2008. "There will be no newspapers, no magazines that are delivered in paper form. Everything gets delivered in an electronic form."[13] Others who studied the future of news media were only slightly more optimistic in their prognosis for newspapers. "We think they have 20 to 25 years," said Jeffrey Cole, director of the Center for the Digital Future at the University of Southern California.[14]

Newspaper Death Watch

Thus began a macabre death watch. Some Internet aficionados tracked ailing dailies with schadenfreude and appeared almost to cheer each newspaper closure as lustily as journalists lamented it. Technology journalist Paul Gillin started a website he called Newspaper Death Watch to catalogue each new casualty.[15] His list of newspapers under the heading "R.I.P." grew, as did a second list of endangered dailies under the heading "W.I.P." — works in progress. The blogosphere buzzed about who would go next. Soon the doomsaying reached the mainstream media. "What if the *New York Times* goes out of business," chortled the *Atlantic* magazine as 2009 began, "like, this May?"

> It's certainly plausible. Earnings reports released by the New York Times Company in October indicate that drastic measures will have to be taken over the next five months or the paper will default on some $400 million in debt.[16]

The magazine pointed out that the venerable *Times* was more than $1 billion in debt and had been forced to raise cash by borrowing against its new Manhattan headquarters. It had even turned for a high-interest loan to Mexican billionaire Carlos Slim, and as a result the world's richest man had become a major shareholder in the company. The *Atlantic* pointed to a prediction made by the Fitch rating agency in late 2008. "Fitch believes more newspapers and newspaper groups will default, be shut down and be liquidated in 2009 and several cities could go without a daily print newspaper by 2010," it had warned in rating the debt of two distressed newspaper groups — McClatchy and Tribune — as "junk."[17] Even if the *New York Times* wriggled off the hook this time, the *Atlantic* predicted that it was only a matter of time before the nation's leading daily was forced to exit print for online-only publication. "At some point soon — sooner than most of us think — the print edition, and with it the *Times* as we know it, will no longer exist. And it will likely have plenty of company."[18]

The most likely major dailies to exit print for online-only publication, according to *BusinessWeek*, were the *San Francisco Chronicle* and the *Boston Globe*, in that order. "Executives might be better off wondering at what point the *Globe*'s Boston.com or the *Chronicle*'s sfgate.com — with unassailable market positions, excellent editorial, and massive traffic — will be worth more as a solo digital play than attached to a print newspaper."[19] Even the *Washington Post*, famed for its reporting of the Watergate scandal that forced Richard Nixon to resign as president in 1974, wasn't considered a safe bet to continue print publication. Citing its falling ad revenues and plummeting profit levels, *Fortune* magazine speculated that the *Post* could be forced by sheer economics to go online-only. "What lies ahead for the *Post* seems to be a long and painful transition from print — so important to local advertisers that the newspaper could raise prices almost at will — to the Internet, where competition for readers and advertisers is brutal."[20]

The financial problems of the *New York Times* also imperilled the *Boston Globe*, which it had bought for $1.1 billion in 1993. As news broke that the New York Times Company had lost $74.5 million in the first quarter of 2009, the company threatened to close the *Globe* unless its unions agreed to $20 million in contract concessions, citing projections it would lose $85 million that year. The *Times* was not the only newspaper company to play hardball with its unions in the face of dire economic conditions. Hearst threatened to close its *San Francisco Chronicle*, which it claimed had lost more than $1 million a week the previous year, unless its unionized workforce made contract concessions. The California Media Workers Guild reluctantly agreed to longer work weeks and less vacation time, not to mention the elimination of 150 jobs, or almost one-third of its membership.

As dailies began to wither on the vine all around the U.S. in early 2009, pundits began to speculate about which would be the first American city to see the death of its last remaining daily. "There are candidates all across the country," warned the *New York Times*, which floated a worst-case scenario. "In 2009 and 2010, all the two-newspaper markets will become one-newspaper markets," it quoted industry analyst Mike Simonton of Fitch Ratings as predicting, "and you will start to see one-newspaper markets become no-newspaper markets."[21] The State of the News Media, a comprehensive online report produced annually by the Project for Excellence in Journalism, agreed in its 2009 edition that falling ad revenues could kill off even monopoly dailies. "There is not yet a major city without a newspaper, but that, too, could be coming soon."[22] *Time* magazine concurred that the daily newspaper had become endangered to the point of extinction. "The crisis in journalism has reached meltdown proportions," it observed. "It is now possible to contemplate a time when some major cities will no longer have a newspaper."[23]

Just as Seattle was losing its *Post-Intelligencer* to online-only purgatory, *USA Today* printed a short list of cities that were candidates to see their only remaining daily close. "At least one city — possibly San Francisco, Miami, Minneapolis or Cleveland — likely will soon lose its last daily newspaper, analysts say."[24] The *American Journalism Review* agreed, emblazoning "Cities Without Newspapers" across its cover. "The unsettling possibility looms," it mused, "that some big cities could lose their sole remaining daily newspaper."[25] *Time* decided to publish a list handicapping the field in March 2009.

It ran a list of The 10 Most Endangered Newspapers in America on its website, and with it a warning. "It's possible that eight of the nation's 50 largest daily newspapers could cease publication in the next 18 months," writer Douglas McIntyre predicted, citing an analysis of financial and market data.[26] The list included some of the largest newspapers in the U.S., many of them market leaders or even monopoly dailies:

1. *Philadelphia Daily News*
2. *Minneapolis Star Tribune*
3. *Miami Herald*
4. *Detroit News*
5. *Boston Globe*
6. *San Francisco Chronicle*
7. *Chicago Sun-Times*
8. *New York Daily News*
9. *Fort Worth Star-Telegram*
10. *Cleveland Plain Dealer*

Broken Chains

Drowning in debt and unable to make ends meet, soon even the once-powerful chains that owned newspapers began declaring bankruptcy. The Journal Register Company, publisher of the *New Haven Register* and nineteen other dailies, had long been one of the country's most profitable newspaper chains. Its earnings had been eroded for years, however, by falling ad revenue. It officially went underwater in 2009 when it could no longer afford to make the payments on its $692 million in debt and it filed for Chapter 11 bankruptcy protection from its creditors. So did the MediaNews Group, which published dozens of newspapers, including the *Denver Post* and *San Jose Mercury News*. Freedom Communications, which published the *Orange County Register* and numerous other dailies, had long been owned by the libertarian Hoiles family. A messy family feud saw it take on massive debt to buy out dissident shareholders. That debt became more than it could handle after the 2007–2009 financial crisis and attendant recession, and Freedom was sold out of bankruptcy to new owners. In Philadelphia, the jointly-operating *Inquirer* and *Daily News* were sold three times in the space of six years, with the selling price falling by more than 90 percent. The dailies sold for $562 million in 2006, but by the time they were scooped up out of bankruptcy in 2012 the price was a mere $55 million. In Chicago, the owners of both major dailies were forced into Chapter 11. The Tribune Company, which published the Windy City's leading newspaper and owned seven other major dailies across the country, including the *Los Angeles Times*, was a staggering $13 billion in debt. It entered bankruptcy in late 2008 after an ill-conceived takeover by real estate magnate Sam Zell flopped with the recession. The Sun-Times Media Group, which published the *Chicago Tribune*'s tabloid competition and 58 other Chicagoland newspapers, had been criminally mismanaged by a pair of Canadian takeover artists, who went to prison as a result. It began drowning in a sea of red ink, which included the legal fees of its own malefactors, and entered bankruptcy in 2009.

In Canada, Canwest Global Communications had been a pioneer of the "convergence" model of media ownership that reshaped the country's media landscape at the millennium. Convergence was an idea sparked by the Internet that predicted all media would merge into one online. Enthusiasm for the concept among media owners saw newspapers frantically partner with other media, typically television, in a short-lived bubble. A federal prohibition prevented common ownership of newspapers and television stations in the U.S., but no such barrier existed in Canada, where convergence reshaped the country's media in less than a year. While it had made a fortune with the country's third television network, Canwest went deeply into debt in 2000 to acquire Canada's largest newspaper chain, Southam Inc. The experiment proved disastrous, with Canwest filing for bankruptcy protection in 2009.

Death by a Thousand Paper Cuts

As their revenues plunged, newspapers desperately began throwing people overboard in an attempt to keep their ships from sinking. Cutting costs was the quickest way to bring their expenses back into line with their plummeting revenues, and labor costs were the easiest to cut. In 2008 and 2009, reports of journalists joining the unemployment line seemed unending. Erica Smith, a graphics designer at the *St. Louis Post-Dispatch*, started a website in 2007 that she called Paper Cuts to monitor layoffs at newspapers across the U.S. She counted more than 15,000 jobs that were eliminated in 2008 alone, about half of which she estimated were journalists.[27] ASNE counted 5,900 daily print journalists who lost their jobs in 2008, with another 5,200 shown the door in 2009.[28] The Project For Excellence in Journalism estimated in 2010 that 13,500 newsroom jobs were lost in the U.S. over a three-year period.[29] Its headcount of newspaper journalists fell from 55,000 in 2007 to 41,500 in 2010, a drop of almost 25 percent. The massive loss of journalists left many wondering whether the press could continue to cover the news comprehensively. Paul Starr, a professor at Princeton University, warned that the inevitable result of reduced newspaper coverage of government would be increased political corruption. "Corruption is more likely to flourish when those in power have less reason to fear exposure," he pointed out in an article for *New Republic* magazine. "The lower the free circulation of newspapers in a country, the higher it stands on the corruption index."[30] Even worse, warned Starr, was the likelihood that newspapers themselves would become corrupted out of desperation.

> When they were financially strong, newspapers were better able not only to invest in long-term investigative projects but also to stand up against pressure from politicians and industries to suppress unfavorable stories. . . . A financially compromised press is more likely to be ethically compromised. So the danger is not just more corruption of government and business — it is also more corruption of journalism itself.[31]

American Journalism Review regularly counted the reporters covering Washington and state capitols. In late 2008 it noted that newspapers had eliminated more than forty Washington bureau positions over the previous three years, with most citing "daunting" financial problems as the reason. "In November alone, Copley and Newhouse News Service shuttered their Washington bureaus, and Small Newspapers eliminated the position of Edward Felker, its lone Washington reporter."[32] By early 2009, the exodus had turned into a flood, with AJR reporting "a dramatic decrease in the number of newspaper reporters covering state government full time." Its census of newspaper reporters covering state government found a 32 percent decrease from six years earlier, or what it called "a staggering loss of reporting firepower at America's state capitols."[33] AJR cited academic research that showed negative political consequences when newspaper coverage was reduced. A study by Princeton economists found that the closure of the Cincinnati Post lowered the number of people voting in elections there and increased an incumbent's chances of staying in office. University of Chicago economists also found voter turnout dropped significantly in cities where U.S. newspapers had closed since the 1870s. MIT and Stockholm University researchers found that members of Congress who got a lot of newspaper coverage worked harder for their constituents and were less likely to vote along party lines.[34] In 2014, Portland State University's Lee Shaker published data that showed civic engagement in Seattle and Denver dropped significantly following closure of the Rocky Mountain News and the conversion to online-only publication of the Post-Intelligencer. "Newspapers are vital institutions in our democracy," concluded Shaker, "and their decline warrants our concern."[35]

A Meme is Born

The fate of newspapers suddenly became big news in the spring of 2009, with pundits competing to predict their imminent demise. "It suddenly reached critical mass," noted Rem Reider, AJR's editor and publisher. "All at once, you couldn't go anywhere without somebody talking about the perilous state of America's newspapers." Reider pointed to the enormous losses that newspaper companies reported that quarter — $53.8 million by the Washington Post and $74.5 million by the New York Times — as evidence that democracy itself was on the brink. "The sums that some of our top newspapers are losing are truly staggering — and frightening," noted Reider. "The extent of the carnage has greatly diminished the ability of many news outlets to give readers the information they need as citizens in a democracy."[36] Magazines went to town on the story. In a cover story headlined "How to Save Your Newspaper," *Time*'s former managing editor Walter Isaacson proposed a "micropayment" system similar to iTunes in order to help newspapers gain some revenues from online freeloaders in a pay-as-you-read scheme. "A newspaper might decide to charge a nickel for an article or a dime for that day's full edition or $2 for a month's worth of Web access," he explained. "Some surfers would balk, but I suspect most would merrily click through if it were cheap and easy enough."[37] A pair of liberal commentators went so far as to suggest government subsidies for ailing newspapers. "We need to think about an immediate journalism economic stimulus," wrote John Nichols and Robert McChesney in a cover story for *The Nation*, "and we need to think big."

> Journalism is collapsing, and with it comes the most serious threat in our lifetimes to self-government and the rule of law.... As journalists are laid off and newspapers cut back or shut down, whole sectors of our civic life go dark.[38]

Nichols and McChesney suggested a three-year program of government spending to help newspapers navigate the transition to the brave new world of digital media. They estimated that their plan for subscription subsidies, free postage for small periodicals, and an "exponential" expansion of funding for public broadcasting would cost $60 billion. Included would be a tax credit for every American to cover the first $200 spent annually on a newspaper subscription, similar to what had recently been implemented in France for teenagers upon reaching their eighteenth birthday. "In effect, this means the government will pay for every citizen who so desires to get a free daily newspaper subscription," they wrote. "It would keep the press system alive. And it has the added benefit of providing an economic stimulus."[39] *Los Angeles Times* columnist

Rosa Brooks, a professor of law at Georgetown University, agreed with Nichols and McChesney, saying she couldn't imagine "anything more dangerous than a society in which the news industry has more or less collapsed." Brooks concurred that preserving the press was a matter for urgent public intervention. "It's time for a government bailout of journalism," she wrote.[40] That brought howls of derision from conservatives opposed to government spending, not to mention press freedom advocates who feared any intrusion of government into the operations of the news media. But many in government seemed to consider the situation so serious that they were prepared to consider public subsidies for journalism.

Political Hand-Wringing

Concerned for his hometown *Baltimore Sun*, which was imperiled by the bankruptcy of its owning Tribune Co., Maryland senator Ben Cardin introduced a Newspaper Revitalization Act in March 2009. It would have allowed newspapers to claim non-profit tax status and be supported with tax-deductible contributions, but would have prohibited them from endorsing political candidates. "We are losing our newspaper industry," exclaimed Cardin in a *Washington Post* column. "The business model for newspapers, based on circulation and advertising revenue, is broken. That decline is a harbinger of tragedy for communities nationwide and for our democracy."[41] His legislation went nowhere. Concerned for his hometown *Boston Globe*, which was imperiled by the financial woes of its owning New York Times Co., Massachusetts Senator John Kerry took action in May. Kerry convened hearings into the crisis by the Commerce Subcommittee on Communications, Technology, and the Internet, which he chaired. "Newspapers look like an endangered species," warned Kerry, adding it was vital to "preserve the core societal function that is served by an independent and diverse news media." A parade of all-star witnesses testified in an attempt to get to the bottom of the problem. "The future is to be found elsewhere," said Arianna Huffington, editor-in-chief of The

Huffington Post online news and opinion site. "It is search engines. It is online advertising. It is citizen journalism and foundation-supported investigative funds." That brought a retort from David Simon, creator of the HBO crime drama *The Wire* and a former *Baltimore Sun* reporter. "The day I run into a Huffington Post reporter at a Baltimore zoning board hearing is the day that I'll be confident." [42]

Some in Washington began to think it was time to lift the Federal Communication Commission's 1975 ban on granting television station licences to newspaper owners because of the dire business climate for both. The Bush administration had twice tried to lift the ban, quietly in 2003 before a firestorm of protest prevented the move. A 2007 attempt to lift the ban in only the country's twenty largest media markets was justified in part as a bid to help ailing newspapers. "In many towns and cities, the newspaper is an endangered species," wrote FCC chairman Kevin Martin in the *New York Times* after hurriedly holding the minimum number of public hearings required. "At least 300 daily papers have stopped publishing over the past 30 years. Those newspapers that have survived are struggling financially." [43] The bid was blocked in the Senate, however, by presidential hopefuls Hilary Clinton and Barack Obama, which made the ban's lifting unlikely after Obama was elected president in 2008 and re-elected four years later.

The urge to assist big-city newspapers reached the highest ranks of power in Washington, where some even favored loosening long-standing antitrust laws against mergers that eliminated competition if it would assist their favorite daily. House speaker Nancy Pelosi, alarmed by the possibility that her hometown *San Francisco Chronicle* might be endangered, wrote to Attorney-General Eric Holder at the height of the newspaper crisis. The *Chronicle*'s owning Hearst Corp. had warned that it might have to close the paper if it couldn't make dramatic cost savings. The venerable daily had become encircled by competing newspapers owned by the MediaNews chain, and the possibility of its merger with the *Chronicle* had been raised. That would have eliminated newspaper competition almost entirely in the Bay area and almost certainly would have invited the Department of Justice to block such a merger. Citing

the alarmist *New York Times* article that bruited newspaperless cities, Pelosi urged Holder to "allow free-market forces to preserve
as many news sources as possible." She urged him to take online
sources of news and advertising into consideration when the
Department of Justice calculated newspaper competition in the
Bay Area. "We must ensure that our policies enable our news organizations to survive and to engage in the news gathering and analysis that the American people expect."

> I am confident that the Antitrust Division, in assessing any con-
> cerns that any proposed mergers or other arrangements in the San
> Francisco area might reduce competition, will take into appropriate
> account, as relevant, not only the number of daily and weekly news-
> papers in the Bay Area, but also the other sources of news and adver-
> tising outlets available in the electronic and digital age, so that the
> conclusions reached reflect current market realities.[44]

While politicians in Washington, D.C., considered a bailout for
newspapers, legislators in Washington state took action to assist
them by cutting their business and occupation taxes by 40 percent
through 2015. The measure was estimated to provide newspapers
with more than $8 million in relief. Newspaper executives testi-
fied before the state senate's Ways and Means Committee that their
newsgathering efforts had been hindered by the recession. "Some
of us, like *The Seattle Times*, are literally holding on by our fingertips
today," said *Seattle Times* publisher Frank Blethen. The *Times* had cut
almost 500 positions in the previous year, ordered 500 managers
and non-union employees to take an unpaid week off, and asked its
unions to agree to contract concessions totaling 12 percent. "The
critical challenge that's facing us right now is how do we preserve
content, which also has been cut severely, and how do we preserve
jobs," Blethen said.[45]

Newspapers Without Advertisers

By summer, the calls for federal government action were increasing. In August, former CBS anchor Dan Rather called on Presi-

dent Obama to form a commission to address the perilous state of America's news media. "You don't have to care about media companies or reporters to care about the state of the news, because if it's in trouble — and it surely is — this country is in trouble," Rather wrote in a *Washington Post* column.[46]

Just how much trouble newspapers were in quickly became apparent with the release of advertising numbers by the Newspaper Association of America. The NAA had kept careful count of ad revenue flowing in to newspapers since 1950, and in the Internet age it had posted the amounts for classified, retail, and national advertising on its website every quarter for all to see. From 1975 to 2000, newspaper advertising as tracked by the NAA had increased almost sixfold, from $8.2 billion to $48.6 billion. It slipped somewhat during the recession of the early 2000s, but by 2006 it was still a healthy $46.6 billion. Starting in 2003, the NAA added a category for online advertising, and it soared for the first few years, increasing at rates around 30 percent annually. In 2007, however, print advertising fell 9.4 percent, led by a decline of 16.5 percent in classified ads. It was the largest annual decrease ever recorded by the NAA. The following year, the drop almost doubled, to 17.7 percent. By 2009 it more than tripled, and suddenly there was blood all over the floor. Even online advertising was in freefall that disastrous year, dropping by almost 12 percent while print advertising plummeted 28.6 percent. What was a $49 billion industry just four years earlier was by the end of 2009 a $27 billion industry. That put newspaper revenues back at their level in 1986, but blogger Ryan Chittum did a bit of math to adjust the numbers for inflation, which showed that the situation was even worse. "You have to go back to 1965 to find a year with revenue lower in 2009 dollars than what this year is projected to be," Chittum wrote on *CJR*'s news business blog The Audit. "That year, the industry took in $4.42 billion, which works out to $30.22 billion in current dollars."[47]

Martin Langeveld, a retired newspaper executive, saw the plummeting ad revenues as proof that the newspaper business was doomed if it didn't go digital. Langeveld started a blog he called News After Newspapers to chronicle the industry's demise. "Newspapers are in danger of dropping to a market share level from which no bounceback is possible," he wrote that August. An early convert to digital publishing, Langeveld saw online publication as the daily newspaper's only way out. In 2009, his blog was picked by Harvard University's newly created digital media think tank Nieman Journalism Lab. "Newspapers have stood by while many others have built a world of digital media and digital commerce," wrote Langeveld. "The time for newspapers to become digital news enterprises is now, and it's their only hope." [48]

Circulation Problems

By the time the semi-annual count of newspaper circulation was released in the fall of 2009, all indicators pointed to a full-on disaster for newspapers. Audit Bureau of Circulations figures showed that daily newspaper circulation dropped 10.6 percent in the U.S. from a year earlier, while Sunday circulation was down 7.4 percent. "The two-decade erosion in newspaper circulation is looking more like an avalanche," reported the *New York Times*. "Through the 1990s and into this decade, newspaper circulation was sliding, but by less than 1 percent a year," it noted "Then the rate of decline topped 2 percent in 2005, 3 percent in 2007 and 4 percent in 2008." [49] Some of America's leading dailies dropped the most in 2009:

San Francisco Chronicle	25.8 percent
Miami Herald	23.0 percent
Dallas Morning News	20.8 percent
Boston Globe	18.4 percent
USA Today	17.0 percent
Baltimore Sun	14.7 percent
Houston Chronicle	14.2 percent

Alan Mutter, a former newspaper editor and Silicon Valley CEO who tracked industry fortunes on his blog Reflections of a Newsosaur, questioned whether newspapers still qualified as a mass medium given their recent circulation declines. "Circulation now is lower than it was prior to World War II," he pointed out. "Newspapers today are purchased on average in only 33 out of every 100 American households, as compared with 98 homes in 1970 and 53 households as recently as 2000."

> Publishers who think their businesses are going to live or die according to the number of bellybuttons they can deliver probably will see their businesses die. . . . The undoing of newspapers has been under way for decades and should come as no surprise to anyone who has been paying attention.[50]

The *Columbia Journalism Review* commissioned two of the biggest names in the business to look into the crisis in the news media. Michael Schudson, a sociologist and newspaper historian, and Leonard Downie Jr., a former editor of the *Washington Post*, delivered their report that October. "Newspapers are the source of most local news reporting, which is why it is even more endangered than national, international or investigative reporting that might be provided by other sources," they wrote. Downie and Schudson suggested a range of remedies for what was ailing American journalism, including such innovative ideas as universities picking up some of the slack by getting into the news business. "They should operate their own news organizations, host platforms for other nonprofit news and investigative reporting organizations." They also suggested a national "Fund for Local News," to be paid for by a tax on broadcast licensees or Internet service providers and administered through state Local News Fund Councils.

> Most Americans have a deep distrust of direct government involvement or political influence in independent news reporting, a sentiment we share. But this should not preclude government support for news reporting any more than it has for the arts, the humanities, and sciences, all of which receive some government support.[51]

Mr. Murdoch Goes to Washington

The Federal Trade Commission (FTC) convened hearings in December to examine the perilous state of the news industry.

Some of the biggest names in the media testified, including argu-ably the world's most powerful media mogul, News Corp. boss Rupert Murdoch. "The old business model based mainly on adver-tising is dead," Murdoch told the FTC, and his newly-acquired *Wall Street Journal* reprinted his testimony. "The old model was founded on quasimonopolies such as classified advertising, which has been decimated by new and cheaper competitors such as Craig-slist, Monster.com, and so on."[52] Murdoch also urged the FTC to re-think its cross-ownership prohibition.

> If you are a newspaper today, your competition is not necessarily the TV station in the same city. It can be a Web site on the other side of the world, or even an icon on someone's cell phone. . . . In this new and more globally competitive news world, restricting cross-ownership between television and newspapers makes as little sense as would banning newspapers from having Web sites.[53]

The FTC considered the situation so serious that it convened more hearings in early 2010. In March, it held a two-day sympo-sium called "The Future of Journalism: Is it Time for a Bailout?" Among the speakers was McChesney, who had turned his maga-zine article, co-authored with John Nichols, into a book titled *The Death and Life of American Journalism*. "Journalism as we know it, and to the extent we need it, it will never be profitable again," they warned.[54] In their view, newspapers were in need of government help to navigate their way to a post-corporate ownership form. "We are dealing with a failing industry. It has no viable business model." Their prescription for saving journalism called for $35 bil-lion a year in government assistance. McChesney's testimony to the FTC outlined some of the measures he thought government should take. "There may be an important role for the private sector, but with public goods the government plays quarterback or the game never starts," he said. "We should launch a 'Write for Amer-ica' or 'News AmeriCorps' type program to subsidize thousands of young journalists for a year or two after college working for news media around the country."[54]

The FTC issued a report outlining some of the possible measures government could take to deal with the crisis. "Newspapers have not yet found a new, sustainable business model, and there is reason for concern that such a business model may not emerge," it stated. "Therefore, it is not too soon to start considering policies that might encourage innovations to help support journalism into the future."[56] Included were ideas such as imposing a 5 percent tax on consumer electronics to provide an estimated $4 billion annually to help fund the news; imposing a tax on broadcasters to assist newspapers; and providing tax credits to newspaper companies based on the number of journalists they employed. The reaction was predictably outraged. "I find it dangerous for government to have a role in speech because the government gives and the government taketh away," Jeff Jarvis told Fox News. "It's a power grab by the FTC and it's also an example of one old power structure circling its wagons around another."

> No one is going to support a tax to support old newspapers. They're talking about the future of journalism, but they only talk about the past of journalism. They equate journalism with newspapers strictly. It's too soon to give up on the market, which is what the FTC is doing. Everything you see in that document is an attempt to stifle new competition by sustaining the incumbents.[57]

Jarvis, a journalism professor at the City University of New York, was an ardent advocate of online journalism. He took to his influential blog BuzzMachine to give the FTC's report a big thumbs down. "If the FTC truly wanted to reinvent journalism, the agency would instead align itself with journalism's disruptors," buzzed Jarvis. "But there's none of that here. The clearest evidence: the word 'blog' is used but once in 35 pages of text and then only parenthetically."[58] The FTC quickly issued a press release pointing out that it wasn't actually recommending any of the options outlined in its report. "The FTC has not endorsed the idea of making any policy recommendation or recommended any of the proposals in the discussion draft," it noted. "Recent press reports have erroneously stated that the FTC is supporting and proposing some of the public comments (for example, taxes on electronic devices, favoring one medium over another)."[59]

'Burn the Boats'

There was no shortage of suggestions on how to save newspapers. Most techies urged publishers to abandon print for digital-only publication. Some did so more stridently than others. "Burn the boats," bellowed software pioneer Marc Andreessen on his blog New York Times Deathwatch, invoking Spanish conquistador Hernan Cortes, who torched his fleet upon reaching the New World so there could be no turning back. The Netscape founder urged the *Times* to quit print publication cold turkey for the brave new world of the Internet. "Take acute pain now in order to avoid years of chronic pain," Andreessen advised.[60] Short of a government bailout, others urged government to at least cut newspapers a regulatory break. John Chachas, the investment banker who warned of imminent doom for the newspaper business, was among many who called for "urgent and long overdue regulatory relief" from government. Restrictions preventing the merger of local dailies or preventing newspapers from owning TV stations should be ditched, he argued. Anti-trust laws were "antiquated" in dealing with media competition, he added, as they considered only old media in calculating the diversity of "voices" in a market. "This is nonsense," railed Chachas. "It is as if regulators went to sleep during the Eisenhower administration and woke up staring blankly at an iPhone."[61]

In the halls of academe, there was similar hand wringing. Innumerable conferences on the future of news were convened, with almost all agreeing that print on paper had run its course. The loudest scholarly voices for some reason boomed out from Big Apple universities. "Newspapers should have planned for the date when they would turn off their presses so they would reinvent themselves," argued Jarvis in a *Los Angeles Times* column. "They didn't."[62] Perhaps most influential of all, however, was a much-reprinted doomsday scenario by New York University's Clay

Shirky. His blog entry was ominously titled "Newspapers and thinking the unthinkable." To Shirky, the economics of newspapers had been "destroyed" because the Internet had provided a lost-cost solution to the expensive problem of printing and distribution. "There is no general model for newspapers to replace the one the internet just broke," he wrote. "With the old economics destroyed, organizational forms perfected for industrial production have to be replaced with structures optimized for digital data."[63]

There was only one problem amidst all the punditry. Newspapers didn't go away. They just kept publishing, and publishing, and publishing. They were admittedly publishing slimmed-down versions of the corpulent editions they had produced before technological change and the financial crisis took their toll. But anyone who cared to examine their financial reports in detail, deaf to the hype and the headlines, could only marvel at their ability to downsize in the face of their plummeting revenues and thus keep their heads above water, albeit often gasping for air.

TWO

A Funny Thing Happened
on the Way to the Funeral

Despite the rampant predictions of imminent doom for the industry in 2009, no major North American newspaper exited print publication after the *Rocky Mountain News* and *Seattle Post-Intelligencer* did so in March 2009. The *Tucson Citizen*, the oldest continuously-published newspaper in Arizona, was folded by Gannett in May of that year, but its circulation had fallen to 17,000 from a peak of 60,000 in the 1960s. An afternoon newspaper, it had been propped up for years by a joint operating agreement (JOA) with the morning *Arizona Daily Star*, whose circulation was almost ten times higher. The closest thing to the closure of a major daily was the merger in June 2010 of the dominant *Honolulu Advertiser* and its JOA partner, the *Star-Bulletin*, a struggling tabloid with a circulation of 37,000. Mergers between metropolitan dailies had been a trend for more than a century, however, and the *Star-Bulletin* had been on life support for years. By mid-2010, the clock was ticking down on *Time*'s online prediction that several of the top U.S. dailies could go out of business within eighteen months. Some newspaper people had obviously circled that date on their calendars. "As the 18-month mark approaches, *Time* is not exactly batting 1.000," pointed out *Buffalo News* editor Margaret Sullivan. "More like zero."

Perhaps the magazine had the timetable right — something would happen to newspapers in the next year or so — but the story wrong: Rather than going out of business, many newspapers are beginning to right themselves.[1]

Some claimed that closure of the 45,000-circulation Ann Arbor News in July 2009 fulfilled the prophecy that a major U.S. city would soon lose its last daily newspaper. "Ann Arbor has become the first American city of any size to lose its only full-time daily," lamented Chicago Tribune columnist Eric Zorn when the newspaper he delivered as a boy, which had been in business since 1835, cut back to twice-weekly publication. Zorn was arguably wrong on two counts, however. He and others ignored the fact that a very successful daily newspaper still published in that college town. The 18,000-circulation Michigan Daily at the University of Michigan did a roaring business selling ads catering to the town's dominant demographic. With a population of 114,000 and located forty-five miles from Detroit, Ann Arbor better qualified as a suburb than a city, but it fit almost perfectly the description of what newspaper economists called a "satellite city." Newspapers that were published where people actually lived (and shopped) had flourished in satellite cities at the expense of major dailies published in metropolises where people worked, but had been moving out of for years.

Advance Publications, owner of the News, decided to take a different tack than simply closing the newspaper, as had been done in other cities, or going online-only, as the Seattle P-I had. Instead it sent the News to a special kind of purgatory as an online publication with a print appendage. Advance, which was the tenth-largest media firm in the U.S., announced it would henceforth publish news online at AnnArbor.com, supplemented by a twice-weekly print publication, which would oddly also be titled AnnArbor.com. The new publication was pointedly called a "print product," not a newspaper.[2] "This is an extremely wired, high-tech community that we think is ready for a completely different news and information model," Steve Newhouse, head of digital operations for

Advance, told Zorn when he visited his hometown to investigate.[3] The new venture had fifty-six full-time employees, roughly half of them holdovers from the *News*, and they were paid about 30 percent less than reporters and editors had earned at the daily newspaper. Advance, which owned eight dailies in economically depressed Michigan, announced it was cutting print publication to three days a week at three of them — the *Flint Journal*, the *Saginaw News*, and the *Bay City Times*. Editing and production work for its four remaining Michigan dailies — the *Jackson Citizen Patriot*, the *Grand Rapids Press*, the *Kalamazoo Gazette* and the *Muskegon Chronicle* — would be consolidated in Grand Rapids.

A year later, much had changed, both in Ann Arbor and in the newspaper business. Zorn again returned to his hometown to investigate how the new digital reality was working out there. What had once looked like "a sharp turn on a rocky road to an all-digital future for print news," quipped Zorn, twelve months later looked "more like a small fork." Web traffic to Annarbor.com had increased considerably, but the Sunday newspaper, admitted an Advance executive, was still "the single biggest revenue driver for us, and will be for the foreseeable future." The newspaper business remained in transition, noted Zorn, but predictions of its imminent demise had faded against the obvious persistence of print publication. "The funeral knells have quieted and struggling publications are riding the improving economy out of bankruptcy and into the black." Zorn checked with Erica Smith of the Paper Cuts blog to see how employment in the industry was faring. "Layoffs have slowed dramatically and the papers that have closed this year were very small to start with," she told him. "The dire predictions haven't come true."[4]

In 2013, even as Advance made news across the country by cutting back publication frequency at its newspapers in New Orleans, Cleveland, and Portland, Oregon, it backtracked slightly on its strategy in Ann Arbor. The name *Ann Arbor News* was restored to its newspaper there, which still came out twice weekly. The Ann-Arbor.com website disappeared and its content was folded into MLive.com, Advance's website for its other Michigan newspapers.

"Integrating Ann Arbor with its other media properties across the state enables MLive Media Group to leverage our unified strengths," announced MLive president Dan Geode, "ultimately offering readers a better news experience, both online and in print." Others saw the move for what it was — another example of Advance backing down in the face of outrage across the country from its newspaper readers and even advertisers, who felt robbed of their daily newsprint fix. "You can think of this as the latest iteration of Advance's multi-state, multi-year efforts to manage a move away from seven-day print publication," noted Caroline O'Donovan on the Nieman Journalism Lab website. "What was different in Ann Arbor was abandoning the print brand entirely. Now that's reversing."[5]

Newspaper Stocks On the Rise

Newspaper stocks began to rally in mid-2009 after earnings reports showed that drastic cost cutting had achieved its desired effect of preserving profit levels. Earnings at all newspapers were markedly lower as a result of the recession, but they were all still nicely profitable. Not only were they all still in the black, some were well into the black. The profit levels of most remained in the double digits, with some even topping 20 percent. That was a comedown from previous decades, which had seen newspaper profits routinely over 20 percent and in some cases even into the 30- and 40-percent range. But despite their uncanny ability to remain profitable, newspaper companies were diminished by falling revenues and earnings, which in the U.S. were more than cut in half in only five years.

The historic downturn in advertising revenues was due only in part to the 2007–2009 financial crisis. A "secular" shift of advertising dollars away from print publications to the Internet also contributed to the drastic drop in newspaper revenues. As a result of their reduced revenues, newspapers simply became smaller businesses with fewer employees and often smaller premises. That didn't mean they were dying, however. It meant they were adapting. Their ability to adapt, in fact, suggested that they would continue to remain in business and to publish in print. It turned out that the business model for print advertising, even at lower levels of revenue, was more profitable than the business model for online news media. The economics of online publishing, in fact, were not promising at all.

A comprehensive review done for this book of annual earnings reports filed by all sixteen publicly-traded newspaper companies in the U.S. and Canada from 2006 through 2013 shows that none suffered an annual operating loss during this period. The Washington Post Company came close, but given the arcane nature of its annual reports, it was hard to tell just how close. Parsing the financial statements of some newspaper companies was like reading tea leaves. Most reported their earnings in a straightforward way in the standardized format of EBITDA: earnings before interest, taxes, depreciation, and amortization. Also known as "operating earnings," EBITDA is the measure most investors rely on to determine the value of a company — how much revenue it took in, minus its operating expenses equals its annual earnings. Extraordinary expenses are usually left out of the equation in order to determine how profitable the business is to operate. The way that companies presented their earnings in financial reports was hardly standard, however. Some deducted from their earnings such charges as amortization of property purchases and depreciation on plant and equipment, so those had to be added back on to earnings to determine EBITDA. The Washington Post Company, a conglomerate whose namesake newspaper was actually the least of its holdings, even cryptically listed pension expenses and capital expenditures after its earnings. (See Appendix.) WaPoCo's earnings were boosted for years by its Kaplan test preparation arm until those revenues also went south in 2012 after for-profit education was regulated.[5A]

News reports of the huge losses that were supposedly being incurred by some newspaper companies were similarly confused. They were often misleading because they included large "paper" losses that were simply an estimated decrease in the value of the business, which was called a "writedown" or "asset impairment."

In the newspaper business, this was often referred to as "masthead impairment," which conjured a delicious metaphor for how they were coping because a newspaper's masthead was where its senior executives and editors were listed. More revenue still flowed into their companies in the form of revenues than flowed out in expenses, however, which is the very definition of profit.

A review of the financial statements of selected newspaper companies in other countries showed they also remained profitable, despite falling advertising revenues, rampant predictions of their demise, and no small amount of whinging. Most newspaper companies, in fact, were still recording double-digit profit margins, or more than twice the historical average for Fortune 500 companies of 4.7 percent. Some companies with newspapers in smaller markets that weren't as affected by online competitors seemed to barely notice the historic downturn in the economy and continued to make profits in excess of 20 percent, as the newspaper contagion was mostly confined to large metropolitan dailies. Of the 1,400 or so daily newspapers in the U.S., about 1,300 of them continued to flourish despite the recession because they published in smaller markets where the Internet had not taken as much of their advertising.[6] In fact, it seemed that the smaller the market, the better a newspaper's prospects were. An estimated 7,500 non-daily newspapers were published in the U.S., many in rural areas, and they mostly continued to thrive.[7]

Gannett, which served as a bellwether of sorts due to its enormous size and a commitment to quarterly earnings that once made it the darling of Wall Street, led the recovery in U.S. newspaper stocks. Its share price had fallen below $2 in March 2009, when the doom and gloom about newspapers was at its worst. But when its second-quarter earnings report beat expectations that July, due mainly to the 5,500 jobs Gannett had cut since 2007, its stock jumped 29 percent in one day to $4.50.[8] Its share price was back up to $10 by September when it issued an estimate of its third-quarter earnings that came in well above the expectations of analysts; its share price shot up another 17 percent in one day. Other newspaper stocks were also buoyed by the rising tide of optimism for the industry. Lee Enterprises, which had been in danger of being de-listed from the NYSE because its share price languished below $1 after having traded above $49 in 2004, saw its stock gain 48 percent in one morning, to $3.17.[9] Lee perhaps best exemplified the paradox the newspaper business was becoming. It remained highly profitable through the 2007–2009 financial crisis and accompanying recession, racking up operating margins between 19.8 percent and 24.8 percent from 2006 to 2012, but because its revenues and earnings fell by 40–45 percent during the period, it was in danger of defaulting on its debt and having to declare bankruptcy. Profitability could be deceiving, because it represented a ratio — earnings over revenues — without regard for the magnitude of either. As a business, Lee was very much a going concern, if only it could stay in business. If it couldn't, it would change owners and continue to publish profitable newspapers.

By 2010, newspaper stocks were firmly on the incline, ranking among the market's best performers. "Yes, papers face declining circulations, particularly among the young," wrote stock analyst Dirk Van Dijk in giving both Gannett and the New York Times Co. a top rating. "They are, however, often local monopolies, and advertisers still find them useful."

> While they may never return to their glory days, that doesn't mean that they are all going to go extinct in the near future, either. Most have greatly reduced their costs over the last year, so just a small pick up in revenue should lead to large gains on the bottom line.[10]

In September 2012, a columnist for the popular investment website TheStreet.com wrote a contrarian analysis titled "I'd Rather Own Gannett Than Facebook" that pointed to the newspaper giant's solid fundamentals. "The company wisely cleaned up its balance sheet and paid down debt, which now stands at just under $1.7 billion," noted Jonathan Heller. "The quarterly dividend, which had been cut to 4 cents from 40 cents in early 2009, has been raised back to 20 cents, for a solid 4.9% yield."[11] Ten months later, Heller revisited his prediction to find that shares in Gannett had indeed outpaced those of the social network, gaining 52 percent in value compared to Facebook's 19 percent. "While Facebook has grabbed the headlines, Gannett has quietly gone about its business, successfully resurrecting a company that looked like it might go under just four years ago."[12] By then, *NewsInc.*'s index of newspaper stocks had gained more than 60 percent in a year, triple the increase of the stock market as a whole. Gannett led the way, rising 77 percent to top $26, although it was still down by more than two-thirds from its 2005 high. Lee Enterprises was back from the dead by mid-2013, up more than 300 percent since late 2011 after going through Chapter 11 bankruptcy proceedings.[13]

Doomsayers Have Second Thoughts

Soon the London-based *Economist* magazine, which had been one of the first mainstream news media outlets to pump the doomsday scenario for dailies in 2006 by screaming "Who Killed the Newspaper?" in ransom-note lettering across its cover,[14] had to admit it had been wrong. By 2010, it was forced to recognize what it called the "strange survival" of ink on newsprint. In Europe, where newspapers were less dependent on advertising for revenue, the crisis had been relatively mild. German publisher Axel Springer even recorded the best first quarter in its history in 2010, and the profit margin on its national newspapers was a stunning 27 percent. Elsewhere in the world, the economic downturn had barely caused the profitable press to pause. "In emerging markets one must look hard to find any sign of crisis at all," noted the *Economist*.[15] In fact, research showed that newspapers were doing very well in other countries. "In sharp contrast to the vanishing newspapers in the United States, among other countries, China and India's newspaper markets are thriving," noted one 2010 study.[16] All of which proved, the *Economist* admitted, that the prognosis for newspapers was a lot better than it had once thought. "The recession brought out an impressive and unexpected ability to adapt," it concluded. "If newspapers can keep that up in better times, they may be able to contemplate more than mere survival."[17] It turned out that, because of some peculiarities of the business there, newspapers were really only on the endangered list in the U.S. Their business model proved sufficiently robust, however, that some tweaking resulted in a much brighter outlook.

Even the crypt keeper at Newspaper Death Watch had to admit in 2010 that "setting fire to profitable print operations is the wrong strategy at the moment." Paul Gillin was forced to confess that the moves newspaper publishers had made, from aggressive cover price increases to reductions in discounted circulation, were "turning paying subscribers into a profit engine." The business model that many claimed was "broken" actually turned out to be fairly robust, which was the reason Gillin's R.I.P. list stubbornly refused to grow. "After years of fretting over declining circulation and trying desperately to rejuvenate a dying business, newspaper publishers are finally adopting an intelligent strategy," he noted. But despite all the evidence, Gillin remained skeptical about the long-term prognosis for print on newsprint. "They're milking all they can from their profitable business while trying to manage it down to a level that new models can take over."[18] Declining circulation, which many took as an indicator of imminent doom for newspapers, actually turned out to be a way for them to manage the downturn in advertising revenues.

Far-flung readers tend to be of little interest to local advertisers, and are more expensive for publishers to reach. With advertising melting away, it no longer made sense to truck copies to small towns and satellite cities far from downtown. As a result, publishers deliberately cut back on their circulation by reducing their geographic "footprint" and eliminated many of the promotional copies given away or sold at bulk discounts.[19] In the upside-down economics of the newspaper business, publishers lost money on every copy they sold in the expectation of making it all back — and more — in advertising. Without as much revenue from ads, however, they sought to make up the difference by not only cutting back on printing and distribution, but also by charging readers more. The San Francisco Chronicle, for example, raised its home delivery rate from $4.75 a week to $7.75 in 2009, while the Dallas Morning News hiked its monthly subscription price from $21 to $30. Both newspapers also cut back on distribution. "There are places we used to truck it like Modesto, Lake Tahoe, that we don't, because quite frankly, that's not a market that local advertisers care about," said *Chronicle* president Mark Adkins. The *Dallas Morning News* similarly adopted a policy of not delivering outside a hundred-mile radius.[20]

Media economists had long noted the "elasticity" of demand for newspapers, which meant that readers were usually willing to pay a bit more for their copy. Raising cover prices would thus increase total revenue because relatively few readers would cancel their subscription. "Subscribers are sticking with their papers for longer — and frequently paying more," reported *Advertising Age* in October 2009. "The cancellation rate for newspaper subscribers has plunged pretty incredibly, to 31.8 percent last year from 54.5 percent in 2000 and from 36.6 percent in 2006."[21] That's because newspapers had stopped going after casual subscribers, who tended to cancel and re-subscribe promiscuously in a phenomenon known as "churn." The bigger the newspaper, the bigger the churn of subscribers.[22] Publishers had previously pursued even fickle subscribers ardently with inducements in an attempt to increase their circulation and thus their advertising rates. Instead, they began to focus on their more reliable core readership and saved money on both promotions and television advertising.

The extent to which U.S. newspapers had come to rely on advertising revenue was illustrated by a 2010 report that showed newspapers around the world derived about 57 percent of their revenues from advertising on average. In the U.S., however, newspapers took in 87 percent of their revenue from advertising, which was 10 percentage points higher than in any other country and more than twice what it was in Japan, where newspapers received only 35 percent of their total revenues from advertising.[23] Led by a doubling in classifieds, the percentage of revenue derived from advertising at U.S. newspapers had increased from 71 percent in 1956 to 82 percent in 2000, according to media economist Robert Picard.[24] The boom in advertising that fuelled the newspaper bubble in the U.S. encouraged publishers to sell as many copies as far and wide as they could in order to maximize their ad rates, which were based on circulation. Newspapers became "structurally dependent on sky-high advertising rates," noted the *Columbia Journalism Review* in 2014.

> In [the recession year of] 1990, for instance, newspapers lost more than 6 percent of their ad lineage but also raised their ad rates by more than 6 percent. The *New York Times*, for instance, lost 38 percent of its advertising lineage from 1987 to 1992 but continued to raise rates.[25]

Now that their advertising bubble had burst, newspapers had to take measures to realign their business model. Charging readers more was designed to address the imbalance between advertising and circulation revenues and help restore U.S. dailies to health. Many newspapers also decided to stop giving away their content for free online and instituted "paywalls" designed to not only raise more revenue, but also to stem the tide of readers quitting the print product for the less profitable digital edition.

A Financial Nightmare

In the U.S., where the crisis hit hardest, most newspapers were still nicely profitable even if their owners often couldn't keep their heads above water due to all the debt they had taken on in making ill-timed acquisitions. The newspapers themselves were still making money, just not as much as they once had. With tumbling ad revenues, some newspaper owners weren't making enough to pay the interest on their loans, however. Taking on debt to finance acquisitions had once been a sure-fire way to grow a newspaper company, or almost any business in a growth industry. Newspapers were no longer a growth industry — quite the opposite. In most of the developed world, newspapers had entered a phase of rapid contraction, but that didn't mean they were going out of business. Newspapers once generated so much cash flow that in the U.S. re-investing some of it in buying more newspapers was a good way to avoid paying income tax because of the way tax laws were interpreted there. A bank could usually be convinced to loan most of the money needed to buy a publication, or even a string of them. After all, newspapers had only ever gone up in value, never down. That's because advertising revenues had only ever gone up, not down. Sometimes they went down for a while during a recession, but they always went back up again when the economy improved. Until this time.

While newspapers were usually able to pare their expenses below the level of their plunging revenues and remain profitable, their revenues and earnings had undeniably been reduced. That meant newspapers as businesses were worth less. Not worthless, just worth less than they had once been worth. This caused much confusion and led to widespread predictions of the imminent demise of newspapers as a medium. Accounting rules require publicly traded companies to regularly recalculate the value of their business. If revenues and earnings went down appreciably, that meant that the value of the business went down, because the price an investor would pay for it was usually based on its annual earnings. Selling prices of companies were typically five to ten times its annual earnings. In a growth industry, in which earnings could be expected to increase, it might be more than ten times. In the Internet bubble of the late 1990s, startup tech companies that had never earned a cent sold for millions. In the contracting newspaper industry, expectations were instead that earnings would continue to decrease, which saw some newspaper companies sold for little more than the value of their real estate.

In the arcane world of accounting, any decrease in calculated company value has to come off the books somehow. The company's value is recorded on its balance sheet of assets and liabilities, but any reduction has to be noted in the annual profit and loss statement as an extraordinary loss over and above that year's operating earnings or loss. Other extraordinary items, such as a loss on the sale of an asset, or the cost of downsizing the workforce by making severance payments to laid-off workers, are similarly noted. They are not, however, regular expenses incurred in the company's operations and so do not count against its operating profits. Thus a company could have very healthy annual earnings, but because the calculated value of the business has decreased or other extraordinary expenses have been incurred, a net loss has to be recorded·on its account books. For newspaper companies, this often amounted to hundreds of millions of dollars and overshadowed a company's otherwise profitable year. A multi-million-dollar operating profit could this way turn into a hundred-million-dollar net loss, but only on paper. The sensational nature of the reported annual loss, however, is what news media reports typically focused on.

A 2012 study of coverage of the newspaper crisis by the three national U.S. dailies from 2008–2010 found that it focused overwhelmingly on dramatic year-over-year declines rather than providing a more historical perspective. "Some coverage has exaggerated the scale of the newspaper crisis and ignored the historical context for this phenomenon, creating a false impression that the whole industry is 'dying,'" the study concluded. "Without the proper context, readers might have been led to believe that newspapers were 'dying' . . . when in fact they are doing well in small U.S. markets and even flourishing in many parts of the developing world and among certain age groups."[26] The analysis of coverage in the Wall Street Journal, USA Today, and New York Times found it contained "over-amped drama" and even "tabloidization," with more than a quarter of all stories containing death imagery. "Newspaper journalists often fail to contextualize their reports with a comprehensive understanding of the economics of their industry," noted the study. "They rely too heavily on the views of newspaper publishers and too little on empirical data."

> This was particularly apparent in the extensive coverage given to the shutdowns at the Rocky Mountain News, Seattle Post-Intelligencer, and (to a lesser extent) Tucson Citizen. While these might be noteworthy incidents, the closure of a second newspaper in a city is nothing new. . . . Moreover, the trend toward monopoly actually has contributed to increased newspaper profitability.[27]

Almost two-thirds of the New York Times articles on the Newspaper Crisis were written by one reporter, the researchers noted, "indicating the larger-than-anticipated influence one single journalist may have on the framing of a major issue." The study mused that newspapers perhaps exaggerated the crisis in their own industry in part because it "hit home" for journalists personally. "This might suggest, for instance, that reporters covering the crisis have been influenced by the personal relevance and 'human drama' of fellow journalists being laid off and forced to say 'goodbye to the news.'"[28] Critical scholars who looked at political and economic aspects of news media had long noted a tendency for publishers to over-dramatize any financial challenges facing their industry, usually as a way to win favorable treatment from government. In this way, publishers were often able to turn threats into opportunities and make their businesses even more profitable than before. Producing a daily account of reality turned out to be a valuable way to win political favors.

The Financialization of Newspapers

When the plunging value of a newspaper company became less than what it owed, its lenders usually stepped in, took over the business, and tried to sell it to recover as much of the debt as possible. But little about the newspaper crisis of 2008–10 was business as usual. In the new, highly "financialized" world of speculative investment instruments, corporate debt had itself become an object of investment. Hedge funds and other investors that specialized in preying on distressed companies often bought the debt of over-leveraged newspaper owners from the original lenders at pennies on the dollar. By doing so, they could often engineer what the *Chicago Tribune*, in dissecting the painful and prolonged bankruptcy of its own parent company in 2013, described as a "bargain-priced backdoor takeover."[29] In part, "vulture capitalists" such as Alden Global Capital, Oaktree, and Angelo Gordon were betting that newspapers had a profitable future and that their investment would eventually pay off handsomely.

The *modus operandi* of these bottom feeders was to cut costs as much as possible to make a company's quarterly profit-and-loss statement appear as favorable as possible, then sell it to a new owner for a tidy profit. But costs had often already been cut to the bone at many newspapers, and cutting them further risked producing a product few would care to consume. Even these savvy investors, however, found that they couldn't quickly "flip" their newly-acquired newspapers for a profit and were thus forced to hold on to them until the economy picked up. Often these opportunists faced off in bankruptcy court, relying on high-priced specialty lawyers and professional witnesses to see who could get the biggest slice and thus control of a company. Bankruptcy itself even became an investment instrument, with bondholders and other "preferred" creditors taking part of what they were owed as equity in the reorganized company, and part as reduced debt. If the value of the business continued to sink below what they were still owed, another bankruptcy could be arranged. Some newspaper companies became serial bankrupts, shedding legal obligations such as taxes and pension commitments each time in so-called "strategic" bankruptcies and even emerging on the other side of the Chapter 11 process still owned by the same hedge funds.

The nightmare that visited newspaper companies and their dwindling workforces during the crisis was a microcosm of the financial shenanigans that visited the investment world as a whole and brought on the 2007–09 financial crisis and attendant downturn. The profitability and political influence of newspapers had made them favorites of Wall Street starting in the 1960s, and their "financialization" as investment instruments was symptomatic of the contagion afflicting the system. Newspapers had become the darling of investors because of their high profit margins, which could usually be raised even higher by cost-cutting and increasingly centralized management. What had usually started as small, independent family businesses often ended up being sold by the founder's heirs to large newspaper chains, which raised capital to finance these acquisitions by borrowing and/or selling shares on the stock market. In a perverse push-pull phenomenon, high estate taxes in the U.S. encouraged newspaper heirs to sell at the same time that tax advantages encouraged chains to buy. So-called "public" ownership by listed companies was something of a misnomer, however. Most shares were owned not by members of the public at large but instead by the investor class that made up the "1 percent" vilified by the Occupy Wall Street movement. The trading of shares on stock markets also made newspaper companies subject to the short-term whims of the marketplace and created pressure for ever-increasing earnings to continually inflate the company's stock price. Any commitment to expensive quality journalism was replaced by a "fiduciary" duty to shareholders that saw publishers legally obligated to instead prioritize the financial bottom line. Editors at publicly-traded newspaper companies as a result reported corporate pressure to fatten quarterly earnings, usually by cutting back on journalism by laying off reporters.[30]

The financial success of newspapers was arguably the worst thing that ever happened to them.

The Best-Kept Secret in Newspapering

Even in the face of new competition from online media, the business model for newspapers was far from broken. It had proved robust enough to weather a recession, as long as the owner wasn't foolish enough to get overextended with debt. Newspapers had endured recessions for decades, cutting staff when things got tough and hiring when the economy improved. Rather than the beginning (or middle) of the end for newspapers, the short spate of closures in 2009 was simply a continuation of industry trends that had been ongoing for decades. "Newspapers are solvent and profitable, often quite profitable on an operating basis," noted Rick Edmonds of the Poynter Institute in late 2010. "Only a handful went out of business during the great recession."[32] Others were less tactful when the "death of newspapers" meme turned out to be bogus, such as former Merrill Lynch analyst Henry Blodget. "All this hand-wringing about the 'death of journalism' and the need for 'newspaper bailouts' is just a crock of self-serving b.s.," he wrote on his website Business Insider after the New York Times Co. reported solid financial results in mid-2010.[33]

Metropolitan dailies had been dying for years due to something economists called the "circulation spiral," but that only made the survivors more profitable. Monopoly newspapers had long been cash machines due to their ability to raise advertising and circulation rates without fear of competition. Only the largest cities were eventually able to support more than one daily newspaper, and the recession had dropped Seattle, Denver, Cincinnati, Albuquerque, Honolulu, Tucson, and others from that list. "The only thing notable about these closings . . . is that the papers lasted as long as they did," said industry analyst John Morton. "Weaker newspapers in two-paper markets have been shutting down for more than 50 years."[34] The newspaper crisis was more like a culling of the herd than the extinction of a species. In fact, for the newspapers that survived, prospects actually appeared fairly bright. "I think the crisis can have a positive impact," Axel Springer CEO Mathias Döpfner told the New York Times. "The number of players will diminish, but the strong players may be stabler after the crisis."[35] In Seattle, for example, the elimination of print competition from the Post-Intelligencer had boosted the surviving daily quite nicely. "The Times has improved its prospects by picking up most P-I subscribers and managing to keep them so far," noted the New York Times a few months later. "It says its daily circulation rose more than 30 percent, to more than 260,000 in June, from about 200,000. . . . Times executives say that of those former P-I subscriptions that have expired, 84 percent have been renewed."[36] As for the online-only P-I, without a print edition its pageviews fell by 23 percent.[37]

Newspapers weren't in danger of extinction. Newspaper competition was. This was nothing new, but it showed the power of the press over public perceptions. Even as dailies consolidated and became more profitable in the 1960s, publishers somehow managed to convince lawmakers that the disappearance of competition meant newspapers were an endangered species in need of protection. In the U.S., that brought regulatory relief in the form of the Newspaper Preservation Act of 1970, an anti-trust exemption that then-president Richard Nixon vowed he would never sign while campaigning for the White House. As Ben Bagdikian chronicled in his landmark 1983 book The Media Monopoly, Nixon was lobbied heavily by newspaper publishers to grant them an anti-trust exemption similar to that enjoyed by owners of baseball teams. Newspapers had since the 1930s been entering into local joint operating agreements, under which two dailies shared office buildings, printing presses, and delivery trucks, with one publishing in the morning and the other in the afternoon. The arrangements typically saw the newspapers set their advertising rates and subscription prices jointly, then split the profits. After a U.S. Supreme Court ruling in 1969 found such arrangements illegal, Nixon gave in and granted newspapers an anti-trust exemption. Perhaps not coincidentally, Bagdikian noted, Nixon received the highest modern level of newspaper endorsements for re-election in 1972, despite his unprecedented use of prior restraint against the press in the Pentagon Papers case and a simmering Watergate scandal.[38]

Bagdikian, who was dean of the Graduate School of Journalism at the University of California at Berkeley, had long cast a critical eye on the newspaper business. He had been an editor at the *Washington Post* in 1971 when Daniel Ellsberg leaked the Pentagon Papers outlining the origins of the Vietnam War. After the government went to court to prevent the *New York Times* from publishing the secret documents, Bagdikian obtained them for the *Post* and had a sympathetic congressman read them into the record. He first identified what he called the "myth of newspaper poverty" in a 1973 article for the *Columbia Journalism Review.* "American publishers have always felt obligated to pretend that they are an auxiliary of the Little Sisters of the Poor," he wrote. "This was always amusing, but now that so many papers are owned by publicly traded companies which have to disclose their finances it is taking on the air of slapstick." Publicly, noted Bagdikian, publishers complained about rising costs. "Privately most have had a different kind of problem: how to get rid of profits." Persistent inflation in the early 1970s had led to government controls on profits, wages, and prices, and newspapers had to be careful to fly under the radar. "Gannett plants [have] been painting everything in sight in a crash program to soak up profits that exceed guidelines," noted Bagdikian.

In an almost unprecedented move for newspapers, the Harris papers in Kansas, Iowa, and California actually reduced advertising rates, though their circulation trends didn't force them to; otherwise their profits would have been beyond limits designated by the Government. [39]

Tough economic times in the early 1970s caused newspaper publishers to complain loudly of financial woe, which was used to justify cutbacks in hiring. "This is mostly hogwash," wrote Bagdikian. "American daily newspapers are one of the most profitable of all major industries in the United States. And they were during the 1970-71-72 'Great Recession.'" Precise figures on newspaper profits were hard to come by, noted Bagdikian, because "of all industries, newspaper publishing is the most obsessed by financial secrecy." The increased ownership of newspapers by publicly-traded companies, however, had opened a window into the hitherto secretive world of newspaper finances. A typical metropolitan daily with a circulation of 250,000 was very profitable, noted Bagdikian, even in the depths of a recession. "In 1970 such papers showed a pre-tax profit of 23.5 per cent. In 1971 it was 23.2 per cent [and] authorities agree that 1972 will be better than 1971."[40]

Some long-publishing second-place newspapers had been dying off, noted Bagdikian, which fueled the poverty myth pushed by publishers. Local newspaper competition was in the midst of its historic extinction, but the survivors would prove to be more profitable than ever. Far from being unprofitable, according to Bagdikian, newspaper owners instead became faced with the problem of what to do with their overflowing coffers. Reinvesting as much as possible in acquisitions became the preferred method of dealing with excess profits, which according to Bagdikian was "fueling an already frantic race to acquire communications properties."

Some independent publishers no longer attend the annual ANPA [American Newspaper Publishers Association] meeting because they must spend all their time resisting the embraces of the big chain paper-buyers. One small publisher said he felt "like a virgin stumbling into a stag party."[41]

Bagdikian's suspicions had been aroused a few years earlier after a Senate committee in Canada that was investigating the mass media forced companies to open their books. Its three-volume report described what it found as "astonishing" — media owners were making enormous profits. From 1958 to 1967, before-tax profits at Canadian newspapers ranged from 23.4 percent to 30.5 percent. After taxes, they were 12.3–17.5 percent, compared to 9.2–10.4 percent in other manufacturing and retailing industries. "Owning a newspaper, in other words, can be almost twice as profitable as owning a paper-box factory or a department store," observed the report.[42] The secrecy surrounding their financial success, the Senate report declared, was delicious in its hypocrisy. "An industry that is supposed to abhor secrets is sitting on one of the best-kept, least-discussed secrets, one of the hottest scoops, in the entire field of Canadian business — their own balance sheets."[43] Pointing out that chain ownership of Canada's daily newspapers had grown to 45 percent in 1970 from 25 percent in 1958, the Senate report urged government action to stem the rising tide of newspaper ownership concentration. It recommended a Press Ownership Review Board to examine newspaper sales or mergers that increased concentration, as well as federal subsidies to encourage the founding of alternative publications. After much national debate, neither measure was enacted.

Bagdikian's 1983 book *The Media Monopoly* blew the lid off what he called the "best kept secret in American newspapering" — its profitability.[44] Wall Street fell in love with newspapers not just for their profits, but also for their influence, according to Bagdikian. Profits and influence, in fact, seemed to go hand-in-hand when it came to newspapers. The growth of newspaper chains, Bagdikian pointed out, had led to the industry being dominated by only fourteen companies. Newspaper chains, broadcasting networks, and other media conglomerates were buying up media outlets at an astonishing rate because of the industry's peculiar economics, which created an almost irresistible urge to merge. In 1981, Bagdikian counted forty-six giant corporations that controlled most newspapers, magazines, television stations, and film producers. Within a few years, that number had been halved to twenty-three. If the economic trends that contributed to media consolidation continued unchecked, warned Bagdikian, there might be only one giant media owner by the millennium.[45] His prediction fell a bit short. Instead it was six; and the purchase by the Tribune Company in 2000 of Times Mirror, publisher of the *Los Angeles Times* and a handful of other major dailies, reduced that to five. By then the Internet had entered the equation.

'Have Journalists Gone Mad?'

As the aftershocks of the 2007–09 financial crisis eased, the future of daily newspapers hung in the balance. Not only did advertising revenue not go back up with the halting revival in the economy, but print advertising continued to go down while online advertising revenue stalled. Newspaper companies were thus forced to continue cutting costs and looking for ways to increase their revenues. Some of these initiatives, such as "native" advertising — content that resembled news but was paid for directly by advertisers — grew increasingly dodgy and pushed the limits of ethics and even legality. Some proved the observation by former *Times of London* editor Harold Evans after he took the reins of the *New York Daily News*. "The challenge of the American newspaper is not to stay in business," he said in 1998. "It is to stay in journalism."[46] Led by the *New York Times*' bold move to charge readers to access content online, newspapers across the U.S. and around the world began erecting paywalls in hopes of raising enough revenue to offset the drop in advertising. As newspaper fortunes revived, a few brave buyers even emerged, scooping up historic titles such as the *Boston Globe* and the *Washington Post* for a fraction of their previous values.

Some industry watchers had been confident all along that the venerable daily newspaper would be around for a long time to come. "Newspapers have survived magazines, the telegraph, radio and television," noted *Toronto Star* business writer David Olive in 2009. "They will not only survive but exploit the Internet. . . . These are the greatest days in the history of newspapers, which have never commanded such a vast, global audience." To those who understood the newspaper business, the hysterics of doom-sayers were hysterical. "I see newspaper executives with their hair on fire," wrote Olive, "and they're trying to put it out with a hammer."[47] Few understood the newspaper business better than Robert Picard, a former newspaper journalist who had gone on to become perhaps the world's leading media economist. "Have journalists gone mad?" he asked on his blog at the height of the newspaper crisis in 2009. "In some ways they have. They are panicking at problems in big city media and ignoring the fact that most newspapers are relatively stable and reasonably healthy."

> The only newspapers experiencing serious competitive difficulties are those in the top 25 markets (about 1 percent of the total) and these are joined in suffering by corporate newspaper companies whose executives have made serious managerial mistakes.[48]

Picard testified to the well-being of newspapers later that year at the FTC's hearings into journalism and news media. "The industry is far from collapse and ruin," he said. "Even in the midst of the damaging recession, its financial situation is akin to where it was in the 1970s — a newspaper era in which its operations and the practice of journalism were hardly ruinous for the industry or society."[49] By 2011, Olive was positively crowing about the prospects of newspapers. "Readership is at record levels, despite price hikes imposed by publishers," he pointed out. "And web interlopers haven't laid a glove on the industry's status as society's dominant news-gatherer."[50]

Historians, who took a more long-term view, similarly saw gaping holes in the death of newspapers meme. "If history has anything to teach us — and it does — we should think twice before planning a funeral," observed Kristen Heflin, a communication professor at the University of Alabama. "Technologies do not suddenly emerge and take the place of other technologies." Heflin rejected the crude determinism of technology advocates in favor of a more contextual perspective on media evolution. "Claims that the Internet has somehow caused or is causing the death of newspapers rely on an implicit technological determinism, which downplays if not outright ignores political, economic, and historical context." She found that the same kind of fatalism dominated industry discourse from the mid-1950s to the mid-1970s, when television was overtaking newspapers as the favorite source for news. "Throughout this 20-year period, newspapermen continually addressed the notion that newspapers were 'dying,' but television news never fully replaced newspapers."

> Newspapers survived the challenge of television news because they were not stable, immutable objects that could be easily overtaken. Instead, newspapers (as all technologies) are in flux, continually responding to and shaping society.[51]

The problem was largely one of perception. A lack of historical perspective led to a myopic, short-term view of the changes roiling the newspaper industry. A lack of understanding of newspaper economics left even long-time industry watchers unable to see through the screaming headlines that predicted doom for the medium. A cacophony of voices online — many of whom had been recently displaced from the contracting newspaper business — began pushing the vision of an all-digital future. Even newspapers themselves, long accustomed to emphasizing any challenges that beset their highly-profitable industry, quickly started singing from the same old song sheet. Together these factors combined to produce a powerful mythology about the future of news media. It was one that would not stand up to scrutiny, however, and the more the scenario played itself out, the more the enthusiasm for online media began to look as misplaced as the pessimism for newspapers.

THREE

An Unusual Industry

Newspapers are peculiar commodities, with upside-down economics, vast political influence, loyal readerships, and immense importance to society. Most products or services sell in only one market, but newspapers make their money in at least two distinct markets — selling information to readers and selling space to advertisers — which makes them a unique economic commodity. In a way, as Canadian political economist Dallas Smythe noted in coining the term "commodity audience," that means newspapers actually turn around and sell their readers to their advertisers.[1] This can bring ethical and even economic conflicts. Journalists and media critics often fear that newspapers will "sell out" their readers to advertisers and thus abdicate their responsibility to inform them in an unbiased manner. Some fear that favoring the interests of advertisers over those of readers may diminish a newspaper's most valuable asset of all — its credibility. Once that is lost, they argue, both readers and advertisers will soon fade away. This is often advanced as an economic argument for erecting a wall between advertising and editorial functions of any journalistic enterprise. The purpose of the wall is to prevent a newspaper's economic self-interest from affecting its news coverage. "It's one of the most destructive things a newspaper can do in the long haul," noted Bill Kovach, a former editor of the *Atlanta Journal-Constitution* and co-author of *The Elements of Journalism*. "Any editorial content . . . not designed by an editor to measure up to standards of honesty . . . is dishonesty."[2]

At the managerial level, the arcane economics of the business, with its multitudinous inputs and outputs, could make managing a newspaper something like playing three-dimensional chess, and the advent of the Internet only further complicated things. A newspaper's business practices could be counterintuitive, to say the least. Publishing a bad newspaper, for example, could be more profitable than publishing a good one because most newspapers enjoy a local monopoly and the publisher thus has little or no incentive to invest in improving the product. The upside-down nature of the newspaper business is best illustrated by the fact that selling fewer newspapers could actually be more profitable than selling more, because each copy is sold at a loss. The idea, of course, is to make it all back and more by selling advertising, but sometimes the quest for ad revenue interfered with informing the public, the higher calling to which most journalists aspired.

Newspapers were aided by the fact that in most countries they were the only industry constitutionally protected from government interference by press freedom guarantees enshrined in law. In the U.S., the First Amendment to the Constitution specifically prohibited Congress from regulating the press, and the newspaper industry used this to its advantage for years, especially in evading calls for some of its anti-competitive excesses to be reined in. Even in the U.S., however, regulation of newspapers was considered by many to have become necessary after World War II because the corporate chains that increasingly owned them had grown as irresponsible as they had become powerful. The privately-funded Hutchins Commission report warned of the dangers of the libertarian press model in 1947, and the press moved toward a "social responsibility" model of self-regulation to avoid government regulation. Elsewhere in the world, calls for government regulation of the press have grown louder as a result of scandals such as the

2011 phone hacking affair in the U.K. that resulted in the closing of News Corp.'s *News of the World*.

Most advantageous of all to newspapers was the fact that they were capable of influencing public perceptions. To a considerable extent, that meant they could create their own reality, and their preferred reality was one in which newspapers were far from powerful or even prosperous. It also helped that, through their coverage of politics, newspapers were influential in electing members of the government. Politicians were thus reluctant to act on calls for press regulation. In fact, those who sought favor in the press were usually more apt to give newspapers a regulatory break.

The Birth of Newspapers

From its earliest days, the printing press proved a formidable force. Following its rapid diffusion across Europe in the late fifteenth century, it showed a remarkable ability to spread ideas that were dangerous to those who held power in society, like the church and ruling monarchs. The ability of Martin Luther to mass-produce copies of his theses of protest prompted nothing less than a religious revolution — the Protestant Reformation. When the Catholic Church responded with its campaign for the Propagation of the Faith, the first printed "propaganda" resulted. The earliest printed news was published irregularly in the form of pamphlets or news "books." The first regular newspapers began appearing early in the seventeenth century, first in Germany, then in Holland and Belgium. The first newspapers in English did not appear until 1620, and even then they were published across the English Channel in Amsterdam. The first newspapers in England didn't start printing until the next year, but monarchs kept a tight lid on their content until the Puritan revolution of the 1640s. After Charles I lost his head in 1649, restrictions on the press eased, which led to an explosion in the printing of political pamphlets and newspapers. That resulted in a brief "public sphere" in English coffee houses and elsewhere that for the first time saw a high level of public participation in politics, if only by white, land-owning gentlemen of leisure.

Press freedom didn't last long in England, however, as the Restoration of Charles II to the throne in 1660 led to the re-imposition of censorship and the requirement that newspapers be licensed by the crown. Many of the Puritans fled to the New World, where the king couldn't control the press as easily. In colonial America, newspapers fomented unrest against the crown, especially over taxation, and sparked a nation's founding revolution. The first newspapers in the United States were highly political, often being directly subsidized by political parties and even serving as party newsletters. Low costs of production allowed this "party press" to proliferate, with titles springing from corner print shops equipped with hand-operated presses. Between 1790 and 1820, according to journalism historian Mitchell Stephens, the number of newspapers distributed in the U.S. per capita exploded, growing at a rate of 14 percent a year.[3] That leveled off from 1820–1835 to only 1 percent a year, but technological change and shifting population patterns would soon transform the newspaper business into a mass circulation phenomenon. Steam-driven presses allowed for faster printing just as American cities began growing into megalopolises due to immigration from overseas and migration from farms to the factories of the Industrial Revolution. While only 8.8 percent of Americans lived in urban centers of 2,500 or more population in 1830, that figure had risen to 34.5 percent by 1870.[4]

The Penny Press

The New York Sun was founded in 1833 and pioneered a new business model for newspapers. Pricing its copies at only 1 cent and selling them on the street, compared to the 5 or 6 cents charged for other dailies sold by subscription, the Sun was affordable to all. Its circulation grew to 5,000 within only a few months, and to 15,000 within two years. By focussing on crime and human interest news and eschewing polarizing politics, the Sun sought to appeal to all. Steam presses purchased in 1835 allowed the Sun to print up to 4,000 copies an hour by 1840, and with improvements up to 18,000 copies per hour by 1851. Soon "penny" papers began sprouting up and down the east coast of the U.S. and across the emerging Midwest. Starting in the 1840s, the telegraph provided vast quantities of news from afar, and photoengraving soon allowed pictures to be printed. The costs that came along with these new technologies, however, turned newspapers from small businesses into big ones. As late as 1835, for example, the New York Herald was established for only $500. The New York Times, on the other hand, cost about $70,000 to found in 1851.[5] According to newspaper historian Gerald Baldasty, the increased costs of production propelled a commercialization of news.

> Charles A. Dana, editor of the New York Sun, estimated that starting a new daily in New York City in 1840 would have cost between $5,000 and $10,000 and, in 1851, as much as $100,000. Costs soared after the Civil War, driving start-up expenses closer to $1 million in New York City.[6]

By the 1850s, according to Baldasty, "virtually every family in New York City was buying a newspaper, and circulations soared."[7] The Herald had the highest circulation, at 58,000, followed by the Sun at 50,000, the Times at 42,000, the Tribune at 29,000 and the Evening Post at 12,000. By 1880, noted Baldasty, newspapers in six cities — New York, Chicago, Philadelphia, Cleveland, Boston and San Francisco — printed 51.1 percent of the nation's dailies, with the newspapers in New York alone accounting for 22.8 percent. Most were eight or twelve pages, and many people read more than one so they could get a more rounded picture of reality.[8] Soon reality would be difficult to determine as warring dailies created their own truth, and even their own wars, with which to sell more and more newspapers.

Yellow Journalism

Joseph Pulitzer, who already owned the St. Louis Post-Dispatch, paid $346,000 for the struggling 20,000-circulation New York World in 1883 and introduced numerous innovations that increased the newspaper's popularity — and profitability. According to sociologist and media historian Michael Schudson, Pulitzer changed the relationship between newspapers and advertisers by charging for ad space based on circulation sales. His newspaper welcomed larger illustrated ads, and the profits poured in. Thanks to the growth of department stores in the 1880s, according to Schudson, the ratio of editorial content to advertising dropped from about 70–30 to more like 50–50. While advertising accounted for 44 percent of newspaper revenue in 1880, noted Schudson, it was up to 55 percent by 1900.

Pulitzer pioneered Sunday newspapers, which became wildly popular despite religious disapproval of publication on the Sabbath. An immigrant himself who learned English after arriving from Hungary to fight in the Civil War as a mercenary, Pulitzer ensured that the World was easily understandable, and amply illustrated, in order to appeal to an immigrant readership. The biggest secret to his success, however, was more sinister, and soon it would get out of hand and write the darkest chapter in journalism history. "The innovation most responsible for the paper's success," noted Schudson, "was, in a word, sensationalism."[9] News of crime, scandal, and high society propelled circulation of the World to stratospheric levels. By 1898, according to Stephens, the World was making an annual profit of about $500,000.[10] By then, a newspaper war had turned into a shooting war.

Pulitzer made the mistake of renting office space in his World Tower to a rich young Californian who soon took sensationalism to new heights and built an even taller tower. William Randolph Hearst's father had literally discovered the Mother Lode, and gold money bought his son anything he wanted, starting with the San Francisco Examiner. Moving to New York, the upstart bought the struggling Journal in 1895 and set out to eclipse Pulitzer. Hearst poached most of the World's staff, offering them much more than Pulitzer was paying. Included was the World's popular cartoonist, William Outcault, who drew the first color comic strip, "The Yellow Kid." By the following year, the Journal could boast a circulation of 430,000 to the market-leading World's 600,000. Hearst spared no expense in covering the ongoing insurgency in nearby Cuba against the Spanish colonial masters there, sending in correspondents and artists by the boatload. Much of the coverage was fictitious, however, as Hearst had hired some of the top novelists of the day as "war correspondents".[11] When the U.S. warship Maine blew up in Havana harbor in 1898, the dailies decided it was an act of war instead of the accident a later investigation found more likely. Sensational coverage in the Hearst and Pulitzer dailies railroaded the White House to war, and Spain was quickly routed in Cuba, the Phillipines, Puerto Rico, and elsewhere. At the height of the Spanish–American War, some newspapers were selling more than a million copies a day and could have sold more if they hadn't run out of paper. Sober post-war reflection, however, understood that the conflict was mostly media-driven, and "yellow journalism" got its name from the cartoon character who had coincidentally become the toast of the town.

A backlash against sensationalism ensued, and a more responsible journalism took precedence, as exemplified by the *New York Times*, which built a reputation for accuracy and focused on business coverage of Wall Street. From a circulation of only 9,000 in 1896, which placed it at the back of a field that at one point included seventeen dailies, the *Times* increased its sales through telephone solicitation. It also re-introduced penny pricing in 1898, tripling its circulation within a year from 25,000 to 75,000 by slashing its price from three cents. By 1900 it was selling 82,000 copies daily. By 1910 that was up to 192,000, and by 1920 to 343,000. More importantly from a business standpoint, its advertising soared, from 2.4 million lines in 1896 to 23.4 million in 1920.[12] The pre-eminence of the *Times* was cemented during World War II, when newsprint rationing caused most publishers to cut back on news at the expense of advertising. Not the *Times*, which turned ads away and as a result passed the market-leading *Herald Tribune*.[13]

Press Critics Emerge

In another backlash against "yellow journalism," a brand of investigative reporting emerged in the early twentieth century that began to hold to account powerful institutions in America. Thus perhaps the noblest chapter in journalism history immediately followed the darkest. Dubbed "muckrakers" after the men who scooped horse droppings from the streets, these investigative journalists chronicled economic excesses by powerful business "trusts," blew the whistle on health hazards in foods, drugs, and housing, and brought to light rampant political corruption.

Some even shone a spotlight on the press itself. Upton Sinclair, one of the foremost muckrakers, criticized newspapers for promoting the business interests of their owners, bankers, and advertisers in his 1919 book *The Brass Check*. The bottom line of Sinclair's self-published indictment of the newspaper industry's profit motive was as blunt as it was cynical. "I have yet to see an American newspaper which does not hold money for its god," he wrote.[14] Walter Lippmann, a founding editor of the *New Republic* magazine, drew on his experiences as a wartime propagandist in developing an astounding critique in his 1922 book *Public Opinion* of the press as actually incapable of conveying an accurate picture of reality. George Seldes quit the *Chicago Tribune* in 1927 and became one of the most trenchant press critics in America, publishing a weekly newsletter titled *In Fact* that chronicled the rampant failures of news media. After *In Fact* folded in 1950, blacklisted journalist Izzy Stone began his own newsletter to pick up the slack, publishing *I.F. Stone's Weekly* until his retirement in 1971. A.J. Liebling was perhaps the first regular press critic published in the mainstream media, writing his "On the Press" column in the *New Yorker* magazine from 1945 until his death in 1963.

By then, the first regular journal of press criticism had been founded. Perhaps to atone for his role in fomenting yellow journalism, Joseph Pulitzer left $2 million in his will to Columbia University in New York to start one of the first schools of journalism. It began publishing the *Columbia Journalism Review* in 1961. The competing *Washington Journalism Review* was founded in 1977 and a decade later was acquired by the University of Maryland, which renamed it *American Journalism Review* in 1993. Even some newspapers began covering the media as a regular "beat," with specialized reporters such as Howard Kurtz at the *Washington Post* and David Shaw at the *Los Angeles Times*. A press that scrutinized the ethics and business dealings of others, after all, should also shine a light on its own practices.

Survival of the Fattest

In a bizarre twist, the quest for advertising dollars actually started killing newspapers off, which led to a kind of survival of the fattest. The newspaper industry came to be seen by economists as a "natural monopoly" like telephones or railroads, which had such high start-up costs and large economies of scale that there was usually only room for one in a market. High start-up costs, which economists called barriers to entry — the costs of buying a press, printing equipment, and delivery trucks, not to mention hiring a staff of journalists — tended to keep new competition out. The proprietor of any start-up newspaper had to have deep pockets to afford not only the required plant and equipment, but also to endure years of heavy losses until a profitable advertising base could be built up. Economies of scale also played a role in eliminating competition, as these "savings of size" basically meant that bigger was better in the newspaper business. Newspaper owners found they could reduce their costs and increase their revenues by simply growing larger. Scale economies have fuelled the media's urge to merge ever since. Economists who studied the gradual disappearance of local newspaper competition also noted something peculiar about newspapers, which they dubbed the "circulation spiral." Advertisers, they observed, naturally favored the leading daily in a market. Many readers bought the newspaper as much for its ads as for the news, and they soon gravitated to the leading daily as well. Second-place newspapers thus became endangered, and in most instances were forced out of business. Eventually, under the Natural Monopoly Theory of Newspapers, only one newspaper would be left publishing in each market.[15]

The number of newspapers in the U.S. thus began to dwindle from about 2,400 in 1920 to about 1,700 in 1950 to about 1,400 by

2000. In 1910, nearly 60 percent of U.S. cities had competing daily papers, but by 1930 that figure had fallen to 21 percent, and by 1971 to only 2 percent. In numerical terms, there were more than 500 cities with competing daily newspapers in 1923, but only fifty by 1980, and by the late 1990s there were fewer than ten. Carl Lindstrom chronicled the trend toward disappearing dailies in his 1960 book *The Fading American Newspaper*.[16] To show how appearances can be deceiving, however, the total number of dailies dropped by only 2 percent between 1950 and 1980. "The distorted perception of newspaper mortality," noted Robert Picard and Jeffrey Brody in their 1997 book *The Newspaper Publishing Industry*, "was fuelled by the deaths of a large number of competing secondary newspapers in mid- and large-sized cities as populations moved to new suburban communities."[17] The closures, mostly of trailing metropolitan dailies, were almost entirely offset by the establishment of new suburban and satellite city dailies. The real decline wouldn't come until the 1980s, when the number of U.S. dailies dropped 8 percent, from 1,745 in 1980 to 1,611 in 1990.

As their numbers dwindled, newspapers grew fatter, both in size and profits. From the four pages typical in 1800, newspapers were usually eight to twelve pages by 1900. By 1940, the average U.S. daily had grown to thirty-one pages, and by 1980 it was up to sixty-six pages. The number of dailies people read began to drop as a result. Whereas in 1930 the average number of newspapers read per U.S. household had been 1.3, by 1960 that was down to 1.1. With the popularity of television evening news in the late 1960s, it dropped below one newspaper per household. By 1980 it was down to 0.8, as many households no longer even subscribed to a newspaper. Television news, which expanded from fifteen minutes to a half hour in 1963 and was soon broadcast in color, grew in popularity and killed off an entire genre of newspaper. People who once sat down to read the evening newspaper when they got home from work instead increasingly turned on their television set to get their news. "Death in the afternoon" came to mean more than a bull-fighting novel by Hemingway.[18]

The Rise of the Newspaper Chains

As newspapers grew more profitable, their owners sought to acquire more and more of them. The earliest chains were formed by Hearst and Pulitzer (the original "yellow journalists"), Canadian printer William Southam, and a Midwesterner named E.W. Scripps. Pulitzer added the *Tucson Star* to his flagship *New York World* and original *St. Louis Post-Dispatch*, but otherwise his holdings comprised smaller titles. Hearst created the country's largest newspaper chain, assembling twenty-eight metropolitan dailies by the mid-1920s, but he lost control of his empire in the Great Depression of the 1930s. Scripps, who started the first U.S. newspaper chain in the 1880s with dailies in Cleveland, St. Louis, and Cincinnati, controlled thirty-four of them by the end of the century through a variety of companies. In Canada, contraction of the newspaper industry, concentration of its ownership, and chain building followed the same pattern seen in the U.S. From a peak of 143 dailies in 1911, a rapid fall to 113 was seen by 1921, and then a steady drop to between ninety and one hundred after World War II.[19] Southam may have started the first North American newspaper chain when he bought the *Hamilton Spectator* in 1877, added the *Ottawa Citizen* two years later, and bought dailies across the country over the next half century. After his death, the Southam chain went public with a 1945 listing on the Toronto Stock Exchange to allow members of subsequent generations to more easily sell their shares. Some newspaper companies that went public, like the New York Times Co. and Washington Post Co., created a two-tiered stock system in which control was guaranteed to founding families through their ownership of super-voting "preferred" shares. Southam did not, however, and ownership of the company by family members fell into a minority by the 1980s, which made it vulnerable to a hostile takeover.[20]

Selling shares of ownership on the stock market was also a convenient way to raise capital for expansion, and many newspaper chains took advantage of it. John Knight inherited his father's *Akron Beacon-Journal* in 1933 and four years later bought the *Miami Herald* to start a chain that would comprise fifteen dailies by 1973. It went public in 1969 and merged with Ridder Publications five years later to form Knight Ridder Publications, which was briefly the largest chain in the U.S. It was eclipsed by the Gannett Company, which began as a chain of minor dailies in upstate New York owned by Frank Gannett and grew into a media conglomerate with radio and TV stations in addition to eighty-two dailies. Gannett went public in 1967 and sold shares to finance its rapid expansion. The growth of newspaper chains in the U.S. was fuelled by a perverse push-pull tax phenomenon. As printing technology improved in the 1950s and 1960s, far fewer printers and press operators were needed, reducing labor costs at newspapers. Their profits and thus their value soared, which did not go unnoticed by the Internal Revenue Service, noted historian Elizabeth Neiva.

> During the 1960s and 1970s, when gift and estate taxes hovered near 70 percent, many papers simply did not generate enough cash to pay the government what it demanded. Many families therefore were forced to sell their properties. Between 1960 and 1980, 587 daily newspapers were sold to newspaper chains.[21]

At the same time that estate taxes were encouraging the sale of independent newspapers, IRS rules also created an incentive for chains to buy them. A surcharge on excess corporate earnings that were not paid out in dividends could be avoided if the cash was spent on acquiring additional businesses. "By 1971, Gannett had retained earnings of over $118 million available in its acquisitions war chest," noted Neiva. "In that year, Gannett purchased an average of one newspaper every three weeks."[22] By 1977, 170 newspaper chains owned about two-thirds of the 1,700 dailies in the U.S.[23] In Canada, two-thirds of the English-language dailies were also owned by chains, but in sharp contrast to the multitude of newspaper companies in the U.S., only two or three chains dominated the Canadian market.[24] Restrictions on foreign ownership in Canada prevented U.S. chains from buying newspapers north of the border, which tended to limit the number of chains there. No such prohibition was allowed in the U.S. under First Amendment guarantees of press freedom, however, and as a result Canadian chains such as Thomson Newspapers and Hollinger International became major owners of newspapers there.

Knocking Down the Church–State Wall

Advertising proved much more lucrative than circulation sales, which newspapers started discounting in a quest for the largest possible audience to cash in on the boom. This had an insidious effect on the press, as readers were no longer a newspaper's best customers. In an effort to insulate the integrity of the news from advertising pressure, some publishers erected a "church–state wall" between their newsrooms and advertising departments and named it after the historical separation of religion from government. *Time* magazine publisher Henry Luce is thought to have been the first to introduce a formal separation of editorial and advertising, but according to historian Richard Clurman, the wall could be a porous one even at *Time*. "Like much of Luce's theorizing," noted Clurman, "the hierarchy of journalists leading and their business partners following was more a concept than a reality."[25] Another major proponent of a church–state wall between advertising and editorial departments was *Chicago Tribune* publisher Robert McCormick, who famously had separate elevators installed for journalists and business staff when his iconic Tribune Tower was built in 1925. "There was a virtual caste system of elevators," recalled James Squires, who was editor of the *Tribune* from 1981 to 1989.

> One set, accessible only with a special security pass, sped directly to [McCormick's] old office on the top floor; a second set serving all floors below except one — the fourth floor; and a third set exclusively for the fourth floor, where the editorial department is located.[26]

Despite the mythical wall, however, many newspapers tailored their content more and more to fit the interests of advertisers in order to increase their revenues. For example, as Ben Bagdikian pointed out, they ignored evidence of the dangers of cigarette smoking for decades because much of their ad revenue came from tobacco companies. In fact, bad news was to be avoided generally because it didn't put readers in what Bagdikian called a "buying mood." Most of the increase in newspaper size was thus devoted to what he called "fluff." Hard news comprised four pages of the average daily in 1940, according to Bagdikian, but had only grown to five pages by the time they had more than doubled in size forty years later. "Most fluff is wanted by advertisers to create a buying mood," he noted. Surveys showed readers wanted more hard news, but according to Bagdikian that wasn't what advertisers — and therefore publishers — wanted. "An article on genuine social suffering might interrupt the 'buying mood' on which most ads for luxuries depend."[27] International news suffered worst of all, as it was both expensive to gather and concerned people in faraway lands, about whom Americans knew little. That didn't fit the corporate paradigm which had captured news media, especially in the U.S., and foreign news became the victim of cutbacks both at newspapers and on television.[28] The chickens came home to roost in 2001 with the terrorist attacks of 9/11, when most Americans struggled to understand why many around the world disdained their way of life, even hated them.

Whole new sections of newspapers instead became devoted to such topics as fashion, food, travel, and real estate in order to attract advertising, and they began to blur the line between advertising and journalism. According to Bagdikian, they were simply "advertising bait." Journalists derided such special sections as "advertorials" and balked at providing their content, which was instead usually produced by advertising departments. Sunday newspapers, published on the day that most people devoted to leisure activities such as newspaper reading, grew fat with these special sections. Travel sections were filled with ads for exotic destinations, motoring sections with ads for cars, and real estate sections with ads for property. Car dealers had long been notorious for putting pressure on newspapers to look the other way on their sometimes shady business practices.[29] Real estate advertising was even more problematic for newspapers, however. The sheer volume of advertising dollars available, according to the *Columbia Jour-*

nalism Review, made this the area where "papers are most tempted to sell their soul. . . . few advertising sources are more lucrative."[30] Newspapers had an ambiguous relationship with real estate, noted *CJR*, because "they are intrinsically boosterish, favoring development because it brings higher circulations and revenues. And real estate profits translate directly into newspaper profits." Its investigation by writer Mary Ellen Schoonmaker found that competitive pressures often made it impossible for newspapers to draw the line. The *Dallas Times-Herald* tried to make its real estate section more critical starting in 1980 with articles written by actual journalists, noted *CJR*, but an advertiser boycott ensued. "The advertisers were unhappy from the start," noted Schoonmaker. "For one thing, they didn't like stories that said sales went down." A withdrawal of advertising by realtors, she noted, cost the newspaper more than $2 million a year and ultimately "broke the paper's will."

> The paper, owned at the time by the Times Mirror Company, which was making a real effort to bring provocative daily journalism to the city, held out for two years before caving in and bringing back the advertorial format. The price was just too high.[31]

The boycott dropped the *Times-Herald*'s share of local real estate classifieds from 48.9 percent to "the low 20s," noted Schoonmaker, and led to the newspaper's demise. While it had once raced neck-and-neck with the competing *Dallas Morning News,* by 1986 circulation of the *Times-Herald* had dropped to 245,000, compared to 390,000 for the *Morning News.* Times Mirror sold it to local upstart Dean Singleton, who was then starting his MediaNews empire, but the *Times-Herald* couldn't escape the circulation spiral in which it was trapped and folded in 1991.

Consumer reporting, which investigated the pitfalls of products and often exposed unethical business practices, gradually disappeared from newspapers. "Hardhitting consumer reporting is withering at most dailies," noted Trudy Lieberman in 1994. "It isn't even a beat anymore at most papers."[32] Consumer reporting had been energized by an active consumer movement in the 1960s and 1970s, noted Lieberman, a senior editor at *Consumer Reports* magazine. A count taken in 1970 found at least fifty full-time consumer reporters and twenty-five newspaper "action line" columns whose mission was solving consumer problems. Two decades later, noted Lieberman, consumer reporters had all but disappeared and consumer stories were instead usually covered on an ad hoc basis by general assignment reporters who lacked both contacts and expertise. "Spreading consumer stories around has the effect of making them less visible and less likely to attract the attention and the wrath of advertisers and other powerful interests who pound on the publisher's door." Consumer reporting was increasingly replaced by coverage of personal finance, noted Lieberman, which was "a safe topic that usually doesn't pinch the holy trinity of media advertisers — car dealers, supermarkets, and real estate brokers."

> Much of what is called consumer reporting (reincarnated as personal finance coverage on newspapers) has found a home on the business pages, a place that almost guarantees that it will not be hardhitting and confrontational.[33]

The shift from consumer reporting to personal finance was symptomatic of the financialization that was by then gripping both media and society. Investing had been largely the reserve of elites until the 1980s, when a decade of deregulation in the U.S. fuelled a bull market that saw ordinary Americans jump into stock ownership. "As late as 1980, only 13 percent of the country owned stocks," noted Dean Starkman in his 2014 book *The Watchdog That Didn't Bark*. "But by 1989, the figure had soared to 32 percent, and by 1998 more than half the country, 52 percent, owned either stocks or equity mutual funds."[34] Increased coverage of personal finance, and even special sections on the topic, was not surprising given the rewards, noted the *Columbia Journalism Review* in 1998. "While reader demand for articles on investing is unquestionably strong, advertiser support is so luxuriant as to make any publisher weak in the knee."[35] Unfortunately, coverage of investment news saw a turn away from investigative reporting on business, according to Starkman, toward "access" reporting that instead focused on inside information about mergers and acquisitions. Investigative reporting fell by the wayside at most newspapers because it was expensive to produce, with reporters often tied up for months on stories.[36]

Joint Operating Agreements

As competing dailies fought it out for first place in a market and thus survival under the Darwinian economics of the newspaper business, some decided to declare a truce, go into business together, and form a "joint operating agreement" (JOA). One would use the press during the day to print an afternoon newspaper, while the other used it at night to print the morning daily. They set advertising rates and circulation prices jointly and split the profits. The first JOA was formed in Albuquerque in 1933 and was soon followed by similar arrangements between publishers in El Paso and Nashville. In Canada, newspapers in Vancouver combined operations in the 1950s. There was only one small problem with this type of arrangement — it was strictly illegal under anti-trust laws. Government watchdogs in the U.S. looked the other way for years, and in Canada anti-combines regulators proved ineffective in preventing such combinations. Hearings were held into the Pacific Press partnership of the *Vancouver Sun* and *Province*, which found the combination to be an illegal restraint on trade but allowed it to stand as an "economic necessity" given the circulation spiral.[37] The U.S. Justice Department eventually sued to stop one such combination, and in 1965 the Supreme Court ruled the arrangement illegal, which put more than a dozen similar partnerships in doubt. The Newspaper Preservation Act of 1971 changed that, but critics of such arrangements claimed they did more to keep competition out than to preserve it.

Other countries used different measures to keep newspaper competition alive. In Scandinavian countries, government subsidies were given to trailing dailies to help keep them in business. Sweden had experienced the same type of decline in the number of newspapers published that other countries had seen since radio was introduced in the 1920s. Starting in 1971, second-place newspapers there were given subsidies funded by a tax on print advertising. These newspapers were required to cover politics and to produce a majority of their own content. While subsidies accounted for less than 5 percent of all newspaper revenues in Sweden, for some trailing dailies they amounted to more than 35 percent.[38] In 2006, Swedish press subsidies amounted to US $65 million. In Norway, press subsidies to second-place newspapers resulted in 625 copies of newspapers being published daily per 1,000 population, compared to only 225 in the U.S.

Newspapering 2.0

In the second half of the twentieth century, two trends combined to make newspapers even more profitable — if they survived the industry's arcane economics to achieve a coveted monopoly or, in the case of a JOA, a duopoly. Technological advances began to eliminate many of the production jobs at newspapers, which resulted in huge cost savings for owners. While once printing plates had been composed by hand out of individual letters assembled by armies of highly-skilled printers, automated Linotype machines were introduced in the twentieth century that easily composed lines of type out of molten lead by a printer using a keyboard. Starting in the 1950s, photocomposition machines were introduced that set columns of type photographically. Soon even those jobs would be eliminated, as computerized word processing systems were introduced in the 1970s that did not require content to be re-typed by a printer or even a typist. Once a reporter typed a story into the newspaper's computer system, it could be edited on another terminal and then transmitted electronically to a photocomposition machine.[34]

Printers once had one of the most powerful unions in the newspaper industry, but by the 1970s they became redundant. The jobs of press operators were similarly reduced by automation. Neither went quietly, however, going on strike at many newspapers to save their jobs. The multitude of New York dailies had already been reduced by economic forces to a half dozen by 1966 when a strike closed the *Herald Tribune*, the *World-Telegram & Sun*, and the *Jour-nal-American*, leaving only the market-leading *Times* and two tab-loids — the *Post* and the *Daily News*. In England, the Canadian chain Thomson Newspapers closed the legendary *Times of London* in 1978 for almost a year rather than give in to union demands. By the mid-1980s, however, most London dailies had moved out of Fleet Street to non-union plants across the Thames to escape their labor prob-lems. In some monopoly markets, however, newspaper owners grudgingly gave in to the demands of unions and granted job guar-antees so they could keep publishing profitably.

Publication disruptions caused by labor disputes had a negative effect on newspaper circulation, as dailies lost readers each time they stopped printing for any significant length of time. The rela-tionship between readers and newspapers has been studied by scholars since the 1940s. The highly-competitive New York mar-ket was the crucible for some of the most interesting research, starting with a strike in 1945 that sent many people into newspa-per withdrawal. The study by researchers at Columbia found that newspapers, more than simply a source of information, also satis-fied important social and psychological needs. "The newspaper is missed because it serves as a (non-'rational') source of security in a disturbing world," it noted, and "because the reading of the news-paper has become a ceremonial or ritualistic or near-compulsive act for many people."[40] When readers were deprived of their daily newspaper fix, they actively sought to replace it and would substi-tute other media. A replication of the research during a 1958 news-paper strike in New York City found that new media — radio and television — did not adequately fill the void.

> People seemed to feel drawn to the news as it appears in a newspa-per without fully understanding what they get out of it ... A printed record can be screened when the moment is convenient and stories of interest can be examined at length. Furthermore, it is a process in which the reader participates actively.[41]

The other trend that benefitted newspaper owners was an explo-sion of advertising revenues in the post-war period. From $2 billion in 1950, they grew in the U.S. to $3.7 billion by 1960 and to $5.7 billion by 1970. Then the real growth began. Newspaper advertising revenues more than doubled in the 1970s to $14.8 billion. Fuelled by growth in classified advertising in the 1980s, which almost tripled during the decade, they more than doubled again, to $32.3 billion by 1990. The recession of the early 1990s proved a bump in the road, with a 6 percent drop in ad revenues in 1991, but by the turn of the millennium newspaper ad revenues had recovered nicely to peak at $48.7 billion. Classified advertising revenues increased almost tenfold from $2.1 billion in 1975 to $19.6 billion in 2000. From 26 percent, classifieds grew to account for 40 percent of newspaper advertising revenues. Those revenues were almost pure profit, as newspapers only had to hire enough staff to answer the telephones and then count the money that poured in.

MBAs in the Newsroom

By the 1970s, not only was television eating into newspaper readership, but shifting population patterns were also causing the circulation of metropolitan dailies to decline. Families fled the crime of inner cities and moved out to the safer suburbs. People began increasingly moving from place to place for work, which loosened community ties. Women were working more, which gave them less time to read newspapers. People increasingly spent their leisure time watching television instead of reading the newspaper. In an effort to keep circulation up, according to former *Seattle Times* reporter Doug Underwood, newspapers turned to marketing experts. "The late 1970s and early 1980s saw a virtual stampede by the industry to become more marketing smart," noted Underwood in his 1993 book *When MBAs Rule the Newsroom*.[42] Because journalists made notoriously poor managers, many of those put in charge of newspapers were chosen not for their expertise as journalists but for their training in business school techniques. Those techniques might have worked well in other industries, but didn't necessarily work in the arcane newspaper business. Newspapers soon became more "audience-based," giving readers what they told marketers they wanted to read about instead of what editors thought they needed to know. Surveys and focus groups increasingly dictated content, much to the chagrin of many journalists.

At some newspapers, marketers began to take precedence over editors. At the *Philadelphia Inquirer*, for example, the paper's editor was put in charge of circulation and promotion in the mid-1980s and was also made president of its parent company. It was "an unusual move that broke through the traditional wall between the editorial and business sides of the organization," noted media scholars Stephen Reese and Pamela Shoemaker.[43] The net effect of elevating corporate values over journalistic ones, they concluded, changed the organizational culture and the relative influence of those values.

> If the editor controls both the editorial and business sides of the paper, the relative power of the journalistic division is less. The person making decisions primarily on journalistic grounds occupies a place somewhere below the editor in this case.[44]

Marketers Take Aim

One of the business school techniques that newspapers began to adopt in the 1980s was target marketing, which advertisers had started in the mid-1970s in a move away from mass marketing.[45] Advertisers had long targeted audiences by breaking them down into demographic categories, such as age, race, gender, income, and education level. More affluent neighborhoods had been targeted since the 1960s by free-distribution "shoppers" or "penny-savers," so-called because they were light on news and heavy on advertising.[46] Some chains, such as Journal Register in the eastern U.S., Tribune in the Midwest, and Harte-Hanks in the West, specialized in such giveaways because of their high profit margins. In some metropolitan areas, they posed serious competition for local advertising dollars, especially lucrative classified revenue. In St. Louis alone, according to the *Wall Street Journal*, there were thirty-six such free papers by the mid-1980s, some of them more than 200 pages thick, with a combined circulation of 834,000, compared to about 250,000 each for the two dailies. "In many cities, including Los Angeles, Philadelphia and Chicago," noted the *Journal*, "the dailies are fighting back with their own weekly supplements, filled with local news and geographically zoned to attract advertisers."[47]

By the 1980s, however, target marketing had gone beyond crude demographic categories to segment audiences by common interests, values, and lifestyles. Radio and television had been able to appeal to advertisers by narrowly targeting their audiences with content that appealed to them. The new buzzword on Madison Avenue became "psychographics."[48] By using sophisticated surveys and focus group research, in which consumers were brought together for group interviews, marketers were able to segment audiences qualitatively instead of just quantitatively. By using computerized "clustering" programs, researchers at the Stanford Research Institute (SRI) categorized consumers into four groups, then subdivided them into nine lifestyle types. SRI's Values and Lifestyles Program (VALS), noted United Press International writer Mark Schwed, also assigned catchy names to each category.

> Sustainers drink more instant-breakfast products than any other group. Emulators read more classified ads. Belongers drink beer and watch *Dallas*, while the Societally Conscious prefer *Hill Street Blues* and mixed drinks. Experientials attend more high school and college sports events than I-Am-Me's, but just as many professional sports events. Achievers play golf, drink cocktails before dinner and have a lot of credit cards.[49]

Newspapers looking to boost their sagging circulations increasingly turned to target marketing and psychographics. The *Vancouver Sun*, for example, hired a consultant in the late 1980s to define the newspaper's target audience. It divided the *Sun*'s potential audience into groups ranked by their potential to boost the newspaper's sagging circulation. These ranged from what it called "middle-class joiners," to "home bodies," to "post-literate hedonists." Most desirable to advertisers, however, was a group it dubbed "literate acquisitors," who were notable for their disposable income. Former *Sun* reporter Ian Gill detailed the report's findings about the *Sun's* new target audience for Vancouver magazine.

> "Psychographics" reveal them to be readers and experimenters, neither traditional nor conservative, who are unlikely to see TV as a major source of entertainment, have good self-esteem, do not worry about finances, and possess strong social responsibility.[50]

By diving into target marketing, however, newspapers discovered what many in the advertising business had known for some time — less is more. These strategic shifts in both the newspaper and advertising businesses combined to provide a new direction for newspapers. In a game-changing decision, many publishers decided to pull back from their traditional strategy of selling as many copies as they could and instead began targeting their product at a higher-quality audience. "After twenty-five years of losing audience and advertisers to television and other media, newspapers decided that there were structural limits to how much circulation they could have in the video age," noted Bill Kovach and Tom Rosenstiel in *The Elements of Journalism*. "Newspapers, in effect, decided they were a niche medium for the better educated."[51] Advertisers decided that the better educated, more affluent customers who tended to read newspapers were exactly the audience they were trying to reach. As a result, readers in more affluent neighborhoods began to take precedence with publishers, which had consequences for a newspaper's journalism as well as for its business. "Writing off certain neighborhoods," noted Kovach and Rosenstiel, "also meant not having to invest heavily to cover them."[52] Distribution to less affluent neighborhoods was often curtailed, and news from them — other than crime news — tended to recede.

The implications for newspapers were enormous. They had come full circle from their heyday a century earlier when newspapers targeted a poor, largely immigrant audience. Their new, more upscale journalism also disenfranchised younger readers, as many newspaper articles went over their heads. "Stories were long, sophisticated," noted Kovach and Rosenstiel, "and often required college degrees to follow."[53] According to Squires, "the camel's nose had gotten into our tent" when newspapers began target marketing. "Nobody thought much about this at the time because the traditional walls separating the church and state of the press – editorial from advertising — were still firmly in place," he wrote in his 1993 book, *Read All About It! The Corporate Takeover of America's Newspapers.* "But it was a critical development."[54]

> By the time I left the *Tribune* ... the hallowed separation between church and state was hardly more than a pretense. For this, no one was more responsible than I. And for the ease with which I let it happen, I can only offer the lamest of excuses, "I really didn't know at the time what I was doing."[55]

FOUR

Money Lust

Things changed dramatically in the newspaper business during the 1990s. The decade began with a crushing recession and ended in a serious journalistic soul-searching. A defining question soon came clear. What business were newspapers in? Was newspapering about journalism or, as many increasingly believed, was it more about making money?

Fundamental shifts in media, retailing, and marketing in the 1980s had taken a toll on newspaper fortunes. The advent of 24-hour cable TV news, with its non-stop barrage of information, and the looming spectre of the Internet, which combined the speed of broadcasting with the depth of newspapers, led many to predict a bleak future for print on paper. Newspaper publishers became increasingly desperate. Their willingness to co-operate with advertisers, which had grown throughout the 1980s, turned into outright collaboration in the 1990s. The result was the biggest black eye yet for the newspaper business. The mantra of Wall Street, as espoused by the eponymous 1987 film, was "Greed is good." Because newspapers were increasingly owned by stock market investors, it seemed that their values were infiltrating newsrooms at the highest levels. In the eyes of many, Mammon began to replace Truth as the new god of many publishers. The result was a brazen assault on the church–state wall, the nominal separation between newsrooms and advertising departments. By the turn of the millennium — Y2K in the jargon of the day — newspapers were more prosperous than ever, perhaps as a result of selling more than a small slice of their souls.

A recession that began in mid-1990 threw newspaper publishers into a panic because, for the first time since World War II, their advertising revenues started going down. A decline of less than 1 percent in 1990 was followed by a plunge of 6 percent the following year. Department stores, which had long been major newspaper advertisers, were being put out of business by discount retailers, such as Wal-Mart, which were not. Other major advertisers, such as supermarkets, began deserting newspapers for new promotion strategies like direct mail — flyers delivered to every doorstep in a neighbourhood. Niche publications for cars and real estate began siphoning off the rich classified advertising that flowed into newspapers. Lou Ureneck wrote a 10,000-word analysis at decade's end of the changes seen in the newspaper business during the 1990s for *Nieman Reports*, the magazine of the Nieman Foundation for Journalism at Harvard University. "During the last decade, the business of newspapers has become significantly more difficult even as pressures to perform financially have grown more intense," noted Ureneck, a former editor at the *Philadelphia Inquirer* who studied the newspaper business and taught at Boston University. "It no longer is a business, as publishers once joked, in which even the brain dead could make money."[1] Declining market penetration, a failure to attract young readers, and increased competition from new media converged to create a dilemma for the newspaper industry, according to Ureneck.

> Confronted by these trends and by steep advertising revenue declines in the early part of the decade, newspaper companies have had to make a choice: Either accept lower profits in the short term, while looking for new ways to grow, or cut costs, restructure and try to maintain historically high profit margins. Most newspapers chose to maintain profits and cut costs.[2]

Publishers responded to the hard financial times that began the 1990s in the ways that Wall Street favored most. Cost-cutting, consolidation, and collusion were top of the list. Financial incentives, such as stock options and profit-sharing bonuses, served to get publishers increasingly onside with the newspaper industry's new realities. The strategies designed to attract readers and advertisers — and to hang on to the ones they still had — were questioned by many, however. Stories began to be selected by editors at many newspapers not for their importance, but because marketing research showed they were likely to attract readers who were of interest to advertisers. Following the successful formula pioneered by Gannett with USA *Today*, such stories were increasingly light, bright, and trite. This amounted to what serious journalists considered pandering to the audience. Measures to attract advertisers were considerably worse in the eyes of news purists. "There is mounting evidence that advertisers nationwide are increasingly taking advantage of weak newspaper ad revenues to pressure papers into more positive coverage of their activities," reported the *American Journalism Review* in 1991. "It's a development that is raising questions about the lengths to which recession-battered publishers will go to court advertisers."[3] The strategies worked, however, and Wall Street couldn't have been happier. Profit margins, which had fallen into the teens on average in the early part of the decade, according to Ureneck, were back above 20 percent by the end of the 1990s as a result of the measures taken by publishers. The price their newspapers paid, however, was a heavy one journalistically.

> There is evidence that cost cutting, in place of product investment, may have weakened readers' connection to newspapers as an object of trust and authority. Perhaps sacrificed by these business decisions had been the maintenance of a public trust, both in terms of newspapers' quality of coverage and their reach into the community.[4]

John Morton, a former newspaper reporter who published a stock newsletter and also analyzed the media business in a regular column for the *American Journalism Review*, shared this concern. His scrutiny of annual reports and quarterly earnings statements showed that newspaper companies took unprecedented fiscal measures to deal with the downturn brought by the recession. "Newspapers' response to the decline in advertising revenue and lower profits in 1991 was much more aggressive than actions taken in earlier recessions," noted Morton. "Newspapers previously had not laid off significant numbers of employees for economic reasons, but this time layoffs were common."[5] By mid-decade, Morton had begun to fear for the future of newspapers, and he expressed his concerns ten times a year in his back-page *AJR* column. When stiff hikes in the price of newsprint prompted publishers to cut back on the size of both their pages and their staff in mid-decade, Morton worried that newspapers were "eating the seed corn," as farmers had been forced to do during the Great Depression. "The worst thing any business can do when faced with so many negative trends," he warned, "is to cut back on the quality of product and level of service."

> Indeed, strategically, a more compelling argument can be made for increasing rather than cutting expenses. Improving and expanding the newspaper product resists negative trends eroding the industry's fundamental strengths. Shrinking newspaper efforts — eating the seed corn — feeds the negative trends.[6]

Reinventing the Newspaper

The hard times faced by newspapers in the early 1990s led to a movement to "reinvent" the newspaper by taking the marketing measures adopted in the 1980s another step further. This led to a culture clash between the financial values of Wall Street and the journalistic values in most newsrooms. *Wisconsin State Journal* editor Frank Denton saw the problem as "journalists' traditional beliefs that they really are the newspaper, that the commerce of the newspaper is potentially evil and intrusive (or at least threatening)."[7] Denton's 1992 treatise on newspaper marketing was published by the Twentieth Century Fund think tank. "Suddenly, within the past half-dozen years and intensifying in the 1990–92 recession," it noted, "everything is changing."[8] Newspapers, and especially journalists, needed to change in response, according to Denton.

> Newspapers need a new attitude of wholism, an understanding that their organic whole can be more than the sum of their separate functions. ... The journalists — without any compromise of their independence, integrity or mission — can work side by side with their advertising and circulation counterparts to find or develop markets they can serve, to their mutual benefit.[9]

Newspapers, according to Denton, were a mature industry facing the final stage of any product's life cycle — decline. The industry had suffered from three "body blows," he noted, including the recession, the shakeout in retailing, and a move away from mass-circulation advertising to promotion strategies that did not involve newspapers, including television advertising and billboards. "Newspaper people must free themselves from useless constraints of tradition and become more thoughtful, analytical, professional, realistic, methodical, and open-minded about their ... product."[10] (Ellipsis in original.) Jack Fuller, who replaced James Squires as editor of the *Chicago Tribune* in 1989, became a leading evangelist for the new corporatism of newspapers in his 1996 book *News Values*, in which he responded to the published criticism of his predecessor. "The basic argument critical journalists make against the corporate form is that corporations have taken money out of newspapers at a far higher rate than private owners did."[11] Not so, according to Fuller.

> In the 1920s during the *Tribune's* heyday ... the company turned out more profit per dollar of revenue than at any time during the high-flying, cost-cutting, corporate 1980s. The operating margin reached almost 29.8 percent in 1929, compared with 24.6 percent at its highest afterwards. Even during the Great Depression, the newspaper's margins never dropped into single digits.[12]

According to Fuller, who echoed what some of the loudest political and economic voices of the day were advocating, the free market should be a guiding light for journalism. "The market provides some measure of whether a newspaper is successful in communicating," he insisted. "A newspaper that reaches people with information they want and need will attract advertising and, unless otherwise mismanaged, will turn a nice profit. A newspaper that pleases its writers and editors but is not a vital part of the community's life will be a commercial failure because it is a rhetorical failure."[13] The infiltration of market forces into newsrooms was something new in North American journalism. According to Ureneck, this development led to "nothing less than a remaking of the culture inside newspaper organizations."

> The independence of the newsroom, once considered a market asset, is now considered by some to be a business impediment. At some newspapers, the diminished commitment to news coverage at a time of rising profits reflects a loss of confidence in the long-term prospects of the newspaper business.[14]

Meet the New Boss

The increased ownership of North American newspapers by stock market investors in the 1990s led to a more market-driven journalism — in more ways than one. In addition to being designed to woo readers and advertisers, newspapers began to be operated to boost their share prices by attracting investors. Ben Bagdikian had long warned that the stock market was a third market for which newspapers had to account. "The impact of trading newspaper corporate stock on the stock market has meant that news companies must constantly expand in size and rate of profits in order to maintain their position on stock exchanges," he observed in 1980. "Instead of the single master so celebrated in the rhetoric of the industry — the reader — there are in fact three masters."[15] With funding from George Soros's liberal think tank, the Open Society Institute, a trio of University of Iowa scholars began a two-year study in 1997 of the seventeen publicly-traded firms that then controlled just over 40 percent of U.S. daily newspaper circulation.

They examined detailed financial information that the Securities and Exchange Commission required the companies to make public, and they interviewed more than one hundred journalists, newspaper executives, and stock analysts. "News has become secondary, even incidental, to markets and revenues and margins and advertisers and consumer preferences," concluded Gilbert Cranberg, Randall Bezanson and John Soloski in their 2001 book, *Taking Stock.*

> At its worst, the publicly traded newspaper company, its energy entirely drawn to the financial market's unrealistic and greedy expectations, can become indifferent to news and, thus, ultimately to the fundamental purposes served by news and the press.[16]

Financial incentives for both editors and company board members — many of whom had no journalism experience — were changing the direction of newspapers, they concluded. "The publicly traded newspapers companies have been 'incentivized' from top to bottom in order to assure that policies, decisions, and corporate behaviors conform to the performance demands of the securities markets."[17] They recommended government change some of the rules involving newspapers, including removing the antitrust exemption granted to publishers in the Newspaper Preservation Act. "Government policy toward newspaper competition should be changed from one that protects newspapers against competition to one that encourages, permits and even fosters competition."[18]

The Three-Man Newsroom

In Canada, an even worse scenario was playing out as a result of widespread stock market ownership of Canada's largest newspaper chains. Concentration of newspaper ownership there was much higher than in the U.S., mainly because foreign ownership was discouraged through tax measures. Some newspaper owners were unfortunately not just intent on pumping as much profit as possible out of newspapers, but on also using them to promote an ideological agenda. Conrad Black had been born into money and grew up idolizing William Randolph Hearst, yet he made his disdain for journalists well known. "My experience with journalists authorizes me to record that a very large number of them are ignorant, lazy, opinionated, intellectually dishonest and inadequately supervised," he told Senate hearings into the country's mass media in 1969, shortly after he bought his first newspaper.[19]

Black and his partner David Radler built Sterling Newspapers into a modest but highly profitable chain by the 1980s. The secret to their success, Radler told hearings held by the Royal Commission on Newspapers in 1980, was "the three-man newsroom, and two of them sell ads."[20] Black had been shut out of acquiring major dailies, however, by newspaper owners who scorned his neoconservative politics, which he promoted relentlessly in his newspapers. He was outbid in 1980 for FP Publications, the country's second-largest chain of dailies, by Ken Thomson, who had recently become Canada's richest man upon inheriting his father's media empire. Black was similarly thwarted in a 1985 takeover bid for Southam Inc., the largest newspaper chain in Canada, which had become vulnerable when family ownership of its shares fell below 30 percent. In a panicked reaction to the thought of Black acquiring the historically liberal dailies, Southam reached for some "shark repellant." It executed a share swap or near merger with the Torstar Corp., owner of Canada's largest-circulation daily, the *Toronto Star*. It issued Torstar new shares worth 20 percent of Southam in exchange for 30 percent of the smaller company, which made a takeover impractical. Black instead turned his attention overseas and built his Hollinger International into the world's third largest newspaper company by the end of the 1990s. He bought the *Telegraph* in London, the *Jerusalem Post* in Israel, and an interest in Australia's leading chain, Fairfax Newspapers. He and Radler also began acquiring small newspapers in the U.S. with a regular classified ad in the trade magazine *Editor & Publisher*. Radler became known as the "human chain saw" for the cost-cutting technique he applied to each new publication acquired, which he once explained to a writer.

I visit the office of each prospective property at night and count the desks. . . . That tells me how many people work there. If the place has, say 42 desks, I know I can put that paper out with 30 people, and that means a dozen people will be leaving the payroll even though I haven't seen their faces yet.[21]

In the space of a decade, their U.S. subsidiary American Publishing Co. grew into a chain of 340 small newspapers, for which Black and Radler paid more than $400 million in more than one hundred purchases. They then set their sights on bigger fish. The *Chicago Sun-Times*, then the eight-largest U.S. daily by circulation, had fallen on hard times by 1993 when Black and Radler acquired it for $180 million. Radler applied his cost-cutting prowess and soon doubled the paper's profit margin to 15 percent by cutting 20 percent of its staff. That prompted the departure of no fewer than eight senior editors within a year. Turning off power to their building's escalator to save on electricity costs especially irked staff. Black then returned his attention to Southam, persuading Torstar to sell him its 20 percent stake in the company at a hefty premium in 1992, which made him the company's largest shareholder. He gradually acquired majority control and revelled in his conquest. "If Southam management had been a little more courageous," Black crowed at the company's 1996 annual meeting, "it might still be a family-controlled company."[22] He used the company's nationwide newspaper resources to found a new national daily in competition with the *Globe and Mail*, which he considered dangerously liberal. The *National Post* trumpeted conservative causes from its first issue in 1998, which featured a banner headline urging Canada's fragmented opposition parties to "Unite the Right." Within a decade, Canada would have a more conservative government that the U.S.

Synergy City

Such was the upheaval in the newspaper industry in the 1990s that the *American Journalism Review* commissioned an eighteen-part series of case studies in 1997 called The State of the American Newspaper. Underwritten by the Pew Charitable Trusts, it was an initiative of the Project for Excellence in Journalism, a Washington-based group led by media critic Tom Rosenstiel. It would run to more than a quarter of a million words and, going the muckraking tradition one better, would be published as not one but two books.[23] "The Project's goal was simple," recalled the first book, *Leaving Readers Behind.* "Hire some of the nation's top journalists to apply the same scrutiny to the newspaper industry that newspapers have historically applied to other business sectors."[24] Its first installment was written by Ken Auletta, who had assumed A. J. Liebling's mantle as press critic for the *New Yorker* magazine in 1992. Auletta's 15,000-word dissection of the Tribune Company revealed a firm that had been practically enslaved by Wall Street. "Tribune has become a prototype for the cutting-edge newspaper company of the future," noted Auletta. "Tribune's profit margins, not Gannett's, lap the industry." Its newspapers, including the *Orlando Sentinel* and *Fort Lauderdale Sun-Sentinel* in Florida, as well as the *Daily Press* in Newport News/Hampton Roads, Virginia, were extremely profitable, boasting a collective profit margin of 24 percent. In the age of stock market ownership, however, profits were almost secondary. The real money was to be made in the inflating of stock prices.

> Tribune executives focus unapologetically on their stock price. . . .
> They do it, says [Chief Financial Officer Donald] Grenesko, by carefully talking to Wall Street and gauging its response. "The operating committee decides the goal — say, $2.40 a share." Then, he says, they tell the divisions, "This is what Wall Street is expecting from you."[25]

In the digital age that was emerging in the 1990s, however, Tribune wasn't just a newspaper company, noted Auletta. It also owned sixteen television stations, including outlets in eight of the nation's top eleven markets. Its TV holdings were putting it in a bind with the FCC's cross-ownership prohibition, however. While its ownership of WGN-TV in Chicago had been allowed to remain when the FCC imposed its ban on newspaper publishers holding TV licences in 1975, Tribune's expansion into TV around the coun-

* WGN-TV's call letters, like those of WGN radio, stood for "World's Greatest Newspaper."

try had to avoid overlap with its newspaper holdings elsewhere.* When Tribune acquired Renaissance Communications and its six television stations in 1997, including WDZL in South Florida, it was ordered by the FCC to divest either that station or its *Fort Lauderdale Sun-Sentinel*. Tribune went to court asking to be allowed to keep both, and the FCC granted a waiver for it to retain the station while the FCC revisited its ownership rules. "If the company means to prosper from multimedia synergies between newspapers and TV stations," noted Auletta, "the rules will have to change."[26]

With the advent of the Internet, according to Tribune and many other media owners and experts, the future of media was multimedia. The early buzzword for multimedia ownership was "synergy," which signified collaboration both within and between media. By owning outlets in different media, synergy could be achieved through cross-promotion and the sharing of content. "Executives — and editors, too — go on about synergy and brand extension," noted Auletta, "about how their individual companies are not mere newspapers, broadcast stations or Web sites, but partners and information providers."[27] Tribune was "miles ahead of other companies that moved early into the electronic realm," according to Auletta. "Its newsrooms were the first to blur the lines separating print, TV, radio and Web sites."

> Unlike most newspaper companies, which are reliant on print, its non-newspaper revenues account for more than half its profits. Its newsrooms are multimedia models, with robotic cameras, digital audio and video equipment and a central command desk shared by editors from TV, cable, the Internet and radio.[28]

There was another meaning for the word synergy in the newspaper world of the 1990s, however. In addition to co-operation between media outlets, it also meant co-operation between departments in each outlet, which meant breaching the traditional newspaper wall between editorial and advertising. "The church–state issue intensified at the *Tribune* as its focus grew increasingly local," noted Auletta. "The wall has been chipped at everywhere." The *Tribune*'s managing editor, he noted, headed the paper's "branding committee" and sat in on reader focus groups to determine, in the words of *Tribune* publisher Scott Smith, "what they should be writing about."[29]

Profit and Peril

Not to be outdone by its rival publication at the University of Maryland and its State of the American Newspaper series, *Columbia Journalism Review* featured an over-the-top package in mid-1998 under the headline "MONEY LUST" in block letters on a black cover, with the words in gold except for the blood-red barbed tip of the S. "A new era has dawned in American journalism," it concluded. "A *New York Times* editor describes its hallmark: 'A massively increased sensitivity to all things financial.'"

> As editors collude ever more willingly with marketers, promotion "experts," and advertisers. . . . as editors shrink from tough coverage of major advertisers lest they jeopardize ad revenue . . . the broadly-felt consequence of those factors and many others, collectively, is a diminished and deracinated journalism of a sort that hasn't been seen in this country until now.[30]

News had been hurt by a "heightened, unseemly lust at many companies for ever greater profits," concluded Neil Hickey after an extensive investigation. "In the service of that ambition, many editors are surrendering part of their birthright to marketers and advertising directors, and making news judgments based on criteria that would have been anathema only a few years ago."[31] The introduction of stock options and profit-sharing bonuses into compensation packages for editors were "often a heftier source of income than their salaries," noted Hickey, and tended to skew editorial judgments toward what would increase profits and stock prices. "Bonuses tied to profits tempt both editorial and business-side executives to trim costs, often to the detriment of news processing."

There are major implications when the bonuses of media executives depend solely on the economic — and not the journalistic — performance of their publications. With a direct interest in his paper's profits, can the editor truly exercise uncontaminated judgment in covering controversial subjects or advertisers that might take offense and defect?[32]

One of the first things to be cut in pursuit of higher profits, Hickey found, was expensive foreign coverage, which at many newspapers had declined drastically as a percentage of the news hole. "Result: the public is being drastically shortchanged in its capacity to learn what's going on in the world outside the U.S.'s borders." News executives, noted Hickey, pointed to market research that indicated the public wasn't interested in the rest of the world and was "narcissisticly fixated on life at home in the U.S. — its economy, celebrities, scandals, fads, and folkways." That may or may not have been true, but it was foreign news that perhaps best exemplified the duty of a constitutionally protected free press to adequately inform Americans. "It's no good to say that people now are not interested in consequential news," former *Time* magazine managing editor Ray Cave told Hickey. "The general public has never been truly interested in it. But we delivered it, like it or not. By so doing, we piqued public interest in the very matters that must, to some degree, interest the citizens of a democracy." In a booming economy, Hickey noted, the newspaper business was doing better than ever as a result of its growing corporatization.

Last year (1997) was a watershed for two big reasons: trafficking in papers was at an all-time high; and profits boomed, even as circulation continued to slide. It was dubbed The Year of the Deal: 162 dailies out of 1,509 changed hands, up 37 percent from the year before. Transactions for the year hit a record $6.23 billion. As of February 1, 81 percent of those 1,509 dailies were members of a chain or group.[33]

A sharp decline in competition, however, had "damaged the quality and squeezed the amount of reporting" in the country's newspapers. "Studies show that in cities where competition is hot, the news holes tend to be larger and there are more reporters to fill them," noted Hickey. "Complaints abound from editors of large chain papers that the investment they require to produce a superior paper is being drained away to meet owners' profit demands." The trend toward bottom-line journalism, if it persisted, would result in "a fatal erosion of the ancient bond between journalists and the public," warned Hickey. Cave called it "the biggest story in American journalism." Added Hickey: "Regrettably, it's also the least reported story in American journalism." He concluded with a riddle: "The big question: What doth it profit a media company to demand, unremittingly, steadily higher profit margins year after year and, in that very pursuit, lose its professional soul?"[34]

'Cheapskate' Journalism

For William Dean Singleton, the newspaper business was about clustering, cost-cutting, and co-operating with his "competitors." Scratch that. "I don't think Dean has competitors," quipped David Cole, who published the industry newsletter *NewsInc*. "Dean has business partners who he hasn't done business with yet."[35] Singleton was known as "Lean Dean" for his cost-cutting prowess. The *New York Times* called him "the industry's leading skinflint."[36] *Forbes* magazine called him "the notorious bad boy of cheapskate publishing."[37] Former *Chicago Tribune* editor James Squires swore Singleton could "wring blood from a turnip."[38] Nicholas Coleridge identified the emerging mogul's simple formula for profitability in his 1993 book *Paper Tigers*.

1. Buy newspaper
2. Cut staff
3. Cut quality
4. Cut objectivity
5. Hike advertising rates.[39]

Singleton bought his first newspaper when he was only 21, but the boy wonder Texan never once invested a penny of his own in MediaNews, which he built into the fourth-largest newspaper chain in the U.S. Instead, he always managed to persuade others to bankroll his ambitions. After starting in the newspaper business at the age of fifteen as a part-time reporter for his hometown *Graham Leader*, the baby-faced college dropout worked his way up to a copy editing job at the *Dallas Morning News*. His aggressive style was evident to others, and in 1972 he was approached by a pair of investors who wanted to start a newspaper in the small West Texas town of Clarendon. They financed the operation and gave the twenty-one-year-old half ownership just for agreeing to run it.[40] Singleton put together a modest chain of eight small weeklies by 1975, when he bought the *Fort Worth Press* from Scripps for the bargain price of $100,000. It was fighting a losing battle against the market-leading *Star-Telegram*, however. The war would be over less than three months later when the *Press* folded after losing a reported $1 million for Singleton, who had to sell his weeklies to pay off his debts.

Singleton went to work for Allbritton Newspapers, where he rose to vice-president by age twenty-seven. He soon linked up with retired newspaper publisher Richard Scudder, who was one of Allbritton's newsprint suppliers. Scudder loaned Singleton $200,000 as a 40-percent stake in a company they called Garden State Newspapers. They bought the *Gloucester County Times* in Woodbury, NJ, and tripled its cash flow in two years.[41] Scudder then cut a deal with the Media General chain that would propel the newly-formed MediaNews into the big leagues. The *New York Times* reported details of the arrangement in 1987.

> Media General agreed to provide all the cash for down payments on newspaper acquisitions — usually 20 to 30 percent of the purchase price — in exchange of 40 percent of the ownership of the papers. Mr. Scudder and Mr. Singleton equally divided the remaining 60 percent.[42]

Singleton began buying newspapers as fast as he could. In 1986 alone, he bought thirty-five of them, including the *Dallas Times-Herald* from Times Mirror for $110 million. It trailed the market-leading *Dallas Morning News*, but Singleton was convinced he could make a go of it. "Singleton cut the news staff to about 250 from 320, and eliminated bureaus in El Paso, Tyler, and Lubbock, as well as New

York," noted the *New York Times*.[43] The following year he picked up the *Houston Post* from the Sun Media chain in Canada for $100 million and the *Denver Post* from Times Mirror for $95 million. Both were also trailing dailies. The acquisitions put MediaNews on the cusp of the Top 10 newspaper chains in the U.S. with twenty-eight dailies, but they also came on the eve of a severe recession. Singleton was fortunate to unload the *Times-Herald* in 1988, a year before it folded. Buying the *Houston Post* put MediaNews into direct competition with Hearst's market leading *Houston Chronicle*. When the *Post* proved unable to overtake the *Chronicle*, Singleton sold the *Post* for $120 million in 1994 to Hearst, which closed the paper and had the Houston market all to itself.[44]

Singleton liked to buy newspapers in "asset sales," in which he acquired only their property and equipment without any obligation to continue employing their workers. When he bought the *Oakland Tribune* in 1992, for example, 60 percent of the newspaper's 630 workers were soon unemployed.[45] When he bought the *Long Beach Telegram* in 1997, he quickly cut 200 names from its payroll.[46] At the *Berkshire Eagle*, a 30,000-circulation daily in Pittsfield, Massachusetts, which Singleton bought in 1995, he dropped a quarter of its employees and paid the survivors about 30 percent less. "*Eagle* employees, regardless of rank or seniority, were directed to start interviewing for jobs with the new company," noted the *Columbia Journalism Review*.

> The procedure was as efficient as it was gut-wrenching. First, people were told whether they had a job or not. If they did, [the new editor] handed them a piece of paper that described the basic terms and their new salaries, sometimes as an hourly rate. People were expected to read the paper and put their initials next to the words "accept" or "reject" on the spot. There were virtually no negotiations.[47]

Singleton was only cleaning out "deadwood," he explained to *Editor & Publisher* in a 1999 interview. As for labor-intensive watchdog journalism, to him it was highly overrated. "We, as an industry, got carried away with investigative reporting," he told *E&P*. "We investigated everything that moved, while circulation plummeted because our readers didn't want it. Some people say we owe it to readers to give them what they need. Bullshit."[48] Much of the editing work on newspapers Singleton bought was outsourced to India, where it could be done for a fraction of the cost.[49]

One of Singleton's favorite business partners was the Times Mirror chain, which owned the *Los Angeles Times*. He bought three suburban L.A. newspapers in 1996, added the *Long Beach Telegram* the following year, and effectively had the *Times* encircled. The deal that Singleton did next, however, was the height of audacity. When the second-place *Los Angeles Daily News* went up for sale in 1998, Times Mirror wanted to block certain less co-operative competitors from buying it and possibly starting a newspaper war. Instead it made a deal with Singleton, noted the *Columbia Journalism Review*, who proved very co-operative indeed.

> For antitrust reasons, Times Mirror could not purchase the Daily News, and it was concerned about who might; its executives didn't want a fierce competitor — like Rupert Murdoch — in their core market. A creative solution was found: Times Mirror lent Singleton $50 million of the $130 million-dollar purchase price to buy the Daily News. Moreover, Singleton and Times Mirror forged a plan to sell preprint advertising together.[50]

The DOJ investigated their deal for a year before finally issuing an approval. "We have very savvy lawyers, as does Times Mirror," Singleton told the *American Journalism Review* in 1999. "We both have been in this business long enough to know what you can and can't do."[51] What wasn't known publicly at the time, however, was that not only did Times Mirror loan Singleton $50 million to buy its rival, it also paid MediaNews $2.4 million for a twelve-year option to buy the *Daily News*.[52] In the San Francisco Bay area, Singleton steadily built a small empire. He bought three dailies in 1985 to form the Alameda Newspaper Group (ANG) and encircle Oakland. He added the *Oakland Tribune* in 1992 and the *San Mateo County Times* in 1996. Editorial functions for the "cluster" of dailies were centralized in Pleasanton, which a writer for the *American Journalism Review* toured in 1999.

In a large second-floor room that approaches the size of a basketball court, dozens of copy editors, grouped in units of three to six, sit at their terminals. They're doing the usual things — polishing copy, writing headlines and captions, laying out pages. But not for one newspaper — for five. Simultaneously.[53]

The Nature of the Business

While still largely a secret to the general public, the high level of newspaper profits became a subject of fascination for a few media scholars and industry insiders in the 1990s. "Why Are Newspaper Profits So High?" demanded the headline atop a 1994 John Morton column in *American Journalism Review*. The subheading conveniently answered the question: "The nature of the business, not greed, is the reason." Morton, who closely tracked the profitability of news-paper companies, found they averaged 15 percent profit margins in 1993, or triple the Fortune 500 average, and ranged from 7.1 per-cent for Times Mirror to 34.6 percent for Warren Buffett's *Buffalo News*. "Even during recessions, when the profits of many other businesses fall sharply or disappear, newspapers usually still post more-than-respectable earnings," marvelled Morton.[54] While some critics pointed to greed as the reason behind such exorbi-tant profit levels, Morton had a much more benign explanation. In short, they just couldn't help themselves. "Greed may be a factor at some newspapers, but the real reason newspaper profitability is high is how a newspaper is organized."

> To a large extent, a successful newspaper cannot help having higher profit margins than most other businesses because newspapers, to use economic jargon, are more "vertically integrated" than most other businesses. ... Almost everything else that adds value to the final product — news and advertising content — is created in-house [and] it also retails its manufactured product — the newspaper — directly to its customers.[55]

Vertical integration had long been identified by economists as a main culprit behind the lack of newspaper competition, as control of a printing press especially determined who could circulate a daily on a city's streets. Some proposals for increasing competition in the industry had even called for newspapers to be prohibited from owning presses, which would instead be shared among several competitors.[56] Morton pointed to department stores as an example of a business that had to acquire its goods for resale from a whole string of middlemen, from manufacturers to wholesalers to distributors, each of which had to make a profit of its own. "Now consider a newspaper. The only materials it needs to acquire on an ongoing basis are newsprint, which it normally gets directly from the manufacturer, and newswire and feature services, which are minor cost items." As a result of buying directly from manufacturers and selling directly to customers, newspapers were able to cut out numerous middlemen and keep their profits for themselves. "Newspapers earn most of the various profit margins that drive up the operating costs of most other businesses," argued Morton. "It is not logical to condemn them for something that in fact is dictated by the very nature of the business."[57]

A study of publicly traded U.S. newspaper companies from 1984–94 didn't let them off the hook so easily and even deemed their profits excessive. It found they averaged 15–17 percent profit margins prior to the recession of the early 1990s, which dipped to 10 percent in 1990, 6 percent in 1991, and 10 percent in 1992 before recovering into the teens. Despite the recession, all but one company earned profit margins over the period in excess of 9 percent. Compared with book publishing companies, newspaper profits were 90 percent higher, according to Hugh Martin, and they were 53 percent higher than the return on corporate bonds. "Newspaper companies averaged normal profits in just three comparisons, all as newspaper profits declined during the recession year of 1990."

Newspaper companies . . . earned excess profits throughout most of the study period despite the effects of what one analyst called "the biggest advertising recession since World War II." Newspaper companies apparently had enough market power to return to pre-recession profit levels in three years. . . . Critics who accuse newspapers of protesting too much about their financial situation may have a point.[58]

The 'Cereal Killer'

Otis Chandler was only thirty-three when he was named publisher of his family's *Los Angeles Times* in 1960. He turned a newspaper that had made *Time* magazine's list of the ten worst newspapers in 1957 into one that made its list of ten best newspapers in 1964. Soon, the *Los Angeles Times* stood second on that list to only the *New York Times*.[59] "No publisher in America improved a paper so quickly on so grand a scale," noted David Halberstam in his 1979 book *The Powers That Be*.[60] On Chandler's watch, the *Los Angeles Times* invested heavily in journalism, expanding from two bureaus to thirty-four and winning four Pulitzer Prizes during the 1960s, more than it had won in the previous nine decades combined. Its holding company Times Mirror expanded in the 1960s into cable television and magazines, including *Popular Science* and the *Sporting News*. It began acquiring other newspapers in the 1970s, including the *Dallas Times-Herald*, Long Island's *Newsday*, the *Denver Post*, the *Baltimore Sun*, and the country's oldest daily, the *Hartford Courant*. It got into broadcast television with stations in Dallas, Austin, St. Louis, Birmingham, Harrisburg, Syracuse, and Elmira, NY. Chandler retired abruptly as publisher in 1980, apparently fed up with squabbling from myriad cousins and their demands for a greater financial return from the family business. He took a seat on the Times Mirror board of directors, turned the company over to professional management, and bowed out completely a few years later. The recession of the early 1990s hit Southern California and its aerospace industry especially hard, however, and dropped the company's revenues sharply. By 1994, its profit margin had fallen below 10 percent from the mid-20s, its stock price was down to $18 from $42, and circulation of its flagship Times had fallen almost 20 percent. To boost Times Mirror fortunes — and their own — the Chandler family hired Mark Willes as CEO in 1995.

A PhD in Economics, Willes had been a university professor, a bank president, and for fifteen years vice-chairman of General Mills, a packaged food company that manufactured Cheerios, Cap'n Crunch, and Hamburger Helper, among other brands. He had no previous newspaper experience. Willes, a Mormon whose uncle Gordon Hinckley headed the church, was given huge financial incentives to boost profit, and he quickly took drastic measures to do so. He eliminated 700 jobs at the *Times*, including 150 in the newsroom, and cut 2,300 more at other Times Mirror properties. "Expenses at the *L.A. Times* are higher than at other newspapers," Willes told *Time* magazine. "To get our returns back up to a competitive level, we have to get staffing down."[61] He closed the money-losing Manhattan edition of *Newsday* and the evening edition of the *Baltimore Sun* and sold off non-core assets, such as the company's medical and legal publishing units. His cost-cutting brought howls of protest from journalists and earned him the nickname "Cereal Killer" from the *New York Post*, but Willes defended the moves as just good management. "The basic things that we're doing have been done by many first-rate corporations for over 10 years now," he told *Editor & Publisher*. "This kind of restructuring and streamlining and focus on returns, innovation and speed."[62] It worked wonders for the bottom line at Times Mirror, whose stock price tripled, earning the Chandlers an estimated $1 billion in his first year at the helm.[63] For his efforts, Willes received a $1.35-million bonus in 1996 in addition to his $798,000 salary.[64] Even more lucrative, however, were the Times Mirror shares and stock options Willes received. Willes further enriched himself more than $3 million within his first year on the job, according to the *Wall Street Journal*, as a result of options he was granted to purchase more than 300,000 shares of Times Mirror stock.[65]

A consultation with eighty-seven-year-old management guru Peter Drucker in 1996, according to Ken Auletta of the *New Yorker*, convinced Willes that synergy was the key to even greater prosperity at the Times.[66] Willes decided to create interdepartmental teams responsible for — and rewarded according to — profit performance. Some in the newspaper's management were unconvinced that such a scheme would work. Others worried about the ethical perils of tying journalism to profits and remuneration. Both the publisher and editor of the *Times* abruptly resigned within a month of each other. Despite his lack of newspaper experience,

Willes named himself publisher. Although he was the top executive on one of the world's great newspapers, Willes's journalism inexperience often showed. When he wondered why journalists didn't participate in politics, he had to be told that it was to avoid perceptions of conflict of interest. When he suggested that women readers could be attracted by stories containing more emotion, members of his staff objected to the manipulative nature of such a scheme and Willes had to apologize.[67] After he planned a section aimed at Latino readers, more than 100 staff members signed a petition protesting the plan as journalistic "ghettoization" and the idea was scrapped. "Journalists jumped on the idea as manipulative, phony, and distorting of the editorial process," noted the *Columbia Journalism Review*. "Most scathingly, it's seen as a use of editorial content to solve a marketing problem."[68]

Critical journalism began to take a back seat at the *Los Angeles Times* in favor of so-called "service journalism," better known as "news you can use." For example, its coverage of a new L.A. tax and licensing law directed at people working from home was decidedly accepting of the measure. "Writers protested that the licensing provision was unconstitutional," noted the *Columbia Journalism Review*. "The *New York Times* ran the news story . . . but the *L.A. Times* instead ran a service piece on how to apply for the license. The story used a writer as an example of how to get a license, ignoring the constitutional issue."[69]

'I Get a Bazooka'

It was Willes's most radical scheme that drew the loudest protests, however. In late 1997, he announced a plan to partner section editors with advertising executives and demolish the church–state wall that traditionally separated news and advertising. Editors were paired with "brand managers" from the business side of the newspaper and were given bonuses based on the financial performance of their sections. Each section became its own business, complete with profit and loss statements. If it made money by selling more ads, it would be given more pages and more staff. His wall-busting

experiment made Willes a lightning rod for criticism. Morton pro-
phetically predicted that the plan "could turn out to be the dumb-
est thing ever tried with a newspaper. . . . Or it could point the way
to the future."[70] The experiment, noted the *Columbia Journalism Review*,
"reverses the formula that made publishing dynasties out of *The
New York Times* and *The Wall Street Journal*, the two papers Willes cited
when asked to name his journalistic models. Both started with
great journalism and built their businesses around that."[71] Willes
was undeterred, however, telling an industry newsletter in no
uncertain terms that the separation of church and state was over at
the *Los Angeles Times*.

> There has been more than one person who has pointed out the wall
> between the newsroom and the advertising department. And every
> time they point it out, I get a bazooka and tell them if they don't take
> it down, I'm going to blow it up.[72]

Despite the misgivings of journalists, however, the scheme actually worked fairly well, for a while. The *Times*'s business section, for
example, sold so much new advertising that it was given 20 percent
more staff and 15 percent more space in the newspaper. Profit margins continued to soar for Times Mirror. Willes told the *Wall Street
Journal* that he expected the company's 1997 profit margin to hit 14.2
percent, up from 10.7 percent in 1996 and 7.8 percent in 1995.[73] As
a result, Willes saw his salary and bonus rise even higher in 1997,
to $2.9 million. He was also granted options on another 200,000
Times Mirror shares, according to the *Wall Street Journal*.[74] Soon,
however, a business reporter found a note from a *Times* advertising executive in her mailbox requesting prominent placement in
the paper for an attached press release. Editors all up and down
the chain of command took pains to declare that was going too
far. Willes took to the conference circuit to defend his initiative.
"Never once have I interfered with editorial independence," he told
the American Society of Newspaper Editors convention in Dallas.
"We understand there are lines not to be crossed."[75] A few weeks
later in Washington, he addressed the Newspaper Association of
America's annual conference. "We are not confused about the fact

that we have a compact with our readers to tell the truth," he said. "It is why people trust us and why people read us. And it is therefore why we can provide a way for our advertisers to reach the people they want to reach."[76]

Before long, however, the alternative newspaper L.A. Weekly began referring to the Times as "the publication formerly known as a newspaper" after it drew connections between its news coverage and the corporate partnerships it had formed. A joint venture with the Los Angeles Kings hockey team resulted in a quarter-page story on an award-winning teacher who showed "how effective hockey statistics are for honing math skills."[77] Even more blatant, noted the L.A. Weekly, was an advertisement passed off as front-page news on the day after an election. A "breathless" front-page story touted a new service by long-distance provider Sprint that promised to "revolutionize the way people use their telephones."

> Odd, but the New York Times, the Washington Post, indeed most major dailies missed this big news break. The Wall Street Journal relegated it to a couple hundred words, tucked into a corner on Page 3. Even USA Today left it in the business section.[78]

A second article in the Times business section brought total coverage of the "story" to almost 2,300 words. Then came the embarassing juxtaposition. "Follow the front-page story to the jump on Page 14," noted the L.A. Weekly, "and you can't help but notice that the facing page and the preceding page carried full-page ads for . . . ION, Sprint's 'Revolutionary New Network,' as the ad copy puts it." The Times denied any connection. "According to Times spokeswoman Laura Morgan, the ads' placement was 'pure coincidence,' " reported the L.A. Weekly. "'One is clearly an ad and the other is clearly a news story,' she went on. 'Let there be no doubt.'"[79]

Even the Times's own media critic looked askance at the wall-busting scheme. "Many in the newspaper industry question whether Willes can really devise new strategies that have eluded people who have spent their lives running big newspaper companies," wrote David Shaw in early 1998. "More important, reporters and editors at the Times and elsewhere wonder if, in his gut, he realizes that newspapers are a public trust, not just another moneymaking enterprise." Shaw interviewed many of his co-workers and relayed their misgivings about Willes's plan. "Many reporters at the *Times* worry that if their section editors are meeting regularly with general managers and becoming more aware of the identity of big advertisers, of marketing and promotion initiatives, of profit and loss positions, there will inevitably be a greater likelihood of self-censorship, even if only subconsciously." Shaw's three-part, 20,000-word series also examined the situation at other major dailies, including the *Chicago Tribune*, where advertising executives increasingly worked with editors, and the *New York Times*, where such alliances were fiercely resisted. The closest scrutiny, however, was reserved for his own employer and its new publisher. "Will his initiatives lure more readers and more advertisers and generate more revenue to make the paper even better, without compromising its journalistic integrity?" Shaw wondered. "Or will the bazookas he's using to demolish The Wall also demolish the editorial independence and high standards of the newspaper?"[80] Shaw's questions would not take long to answer.

The Wall Crumbles

A late-1990s downturn in the Southern California economy put a crimp in Times Mirror finances. "Profits in 1998 were supposed to increase by 3.6 percent," reported the *New York Times* in May 1999. "Instead, they dropped about 15 percent, to about $165 million, according to two people with access to the company's budget summaries." Help-wanted advertising fell with the economy, and as a result ad revenues finished $20 million behind projections, which under Willes's formula led to cuts in the space allocated for news. "The editorial department has lost about 3 percent of the space it had in 1998," the *New York Times* noted. "The front section and the metropolitan news section have been among the most affected." Its reporter Felicity Barringer interviewed nine of the fifteen managers who had recently left the *Los Angeles Times* on the condition that they not be identified, and their critique of the newspaper's management under Willes was withering. "Their most common criticism was that management operated in a helter-skelter, ad hoc manner," noted Barringer, "with serial strategies that produced one exhausting experiment after another."

> The circulation department had different problems. By one former executive's account, 1998 began with directives to grow at any cost, which were supplanted by directives to grow but cut costs ever more aggressively.[81]

The financial underperformance led to the layoff of another 850 *Times* employees in late 1998, but it didn't seem to dent Willes's compensation. He reportedly pulled in $13.3 million more in 1998, including $9.9 million in unexercised stock options.[82] The *New York Times*'s exposé of managerial blundering at its west coast namesake, however, was quickly followed by a strategic sidestep. "Seventeen days after Barringer's article," noted the *American Journalism Review*, "Mark Willes retreated."[83] In mid-1999 Willes stepped aside as publisher of the *Times* and appointed in his place Kathryn Downing, a lawyer who had headed the recently sold legal publishing division of Times Mirror. Like Willes, she also had no previous newspaper experience.

The scandal that would bring an end both to Mark Willes's time at the helm of Times Mirror and the Chandler family's ownership of the company broke in October of 1999. Early in that month a new arena had been opened in downtown Los Angeles. The Staples Center was named after the office supply company that paid $116 million for the privilege, but as with most major sporting venues, Staples was just the largest of a myriad of corporate sponsors. Arena management recruited another ten companies to help defray the $400 million cost of construction, including the *Los Angeles Times*. In exchange for a contribution of $8 million over a five-year period, including cash, advertising, and proceeds from "joint revenue opportunities," the *Times* would be entitled to place advertising around the building and would also receive access to a luxury box for all arena events. As its first "joint revenue opportunity," *Times* executives agreed to publish a souvenir magazine for the arena's gala opening. They decided to make it a special issue of the newspaper's regular Sunday magazine, which usually ran to about forty-eight pages. Advertising sales were so brisk for the souvenir issue, however, that the magazine soared to 168 pages and contained a record $2.1 million worth of advertising. It was not disclosed until after the issue was published that the *Times* was sharing the advertising revenue with the subject of the magazine, which violated one of the basic ethical principles of journalism.

It took a couple of weeks for the story to get out, first in the alternative press, then in the *Wall Street Journal* and the *New York Times*. The *Journal* quoted John McKeon, senior vice president of advertising for the *Times*, as asking "why can't a promotional vehicle like the *L.A. Times* and Staples Center work on joint promotions with profit we can share?"[84] According to William Prochnau in the *American Journalism Review*, McKeon's misconceived rationalization "was like dropping a match in a tinderbox."[85] Journalists at the *Los Angeles Times* were outraged, and 300 of them signed a petition demanding an apology from management. "We are appalled by the paper entering into hidden financial partnerships with the subjects we are writing about," it read. "The editorial credibility of the *Times* has been fundamentally undermined."[86] An overflow two-hour staff meeting with Downing in the staff cafeteria turned hostile. Downing apologized and blamed the fiasco on her "fundamental misunderstanding" of editorial principles. "Some questions bordered on insulting," reported Prochnau in the eighteenth and final installment of *AJR*'s State of the American Newspaper series. "Downing was asked if she'd consider going back to school to learn journalism."[87] Staff demanded an investigation and Shaw volunteered to conduct it, but management resisted, so a second petition went around. "What happened next," wrote Prochnau, "was one of those moments in newspapering that few will ever forget."[88] Otis Chandler phoned the city desk and dictated a letter that he asked be read to staff and posted on the newsroom bulletin board. He called the paper's decision to split profits with one of its news subjects "unbelievably stupid and unprofessional."

One cannot run a great newspaper like the *Los Angeles Times* with executives in the top two positions, both of whom have no newspaper experience at any level. Successfully running a newspaper is not like any other business.... Respect and credibility for a newspaper is irreplaceable. Sometimes it can never be restored.[89]

According to Prochnau, the newsroom "exploded" in cheering after Chandler's letter was read.[90] Downing issued a statement in response, but editors mercifully cut the last sentences. "Otis Chandler is angry and bitter," they said, "and he is doing a great disservice to this paper and that's too bad because when he was publisher, he did wonderful things. It's too bad when some people get old, they get so bitter."[91] Staff finally got the investigation they had demanded. Shaw worked on it for six weeks, and the resulting 32,000-word package, titled "Crossing the Line," was published in a special fourteen-page section just before Christmas. The section was edited by a retired staff member, and only one *Times* editor was allowed to read it prior to publication. "Times journalists now fear that the very essence of their work — the bond of trust between them and their readers — has been jeopardized," wrote Shaw. "Many in *The Times* newsroom see the Staples affair as the very visible and ugly tip of an ethical iceberg of ominous proportions — a boost-the-profits, drive-the-stock-price imperative that threatens to undermine the paper's journalistic quality, integrity and reputation." The interviews Shaw did with colleagues produced what he called "a tangled tale of ignorance and arrogance" and provided a damning indictment of Willes and Downing.

> Many past and present *Times* executives, and several current *Times* editors and business-side employees, say that Willes and Downing are not receptive to criticism or cautionary advice; with Downing in particular, they say, subordinates who offer such comments with any frequency are made to feel unwelcome. Willes is more civil and subtle about it, they say; her management style is often described as "my way or the highway."[92]

"Money is always the first thing we talk about," managing editor Leo Wolinsky told Shaw. "The readers are always the last thing we talk about." Bill Isinger, a retired senior financial officer of the *Times* who was Downing's assistant in 1998, was also highly critical of the top executives. "They don't take any counsel," he said of Willes and Downing. "They thought they could drive the paper where it should go without knowing anything of the traditions of the newspaper business ... and why the newspaper business is so different from any other business — why dissent and independence are so prized among journalists and why a journalist's primary loyalty is not to his editor or his publisher or his CEO or even to his newspaper, but rather to the bedrock principles of the profession."[93]

The End of an Error

As the next millennium dawned, the newspaper business had been irrevocably changed. Few, however, could have guessed how much more it would change. Most agreed that the future was multimedia, but with newspapers still playing a leading role. A few smart ones were beginning to think that maybe it was a good time to get out of the newspaper business. Among them were the Chandler family, who had been stung badly by the Staples Center scandal. In a deal made without the knowledge of Willes or Downing, they agreed to $5.9-billion takeover offer from the Tribune Company in March of 2000.[94] Hard on the heels of the $241-billion AOL–Time Warner merger that January, the deal created the country's third-largest newspaper chain by circulation with eleven major dailies, plus a broadcasting empire of twenty-two television stations and four radio stations. The addition of Times Mirror newspapers in Los Angeles, Hartford, and New York, however, put Tribune even farther offside with the FCC, as it also owned television stations in those markets. None of the broadcasting licences for those stations expired before 2006, however, by which time Tribune hoped the cross-ownership ban would no longer be in place.

Willes reportedly wept when informed of the takeover deal executed behind his back. His tears were no doubt eased somewhat by the severance package he received on leaving the company. Under the terms of his contract, his severance pay was reportedly $9.2

million.[95] On top of that, he stood to collect a pension of $970,000 annually starting in 2002.[96] He also picked up a $2 million bonus for 1999, on top of his $900,000 final year's salary. But by far the most lucrative remuneration came from his Times Mirror stocks and stock options, as the company's share price had more than doubled with the Tribune offer of $95 a share. According to the *New York Post*, he stood to pocket almost $33 million from stock options alone. The nearly 700,000 shares he already owned were worth more than $65 million. "Mark Willes will walk away from his Times Mirror empire a very rich professor," noted the *Post*.[97]

FIVE

The Original Sin

It is not true that the newspaper industry failed to foresee the impact of the Internet. This was a freight train that could be seen coming down a thousand miles of track. By the end of the 1970s, noted Keith Herndon in his 2012 book *The Decline of the Daily Newspaper*, publishers had "generally accepted" that technology would alter the marketplace by empowering consumers with newfound control over information.[1] The coming of the Information Society had been predicted for decades, ever since RV-sized computers were programmed with paper punch cards and the precursor networks of the Internet enabled scientists to communicate digitally in the 1960s. "Newspapers will have to decide whether they are printing factories or analysts of daily political and social information," predicted Ben Bagdikian in his 1971 book *The Information Machines*. "If present newspapers do not prepare to become research libraries for political and social information, then the inevitable demand by the consumer for a few subjects pursued in depth will be met by other kinds of organizations."[2] More importantly for their business model, especially for the acres of lucrative classified advertising that poured into newspaper offices daily, computers provided a much more convenient way to search for such necessities as jobs, homes, and cars. "The classified ads (and stock-market quotations) are the bedrock of the press," noted Marshall McLuhan in his landmark 1964 book *Understanding Media*. "Should an alternative source of easy access to such diverse daily information be found, the press will fold."[3]

Some of the largest newspaper companies thus began pouring tens of millions of dollars into computer projects in hopes of capitalizing on the ability to send digital information directly into people's homes. The *Columbus Dispatch* was the first newspaper to go online in 1980, as it was made available on the CompuServe network that was also based in that Ohio city. By 1982, CompuServe had added content from the newspaper co-operative The Associated Press and several of its member newspapers, including the *Los Angeles Times*, *Washington Post*, and *San Francisco Chronicle*. CompuServe was one of the first "walled gardens," to which subscribers could dial in and read stored content online. The service also offered stock quotes, e-mail, classified advertising, and content from *Better Homes and Gardens* magazine. To some, this was a harbinger of the death of newspapers. "I don't mean newspapers will be gone in ten years, but by the end of the century perhaps," Indiana University journalism professor John Alhauser told the *Wall Street Journal* in 1981. Others were more skeptical about the electronic delivery of news. "The electronic newspaper will no more replace the printed one than electronic football will replace football," quipped stock analyst John Morton.[4] The service was expensive, with an hourly usage rate of $22.50 in prime time, which went down to $5 after 6 p.m.[5] Unfortunately for CompuServe, data transmission rates in the early 1980s were much too slow to make online reading viable, even at the off-prime rate, as the *American Journalism Review* noted in 1999.

> State-of-the-art modems of the day could only download content at the paraplegic rate of 300 baud per second, so all the news that would cost you about 25 cents to get in print would cost more than $30 to get online. By June of 1982, this early round of New Media fever went into a fiscally induced remission.[6]

Of more interest to newspaper companies were experiments in the late 1970s by the postal systems of England and France with videotex, a system on which subscribers could call up text on computer terminals. Several U.S. publishers invested heavily in such systems in the early 1980s. First to market and longest to survive was the Fort Worth Star-Telegram's partnership with local computer pioneer Tandy, which launched the Startext online bulletin board system in May 1982 and charged $5 a month for unlimited access. By 1986 it had 2,200 subscribers who were by then paying $9.95 a month. It lasted until 1997, when it was made redundant by the exploding World Wide Web. It survived as long as it did, according to Herndon, because of its low costs and low expectations, "which were never couched in grandiose terms."[7] In 1982 Times Mirror began test-marketing its Gateway system, on which it hoped to sell advertising. It launched in 1984 but folded two years later because, according to Herndon, it was never able to interest enough subscribers to attract advertisers.[8]

But the granddaddy of all the videotex experiments was Viewtron, which was bankrolled by Knight Ridder, then the second-largest U.S. newspaper chain, in partnership with AT&T, then the nation's telephone monopoly. It was launched in 1983, and in addition to providing newspaper content it also allowed subscribers to shop online and "chat" with each other. Unfortunately it only ever managed to attract about 15,000 subscribers and soon found it hard to compete with emerging home PCs. "Only four out of 10 customers who rented terminals continued to subscribe after six months," recalled Roger Fidler, who was involved in the project. "Even when Viewtron finally adapted its service for PC users who paid by the minute, more than 80 percent of the subscribers would become non-users within 13 weeks."[9] The project lost $50 million but made the important discovery, according to Fidler, that users were less interested in reading newspaper content online than they were in interacting with each other. "The interviews and usage data clearly revealed that access to databases of general news, information, and advertising were less exciting to subscribers than the ability to easily communicate with other subscribers."[10]

Despite the heavy financial losses they incurred, the failure of videotex actually had a reassuring effect on the newspaper industry, according to Pablo Boczkowski in his book *Digitizing the News*. "The lack of commercial success of [non-interactive] teletext and videotex systems reassured newspapers that ink on paper was not going to be under attack in the short term," he noted.[11] The foray into electronic publishing, concluded the *Columbia Journalism Review* in 1987, had been purely defensive. "As soon as it became clear that videotex was not going to replace newspapers in the news/information business, these experiments ended." Information retrieval online, it added, simply couldn't compete with the simplicity and serendipity of reading a newspaper.

> Electronic information services require that the informal user develop the habits of a serious researcher. . . . The task of extracting information from a machine demands precision. The act of browsing through a [newspaper] sports section is, by definition, random — and infinitely more enjoyable. In the hackneyed vernacular of the computer industry, a newspaper is more user friendly.[12]

The Tangled Web

By the early 1990s, however, technology had improved to the point where electronic delivery of newspaper content became economically viable, as faster download speeds made online news reading more affordable. The result, according to Boczkowski, was that this was a period of "renewed enthusiasm in electronic publishing."[13] Several newspaper companies struck agreements with proprietary online services such as CompuServe, Prodigy, and America Online (AOL) to provide content for the walled gardens they were growing. AOL revolutionized the business by charging a flat fee for unlimited monthly access, rather than charging by the hour or minute, and it quickly passed the competition. The Tribune Company and Knight Ridder went with AOL, while Times Mirror and Cox Newspapers signed up with Prodigy, and CompuServe continued to offer an array of content providers. This changed very quickly, however.

The advent of the graphical World Wide Web in mid-decade soon created a market for online news that newspapers could exploit directly, as could everyone else. The open web resulted in a stampede to erect websites that were available to anyone who was online. "The World Wide Web is the true Information Superhighway, the equivalent of the Interstate Highway System," declared *Editor & Publisher* magazine in early 1995. "Just about every newspaper in the United States — no, in the world — now has a way to take a giant step into the multimedia future at a very low cost."

> Newspaper people trying to get a handle on their electronic future had best forget about the sprawling two-lane textual Internet and plunge without reservation into the Subset of The Internet known as The World Wide Web. [14]

Development of the web browser Mosaic, which was soon renamed Netscape Navigator, aided the migration by providing a simple graphical interface for readers to surf the web with. "It's a tribute to newspapers and their keen sense of the future that they quickly determined that the online services would never attract the masses they desired," Jack Shafer of Slate observed. "No sooner had newspapers taken up residence on the proprietary online services than they were packing up their pixels and starting their en masse migration to the World Wide Web:"[15] The first to take advantage of the new technology was Knight Ridder's *San Jose Mercury News,* which was conveniently located in the heart of Silicon Valley. "The *Mercury News* became Netscape's first cash customer," noted Shafer, "paying $50,000 for a co-development agreement that granted it access to anything the company came up with in the next year."

> Knight Ridder also took an equity position in the Silicon Valley start-up that in a few months' time produced a $40 million profit. The Mercury News was the first of 29 newspapers that Knight Ridder trundled onto the Web over the next two years.[16]

While only about sixty North American newspapers were offering an online edition in 1995, either on the web or via a proprietary service, by the end of 1996 that number had climbed to 230, noted Herndon. "In May 1998, less than two years later, the number of online newspapers had exploded to 1,749, and most all of them were using the web rather than a proprietary service."[17] A 1996 study of the earliest efforts to sell online advertising found that strategies varied on how much to charge. Seven of the publications it surveyed had no advertisements, while three gave away free ads. "One company priced its ads at $30 for every 3,000 times subscribers hit, or chose to read, the electronic publication," it noted.

> In Florida, one medium-sized newspaper charged $350 to $1,500 a month for advertising, depending on placement and size of the advertisement. The most expensive site was in a major metropolitan area, where the publication charged $100 a day for a one-year contract, or $36,500 a year.[18]

By mid-1999, only two of the largest one hundred U.S. dailies had failed to establish a web presence, according to Boczkowski.[19] The only problem was that a lot of them didn't quite know why they were there. This was at the height of irrational exuberance in the dot-com boom, when the rhetoric all pointed to the Internet transforming society. As Internet start-ups soared in stock market value, the only problem was that few had yet figured out how to make money with this marvelous advance in information technology. "You have all these intelligent people and they don't know why they're doing something other than because everybody else is doing it," University of Illinois journalism professor Eric Meyer told the *American Journalism Review*, "and every day they're saying to themselves, 'If I don't do it, I'll get left behind!'"[20] *AJR* managed to sum up the motivation in one word — fear. Its exhaustive State of the American Newspaper series included an 18,000-word opus on electronic publishing in mid-1999 under the headline "FEAR. COM." Writer Chip Brown nicely put his finger on several of the Web's foibles, including its multitudinous distractions that offered diversions much more interesting than reading the news. As a result, Brown wondered if newspapers had jumped the gun on what some thought might be a fad. "Some critics are starting to argue that newspapers have not been too reluctant to embrace the Web, but too eager," he wrote. "The reasoning goes that it's not their Old Media pasts newspaper people can't escape, but their penchant for pipe-dreaming about a New Media future."[21] The biggest problem was that there didn't seem to be much money to be made in selling either subscriptions or advertising. "I have yet to see any news sites that claim a profit," Meyer told Brown. "Banner ad rates have collapsed."

> They started out at between $35 and $50 per thousand impressions, and now they're around $5, and some of the major national sites are getting around $2 per thousand hits. Subscription sales are the biggest bust of all. Nearly every newspaper that has tried to charge for content ... has stopped.[22]

Only a few publications proved able to make money early on by charging for online access. Slate, the first online-only magazine, was launched by Microsoft in 1996 and briefly tried a $19.95 paid-subscription model in 1998. That lasted only a year before it went free again. Rival Salon adopted a tiered strategy, with an ad-free subscription, a less-expensive paid tier that included some ads, and a model that allowed most visitors to read its content free after viewing a short ad. Some newspapers, on the other hand, had been able to enforce a paywall. "The only ones I know are the *Wall Street Journal* and the *Champagne News Gazette* in Illinois, which charges $4.50 a month just to read the sports pages," Philip Meyer told Brown. "They have some columnist and everybody who went to school at [the University of] Illinois and followed sports likes to keep up with him."[23] The *Arkansas Democrat-Gazette* took a different approach. It began charging $4.95 a month for access to its website when it launched in 1998 and eventually attracted an online subscription base of about 4,000. Publisher Walter E. Hussman Jr. stubbornly refused to lift his paywall even after most other newspapers had ditched theirs, pointing out that the *Democrat-Gazette*'s print circulation had remained steady while that of most other newspapers had fallen. "Why would they buy a newspaper when they can get the same information online for free?" asked Hussman.[24]

Classified Operations

Wired magazine insisted in 1996 that advertising was the only realistic source of revenue for online publishers because the infrastructure needed to impose user fees was still years off. "Subscriptions can only work with the superpremium end of a publisher's audience," predicted writer Hunter Madsen.[25] In their quest for online advertising, newspaper companies launched a number of initiatives. The first and largest, however, demonstrated that their ability to work together against a common threat would be severely limited. In 1995, a consortium of nine newspaper companies including Knight Ridder, Tribune Co., Times Mirror, Gannett, Hearst, the Washington Post Co., and the New York Times Co. created New Century Networks. Their objective was to counter the threat that technology companies such as Microsoft and Yahoo! posed with ventures designed to capture online advertising. Unfortunately, noted *BusinessWeek*, New Century "came to embody everything that could go wrong when old-line newspapers converge with new media."

> New Century had something even William H. Gates III coveted: the content of newspapers throughout the country. Affiliates could use Mardi Gras stories from the New Orleans Times Picayune or Hollywood news from the Los Angeles Times. Separate subject-oriented Web sites would pool stories on everything from health care to sports. And advertisers could run banners on one site or 100 with the push of a button.[26]

The problem, according to *BusinessWeek*, was that the companies had "wildly diverging philosophies about how newspapers should make the electronic leap" and what the role of their new venture should be. "You had private companies and public companies and companies that were risk-averse and those that were risk-tolerant," explained Harry Chandler of the *Los Angeles Times*. "You had big-city papers and small chains. We shared a need. But it was frustrating trying to come together."[27] New Century spent eighteen months hiring a CEO and two years creating a portal to the online content of 140 newspapers. By the time it went online in 1997, noted *BusinessWeek*, "not only was Microsoft ahead with its Sidewalk. com online city guides, but New Century's own partners also had launched competing ventures."[28] Members of the consortium split over whether to take it public and sell shares. "Like nine parents with a new baby, they couldn't even choose a name," said *Business-Week*. "Some wanted news. Others wanted classifieds. Tribune Co. was so exasperated, it joined America Online Inc. in a classified service, becoming a New Century pariah."[29]

Knight Ridder also went its own way, creating its Real Cities network of newspaper web sites in a bid to attract ad revenue. The network of forty websites included online versions of the chain's thirty-one dailies, regional portals such as Charlotte.com, and websites such as Auto.com, which was a web-only supplement produced by the *Detroit Free Press*. In a determined bid to counter its burgeoning online competition, Knight Ridder also moved it headquarters from its flagship *Miami Herald* to the *San Jose Mercury News*. "Relocating to Silicon Valley . . . is part of a determined effort to fend off powerful foes, such as Yahoo! Inc. and Microsoft Corp., that are trying to lure advertising from newspapers to such fast-growing Internet services as CarPoint and Yahoo! Classifieds," noted *BusinessWeek* in early 1999. "In a kind of 'if you can't beat 'em, join 'em' approach, [CEO Tony] Ridder is pushing hard on a Web assault of his own."[30] Unsurprisingly, New Century Networks collapsed in acrimony in 1998 after having lost its member newspapers $27 million.

The biggest threat the Internet posed to newspapers was its ability to siphon off their rich classified advertising revenues through sortable online databases. "Classifieds work better online than they do in print," noted *Fortune* magazine in 2000. "They are searchable, deep, interactive, and up to date, when done right."

Help-wanted ads link job hunters to company Websites. Car ads include photos and detailed specs. Homes for sale offer virtual tours. Best of all, classifieds can be distributed far more efficiently online than in print; no wonder it costs less to place classifieds on the Web than in a big-city paper.[31]

Newspapers were still fat with classified advertising by then, with their revenues having risen in the U.S. from $11.5 billion in 1990 to $19.6 billion by 2000, which made up about 40 percent of their total advertising revenues. Much of that increase in revenue, however, had been achieved not by increased volume but by continually hiking rates, according to Herndon.[32] Rates for classified advertising placed on websites, by contrast, were low or even free, subsidized by display advertising. "It's really hard to cannibalize yourself and trade high-margin revenues for low-margin revenues one second before you have to," David Israel told *Fortune*. Israel was CEO of Classified Ventures, a newspaper consortium that hosted sites such as Cars.com, Homescape, Apartments.com, Rental-HomesPlus, and HomeGain. Newspaper companies understood that they had to change their approach or they would lose the war for online classifieds, he told *Fortune*. "They get it intellectually," he said. "But they struggle with the emotional issues and the financial dynamics."[33]

The largest slice of the classified advertising pie quickly became the most hotly contested. "The biggest push has been to stanch the hemorrhage in the employment portion of the classified market," noted the *American Journalism Review*, "which the NAA [Newspaper Association of America] estimated in 1997 accounted for $12 billion, or 70 percent or more of the entire classified market."[34] Monster.com quickly came to dominate the online job search market, so in 1996 yet another consortium of eight newspaper companies scrambled to set up CareerPath, its own competing website. By late 1999, however, CareerPath was attracting fewer than 900,000 unique monthly visitors, compared to Monster.com's more than 2.7 million. "Monster.com has a big enough lead that it could soon crush its rivals," noted *Fortune*.

> Its site works better than CareerPath's, it generates three times as much traffic, and it boasts that nearly three times as many resumes are posted on its site. . . . In fact, the Tribune Co. and Washington Post Co., which have stakes in CareerPath, are so unhappy that they have launched Brass Ring, a potential competitor that offers online recruiting services.[35]

As it mostly went with the World Wide Web, however, the secret to unlocking its potential came not from corporate boardrooms but from college dorm rooms and citizen programmers, who came up with the best ideas. When Craig Newmark began posting Craigslist out of his San Francisco apartment in the mid-1990s, it would prove the beginning of the end of any chance newspapers had of hanging on to their lucrative classified advertising base. The free online classified service expanded to other cities in 2001, and by 2010 it was available in more than 700 markets in 70 countries. It became the seventh most-visited web site in the United States, with more than fifty million new classified advertisements each month. According to one study, it took away $5 billion in revenue from local newspapers between 2000 and 2007 alone.[36] By 2011, daily newspaper classified advertising revenues in the U.S. had been reduced to $5 billion from their peak of $19.6 billion in 2000.

The Cult of Convergence

The dot-com bubble of the 1990s brought a new buzzword for media — convergence. The term replaced "synergy" as the guiding mantra of corporate media executives. It essentially envisioned all media converging into one new medium online, with text, audio, and video all being delivered digitally in the future. There were actually several different types of convergence, however. Device convergence saw computer, telephone, television, and other technologies converging. Journalistic convergence saw reporters covering stories for print, radio, television, and online media. Corporate convergence saw broadcasters and publishing companies merging with each other and with new media start-ups to capitalize on advances in technology.[37] The seminal convergence event fittingly took place in January 2000, just as the new millennium dawned. In the largest corporate merger ever, old media giant Time Warner married new media powerhouse AOL to create a multimedia monolith with a stock market value of $541 billion. Time Warner was a media conglomerate that had been created by the second-largest corporate merger, of magazine and book publisher Time Inc. with movie and music company Warner Communications in 1989. The company acquired Turner Broadcasting in 1996, adding its numerous TV stations and cable channels, including CNN. Despite Time Warner's massive size, AOL was actually worth more on paper as a result of the dot-com bubble, so its shareholders got 55 percent of the combined company. The merger created a wave of enthusiasm for convergence, but the FCC's cross-ownership ban put a damper on media mergers in the U.S. because it prevented newspapers and television stations from marrying. AOL–Time Warner may have suddenly become the world's largest media company, but one thing it didn't own was a newspaper.

No such cross-ownership ban existed in Canada, however, and by year's end a frenzy of convergence transactions transformed the country's media. Canada's two private television networks partnered with national newspaper properties, as did the largest French-language network in the province of Quebec. CTV, the country's largest private network, was acquired by telecom giant Bell Canada, which then partnered with the *Globe and Mail* national newspaper to create a $4-billion multimedia monolith briefly known as Bell Globemedia. Canwest Global Communications, which owned the national network Global Television, bought Canada's largest newspaper chain, Southam Inc., from Conrad Black's company Hollinger International for $3.2 billion. Quebecor, a newspaper company that started in the province of Quebec but expanded nationwide with its 1998 purchase of the Sun Media newspaper chain, then paid $5.4 billion for Quebec's largest cable company, which owned the French-language TVA network.[38] Convergence became a controversial issue in Canada, however, as journalists at Canwest's newly-acquired newspapers began protesting editorial interference by the Asper family, which owned the company. The episode convinced many Canadians that convergence had concentrated too much political power in too few media owners, and in 2002 a Senate inquiry was called into the nation's media.[39]

In the U.S., media owners stepped up their demands that the

FCC's cross-ownership ban be lifted so they could get in on the convergence game. Under the 1996 Telecommunications Act, the FCC was required to regularly revisit its ownership regulations to ensure they were necessary. The Bush administration that moved into the White House in early 2001 was ardently de-regulationist and it installed a new FCC chair who was dedicated to lifting the restriction on cross-media ownership. The giant Tribune Co. in particular had been put in violation of the prohibition in several major markets with its 2000 acquisition of Times Mirror. FCC hearings began in September 2001 under chairman Michael Powell, the son of Secretary of State Colin Powell. With little news coverage, in 2003 the FCC voted 3–2 along party lines to lift the ban. A subsequent survey found that 72 percent of Americans had heard "nothing at all" about the relaxation of media ownership rules and that the more people knew about corporate media convergence, the more they opposed it.[40] Word of the change spread mostly over the Internet, and a storm of bipartisan protest resulted in more than two million e-mails, letters and petition signatures being presented to the FCC. The protest resulted from a growing concern about the political power of Big Media following the invasion of Iraq on questionable grounds, according to the *Columbia Journalism Review*. "Media had become a political issue," it noted, "as deeply felt as the economy, health care, or education."[41] The protest resulted in a Senate review, which voted 55–40 in September 2003 to overturn the change.

Walled Gardens

By that time, however, the dot-com bubble had already burst with the recession that began in early 2001 and deepened with the 9/11 terrorist attacks. Share prices of converged media companies plummeted with those of other technology stocks. AOL–Time Warner shares fell from a high of $55 to a low of $8.70 as the company reported a record loss of $98.7 billion for 2002. "AOL" was removed from the company's name the following year and the online division was eventually spun off as a separate company.

Convergence quickly fell from favor among media executives as the AOL–Time Warner merger went down as one of the most disastrous of all time.[42] Canwest Global Communications, which was mired in close to $4 billion in debt, struggled with the cost of servicing its loans as advertising revenues fell with the recession. From a high of $22 in 2000, its share price fell below $7 in mid-2002.

The dot-com crash threw the convergence paradigm for a loop. With Internet start-ups falling by the wayside and online advertising rates plummeting, many newspapers wondered if there was any way to make money online. Some worried that they had made a mistake by committing the "original sin" of giving readers free access to their digital content in their quest for online ad revenue. By 2001, noted a study in the *Journal of Media Economics*, the online subscription model re-entered the agenda despite market research having found "little evidence suggesting that users are ready to pay."[43] Suddenly paywalls began popping up again. The *Spokane Spokesman-Review*, for example, started charging $7 a month in 2004, and after a brief drop in traffic, one year later it had about 1,000 online subscribers.[44] The ethos of the Internet, however, was that information wanted to be free, and most web surfers would much rather go elsewhere for news than pay for it. There was no shortage of places to find online information, either, and most of it was a lot more titillating than what stodgy old newspapers had to offer. By 2005, the NAA counted only forty-four online newspapers in the U.S. that charged a subscription fee, out of about 1,500.[45] "After years of experimenting, no business models seem to generate reliable revenue streams for online news services," observed the *Journal of Media Economics* study. "The industry's endeavor in seeking economic viability has become a unique case in media economics, because no other media have had to experiment with so many revenue models as online newspapers have."

By implementing the fee-based model, the online news industry runs the risk of losing the user base that they have tried so hard to build (by giving content away for free). As a result of this, advertisers will turn away. This may create another crisis and may seriously undermine the quality and quantity of online news services offered to the public.[46]

Rates for online advertising, like those for print advertising, were based on how many people were exposed to the ad, and this created a conundrum for online newspapers. In advertising jargon, rates were measured by CPM, or cost per thousand page views, and they went up as readership or circulation went up. Paywalls discouraged readers from visiting a website, which put a damper on readership and thus ad rates. The *Journal of Media Economics* study found that most Internet users were not paying for online news and "did not show a strong intent to pay in the future, suggesting that the subscription model is not working and may not work well in the future."[47] The *Los Angeles Times* stopped charging for its online entertainment listings CalendarLive in 2005, according to the *Columbia Journalism Review*, after two years of "declining page views and modest revenue."[48] The *Sacramento Bee* dropped the paywall around its state news section Capitol Alert, for which it had hoped to find a market among lobbyists in the state capital.[49] The *New York Times* also abandoned a paywall it had erected in 2005 called TimesSelect, which had charged $7.95 a month or $49.95 a year for online access to its columnists and opinion content, plus the newspaper's vast archives. It ended the experiment in 2007 after it decided the revenue gained wasn't enough to offset the lost traffic to its website.[50] "At the end of its two-year run, TimesSelect had 227,000 paying subscribers and was generating $10 million a year in revenue," noted the *American Journalism Review*. "Not too shabby, but the future was limited."[51] Shortly after its paywall was dropped, unique visitors to the *Times*'s website hit 12.7 million a month, almost 38 percent more than a year earlier.[52] The exodus of the *Times* from the subscription model signaled to *AJR* that the paywall was dead. "With no more high-profile practitioners, can we finally stick a fork in the subscription model?"[53] When CNN and the *Economist* tore down their paywalls in 2007, *Advertising Age* similarly declared the second wave of paywalls dead. "The experiment in paid content is over," it concluded. "No sale."[54]

The Ad Invasion

An alternative to charging for online content saw readers fork over something almost as important as cash to publishers — information about themselves. After the dot-com crash cast the entire information economy into doubt in the early 2000s, many publishers turned to registration, asking only for demographic and marketing data. Some put most editorial content in a registration-only area, while others selectively registered users. More importantly, the sites added revenue by monetizing the demographic data they obtained from their users. The data allowed them to work with marketers to target online advertising to consumers based on the demographic information obtained, as they had been doing since the 1980s with their print subscribers. "That demographic targeting is what has long set *The New York Times* apart from its competitors," noted *Editor & Publisher* in early 2003. "Requiring users to register from the very beginning of its Web site in 1996, the *Times* truly is the master of its domain, with 10 million active registrants today."[55]

The magazine surveyed newspapers and found that requiring registration did not discourage readers from frequenting newspaper websites. "In fact, several of these papers now have more online visitors than they had before requiring registration."[56] More importantly, they were able to turn visitors into revenue as a result of registration. "We've gone from zero dollars to seven figures in 2002 — all from sponsored e-mail products," said Eric Christensen of Belo Interactive, which published the website of the *Dallas Morning News*. Belo, which also published several smaller dailies, recorded a 30 percent decline in page views for a few months after requiring registration, but then its traffic began to increase again and within two years was up more than 20 percent.

Newspaper sites that built up registration walls last year have found that readers didn't leave in droves. In fact, several of these papers now have more online visitors than they had before requiring registration. … As word of this and similar successes spreads, more publishers are gearing up to build registration firewalls.[57]

All of the large newspapers that moved to full-site registration were "pleasantly surprised by the overall impact on traffic," reported *E&P*. "Virtually all of the executives contacted say they'd gladly take these traffic declines in exchange for what they've gained (real data about their users, who are more loyal and more active) and what they expect to gain (an advertising payoff)."[58] The *Washington Post*, 80 percent of whose online readers lived outside the DC area, required readers to provide only their age, gender, and location. Traffic to its website continued to grow in spite of registration. Customer complaints amounted to just one for every one hundred registrations at the Belo papers, and only 2 percent at the *Los Angeles Times*. The online edition of the *Chicago Tribune* experienced only a brief 10-percent drop in page views in the first month after registration was introduced. "We were prepared to lose up to 20% to 25% of our page views during a six-month transition period," said Digby Solomon, general manager of Chicago Tribune Interactive. "It was a really short blip, and it was over quickly. It was much better than we expected."[59]

One advantage of registration was reader loyalty. The *Chicago Tribune*'s website was "stuck at an average of 2.5 visits a user each month," noted *E&P*. "Since the advent of registration, the average user comes six times a month." It had also been able to charge advertisers up to $100 CPM by collecting ZIP codes for use in targeted e-mail campaigns and planned to use registration data to begin targeted advertising on its website. "We are getting such a fine degree of detail in terms of targeting that we will eventually be able to target a physical product to a household address, a digital product to the digital user in that household and a mobile product to the mobile user in that household," said Don Meek, president of Tribune365, told *Advertising Age*.[60] The *New York Times* also became more aggressive in its registration questionnaire, asking users more about their occupations and their print subscriptions, noted *Editor & Publisher*.

The ability of software to tailor on-screen advertising to what was known about a computer user provided what would turn out to be the best opportunity to profit from online ads. For decades, advertisers had complained that most of their advertising expenditures were lost on reaching people who had little or no interest in their products. "Half the money I spend on advertising is wasted," Philadelphia department store owner John Wanamaker once complained famously. "The trouble is, I don't know which half." With the advent of online communication, that problem was soon solved. A website could use robot-like "cookies" that infiltrated a user's computer to track its browsing history and thus determine the user's interests. Websites used this data to decide which of a range of advertisements to post alongside their content. As newspapers raced to get in on the game, however, they were quickly eclipsed by computer wizards who would soon dominate the market for this type of advertising.

Newspapers also experimented with what media economist Robert Picard called the "ad push" model of online advertising, which would target users of their websites with email marketing campaigns based on what had been gleaned about their interests. The effectiveness of this type of marketing was limited, however, by its intrusiveness. "Although the model created a revenue stream to support operations, audiences were unhappy with content and service providers who used such systems because they saw it as an intrusion on their mailboxes," noted Picard.[61] Even more intrusive were the "pop up" ads that began to bedevil web surfers, but blocking programs rendered them largely ineffective by the mid-2000s. Less intrusive were the display ads that made up most of a newspaper website's non-news content, and by using demographic information and browsing history, they could be targeted to a user's interests. Unfortunately for online newspapers, a digital juggernaut was already perfecting a system to profit from just this type of advertising.

Programmers of the search engine Google developed its AdSense program in 2003 to target advertising on its pages of search results based on what it was able to find out about a computer's user. The system proved wildly profitable as Google began to dominate the way computer users navigated the web.[62] By itself, that might not have greatly affected the newspaper business, but in the mid-2000s Google developed a new search product called Google News. By linking to the stories that news organizations posted on the web free for all to read, posting their headlines and the first few lines of their content on a page of search results, Google had found a way to attract oceans of eyeballs. It made a killing by selling targeted advertising alongside portions of the news that had been gathered and posted by others. News organizations became alarmed, as this was an unintended consequence of the original sin they had committed of giving away their online content for free. In early 2005, the French news service Agence France-Presse filed suit against Google for $17.5 million, claiming copyright infringement for reproducing portions of its news stories. A settlement was reached that included a licensing agreement under which Google paid AFP a fee for replicating its content. Agreements with several other news services followed, including the Associated Press.

The Battle of the Freesheets

In the early years of the twenty-first century, newspapers of a certain type experienced a curious revival. A worldwide explosion of commuter tabloids had quietly begun with their successful 1995 introduction in Stockholm by Swedish company Metro International. Make that re-introduction. The 19th Century "penny press" dailies in the U.S. had been tabloid-sized and even smaller, designed to be read by riders on the earliest horse-drawn mass transit systems. Tabloids were also popular in the U.K., as exemplified by Rupert Murdoch's *Sun*, which he converted from a broadsheet after buying it in 1969. The format proved so successful that even up-market titles the *Independent* and the *Times* converted to tabloid format in 2003. The *Times* was able to reverse years of circulation declines by doing so, especially boosting its readership by women under forty-four. Tabloids found a niche in Canada starting in 1971, when staff of the folded *Toronto Telegram* broadsheet started the tabloid *Toronto Sun*. It grew into a minor chain of like-named tabloids across Canada in the 1980s, boosted in part by the closure of long-publishing broadsheets in Ottawa and Winnipeg in 1980. Southam even converted its conservative broadsheet *Vancouver Province* to tabloid format in 1983 and found the format attracted advertisers wanting to reach younger readers.[63]

Free commuter tabloids proved so popular in Europe that by 2006 almost half of the newspapers printed in Spain were giveaways. *20 Minutos*, a freesheet owned by Norwegian publisher Schibsted, became the country's largest daily with a circulation of 2.3 million.[64] Metro's giveaway editions boasted a worldwide circulation of 8.5 million, with twenty-one titles in sixteen countries by 2002.[65] It launched in Philadelphia in 2000, in Boston the following year, and in New York in 2004.[66] The infiltration into U.S. markets prompted established dailies to launch their own freesheets to head off the competition. The Washington Post Co. launched *Express* in 2003, while the Tribune Company launched free tabloids called *RedEye* in Chicago and *AM* in New York.[67] "Getting into the free business is a smart and necessary strategy for a graying industry," noted *BusinessWeek* in 2005.

> The move draws in new advertising, from local auto dealers to special cell phone promotions. The giveaways provide the big papers with a scrappy brand that allows them to deliver a young audience to advertisers with discounted rates or packaged offers.[68]

After Metro announced plans to begin publishing a free commuter tabloid in Vancouver and other Canadian cities in 2005, Canwest announced it would give away its own free sheet, dubbed *Dose*, in five cities.[69] Quebecor also got in on the game with a tabloid called *24 Hours* in several Canadian cities. Suddenly, newspaper wars were breaking out all over North America, nowhere more than in Vancouver. Three new titles sprang up there in a market that Canwest had dominated with both dailies, most of the community newspapers, and the dominant television station. There was apparently money to be made with free newspapers. Belo's freebie *Quick* attracted about 200 advertisers that had never bought space in its *Dallas Morning News,* according to *BusinessWeek.*[70] *Quick* soon doubled in size from its initial editions of twenty to twenty-four pages. "Revenues in the fourth quarter of 2004 exceeded $1 million and were 35 percent greater than the revenues in the previous quarter," its general manager told the *American Journalism Review.*[71] *Metro Boston,* a 49-percent share of which the New York Times Co. bought for $16.5 million in 2005, reportedly had revenue the previous year of $10 million.[72] *Metro New York,* noted the *American Journalism Review,* started off printing 250,000 copies a day but soon increased its press run to 350,000 and also hiked its advertising rates by 10 percent. "More than 500,000 people see an average issue, according to a survey done in January by Scarborough Research."

> Fifty-one percent of those are in the golden demographic of 18 to 34 years of age, Metro's target market. By comparison, only 28 percent of the New York Times' readership falls in that age bracket, and 18 percent of the New York Post's, Scarborough found.[73]

In San Francisco, billionaire Philip Anschutz bought the ailing *Examiner* in 2004, which had undergone a messy divorce from the joint operating agreement it had with market-leading *Chronicle.* He converted it to a free tabloid the following year, with home delivery to selected neighborhoods. His company Clarity Media then started *Examiner* editions in Washington and Baltimore and registered the name as a trademark in sixty-three U.S. cities. "Critics can argue about the quality of these papers, but their existence does say something about the prospects for print," noted Paul Farhi in the *American Journalism Review.*[74] Some media critics, however, were not impressed. "Some of the new free tabloids in the Bay Area are taking the commercialization of news to a new level," noted the media monitoring group Grade the News in 2005.

> The line separating journalism from commerce can get so blurred that one local paper, the Palo Alto Daily News, has advertising salespeople write entertainment, restaurant and art reviews — masquer-

ading as journalists while plugging businesses. The Daily News also has a written policy encouraging journalists to write news articles about advertisers, "promoting the business as their own."[75]

Stories in the *Examiner* and the *Palo Alto Daily News*, which was part of a five-freebie chain purchased by Knight Ridder in 2005, tended to be shorter and more superficial than those in the Bay area's broadsheets, according to Grade the News. "The quality of reporting falls well short of the journalism provided by newspapers you purchase," noted Michael Stoll. "The giveaway dailies often push inexperienced, underpaid reporters to churn out short articles that lack context, adequate sources and initiative."[76] But the stories in many of these papers weren't just short, noted the *American Journalism Review*. "There's also a . . . snarky voice designed to echo the lingo of these younger readers and the writing in hipper alternative media." The younger readers at whom these newspapers were targeted were more used to surfing the Internet, and studies showed they actually got most of their news from Comedy Central's satirical news program *The Daily Show*. "We certainly didn't model anything after *The Daily Show*," *Quick* editor Rob Clark told *AJR*. "But it's the perfect example of the sort of thing that gets people talking. I believe that this is a generation of people that craves satire."[77]

Recovery and Folly

With the economy's return to health by mid-decade, some newspaper companies began making acquisitions again. Others with more foresight decided that it might be a good time to get out of the newspaper business. Those that got out did so just in time, while those that took on high levels of debt to bolster their holdings soon found it weighed them down. Among the buyers was the Journal Register Company, which was already highly leveraged. It bought a chain of four Michigan dailies and eight-seven non-dailies in 2004 and thus took on another $415 million in debt. Lee Enterprises, an Iowa-based chain, swallowed the larger Pulitzer, Inc., a chain of fourteen dailies founded in the nineteenth century by Joseph Pulitzer, for $1.46 billion in a 2005 deal that was financed almost

entirely by debt. Those acquisitions were small, however, compared to the ones that followed.

   After Knight Ridder profits fell from 19.4 percent in 2004 to 16.4
percent in 2005, dissident shareholders of the nation's second-largest chain, which owned thirty-two dailies, demanded higher
returns. The former family-controlled firm had neglected to institute two-tiered stock ownership when it went public and it eventually became dominated by professional investors.[78] When higher
returns were too slow in coming, they forced a sale to the smaller
McClatchy chain for $4.5 billion in 2006. McClatchy was the sev-
enth-largest chain in the U.S. before acquiring Knight Ridder, and
was based in Sacramento, where it published the *Bee*. In order to
digest the giant acquisition, it sold a dozen of Knight Ridder's less
profitable newspapers, including both dailies in Philadelphia, and
its own *Minneapolis Star Tribune*, which it had bought in 1998 for $1.3
billion. According to Herndon, the Knight Ridder sale signaled
"that the traditional business model for newspaper companies was
finished."[79] As a sign of the stock market's disapproval, McClatchy's
share price began falling. By the end of the following year it had lost
69 percent of its value, while the market had gained 17 percent.[80]
McClatchy's purchase of Knight Ridder would not be the biggest
newspaper deal to go down before the bubble burst, however, nor
the most foolish.

   In Chicago, the Tribune Co.'s board of directors had become frac-
tured between the company's old guard and the Chandler family
members who had taken a significant position in the company
with its takeover of Times Mirror. In a quest to boost quarterly
earnings, Tribune's absentee management of the *Los Angeles Times*
had seen staff slashed, over the objections of the newspaper's top
executives. Publisher Jeffrey Johnson was fired in 2006 after protesting the cuts, and editor Dean Baquet followed him out the door
a month later after publicly speaking out against further auster-
ity measures.[81] After Tribune's profits fell from 20 percent to 18.5
percent in 2006, Chandler family members demanded out. "The
Chandlers' outrage put enormous pressure on the board to sell
the company," recalled James O'Shea in his 2011 book *The Deal From*

Hell.[82] O'Shea was dispatched from the Tribune Tower to Los Angeles to replace Baquet, but ended up quitting in disgust himself. A buyer was found for Tribune Co. in colorful real estate mogul Sam Zell, who put up only $315 million of his own money in a controversial $8.3 billion acquisition in mid-2007. The other $8 billion was borrowed by the new Employee Stock Ownership Plan that bought all shares of the company, effectively making its retirees (and would-be retirees) part owners.

The following month, Rupert Murdoch acquired privately held Dow Jones and its *Wall Street Journal* for $5.6 billion in a takeover that paid members of its controlling Bancroft family a rich premium over the company's share price. Murdoch coveted the business daily as a platform from which to compete with the *New York Times*. No sooner had the ink dried on the paperwork, however, than advertising revenues began to nosedive. The U.S. economy officially went into recession by year's end, marking the beginning of a long financial nightmare for newspapers, which would never be the same.

'A Disastrous Strategy'

In the *Wall Street Journal*, Murdoch acquired one of the few newspapers that had been able to make an online subscription model pay from the start. It and the *Financial Times* in the U.K. were able to attract scads of paying customers to their websites, so they must have had something that readers were willing to pay for. Not only was their news valuable to investors, but the immediacy provided by the Internet was worth paying for from an investment perspective. The secret to their success, many believed, was that not only were the quality and immediacy of their business coverage worth something to investors, but that the cost of subscriptions was tax deductible as a business expense. The *WSJ* first began charging for its online content in 1997. It had more than 650,000 registered users before that, and when it started asking $49 for annual access to its website, that number dropped by more than 90 percent. Two years later, however, the *WSJ* had about 250,000 online subscribers. It raised its online subscription rate to $59 per year in 1999, but renewal rates were about 80 percent. By 2000, according to one history, it recorded the largest gains in paid circulation in its four year history, reaching 438,000 subscribers.[83]

Despite this success, subscriptions actually brought in a minority of WSJ.com revenue, as advertising accounted for 60 percent. While the *New York Times* could charge advertisers on its website a CPM of $40, noted the *American Journalism Review* in 1997, the *Wall Street Journal* could charge considerably more. "The Wall Street Journal Interactive Edition charges a $55 CPM for a similar buy," it noted. "Search engines like Yahoo! and Excite, by comparison, charge about $20 per thousand impressions."[84] These new revenue streams, the WSJ.com history concluded, were the result of "a variety of programs, ranging from traditional advertising and direct marketing to innovative retail and e-tail efforts to expanded efforts on college campuses."[85] The *WSJ*, noted historian Dan Steinbock, had developed a product with real value to readers. "It was able to create, attract, and retain users, because of its continuous product augmentation, complementary downstream capabilities, and customization and personalization."[86] In the U.K., the *Financial Times* enjoyed similar success, with more than 100,000 online subscribers. It increased the annual fee for its subscribers, two-thirds of whom were located outside the British Isles, from £99 to £149 in 2008.[87]

Despite the *Wall Street Journal*'s success in enforcing a paywall, Murdoch speculated in 2007 about dropping the subscription model at his new acquisition in an attempt to sell even more online advertising. His idea was based on the traditional mass media model of newspapers attracting more ad revenue by bringing in more readers. The fact the *WSJ* was able to make more than $65 million a year from online subscriptions changed Murdoch's mind, however. *BusinessWeek* noted that the *WSJ* was also able to charge much more for its ads than the rival *New York Times*, in part because its readers were considered more desireable by advertisers.

The Journal's readers are seen as business-minded, college-educated professionals with significantly above-average wealth — the sort of audience that advertisers, particularly makers of luxury goods, want to reach. If the Journal were to significantly expand its audience by moving to a free model, it would no longer be able to command the same premium because the audience would be more diverse.[88]

Soon Murdoch became a staunch defender of paywalls, moving to impose them at his other newspapers around the world. He also became a fierce opponent of Google, whose aggregation of newspaper content in its search results was bringing it considerable ad revenue. Despite their declining print circulation, newspapers actually had more readers than ever when online readership was factored in. The only problem was that those extra readers did not bring newspapers much revenue because it was going elsewhere instead, mostly to Google. Advertising started to dry up for newspapers, according to Morton, at least in part because of a major shift starting in 2004 of advertising to websites that were proliferating due to the rapid expansion of high-speed broadband Internet access. "Among the competing sites are aggregators that gleefully pluck newspaper-gathered news there for the taking on free newspaper Web sites," noted Morton in 2011. "Only now are newspapers rethinking this disastrous strategy."[89] Many of the competing websites that proved more successful than newspapers in attracting online advertising were actually filled with newspaper content. In addition to Google and other search engines, websites such as MSN.com and Yahoo! had struck licensing deals with the Associated Press starting in the 1990s to publish its voluminous daily news content to attract advertising. The problem was that the AP was a co-operative owned by its member newspapers, and much of its news service content thus came straight off their pages. "In fact, some of the stories the AP sends out to its digital customers each day are rewritten from newspapers," noted Paul Fahri in 2009. "All of which means that, for years, newspapers have effectively been handing their online competitors one of their chief weapons in the fight for the news audience, the AP wire."[90] The practice dated to the 1980s, when the AP began licensing its content to Internet service providers such as CompuServe and AOL. In 1998, the AP's board of directors compounded the original sin of newspapers by voting to sell its content to Yahoo!, its first open Internet customer. "Over the past decade, digital clients have grown from almost nothing into one of the AP's largest revenue sources," noted Fahri. "Fees from online customers now account for about $125 million annually, or about 17 percent of the $748 million the AP collected from all sources last year."[91] It seemed that newspapers could do nothing right in their bid to capitalize on the Internet. Soon they would be preoccupied with their very survival.

SIX

The Dead

The brief spate of newspaper closures that attended the 2007–09 financial crisis and ensuing recession brought on a panic in the media that quickly spread to the general population. Soon many became concerned for the survival of their favorite daily newspaper, which most had actually stopped reading years earlier, at least in print.

What could be called the Great Newspaper Panic was caused by a bubble bursting in print advertising, which was accelerated by the economic downturn but had actually begun a bit earlier. Advertisers began to capitalize on their ability to reach customers directly via the rapidly-diffusing Internet rather than having to pay media owners to spread the word about their wares. This included ordinary people who could now advertise online for little or no cost rather than having to place an expensive classified ad in their local newspaper.

The Internet was just the latest in a series of technological advances that had eaten into newspaper readership, starting with radio in the 1920s. There was surprisingly little effect on newspaper revenues until the advent of the broadband Internet, however. Newspaper print advertising revenues in the U.S. were a near record $47.4 billion in 2005, just off their all-time high of $48.6 billion in 2000, which was more than double what they had been in 1984, and four times their 1978 total. Newspaper print ad revenues had shot up since 1968, when they first passed $5 billion.[1] Forty years later, the bubble burst.

The newspaper panic was short-lived, however, as most dailies were able to downsize their staffs and otherwise cut costs enough to keep their heads above water. Those that couldn't were on their last legs anyway as either second-place dailies or afternoon newspapers, or both. Their extinction was nothing new and merely continued a trend dating to the 1930s. Few cities in North America had been able to sustain more than one competing daily newspaper, and the latest round of closures added Cincinnati, Halifax, Albuquerque, Madison, Denver, and Seattle to the list of one-newspaper towns. For the dailies that remained, however, their monopoly made them stronger businesses. By examining each market where newspapers disappeared, it is possible to understand their deaths as explainable under the circumstances and not as part of an inevitable extinction that many predicted.

Cincinnati

The newspaper die-off began on the last day of 2007, when the *Cincinnati Post*, an afternoon daily founded in 1881, printed its last edition. Its death was hardly a surprise, however. The rival *Enquirer*, with which the *Post* had cohabited since 1977 in a joint operating agreement (JOA), announced in early 2004 that it would not renew the agreement when it expired at the end of 2007. The *Post*'s circulation had dropped from a high of 275,000 in 1961 to just 27,000 by the time it closed, most of it in northern Kentucky, where it published as the *Kentucky Post*. So routine was the *Post*'s closure that it gained almost no attention in the national press, and none in the journalism reviews. Its death only became relevant as the body count of deceased dailies grew over the next year or so. In hindsight, however, the closure of the *Post* was a result of many of the factors that conspired against newspaper competition. It was both an afternoon daily and running in second place, which under the circulation spiral and the Natural Monopoly Theory of Newspapers made it a prime candidate for closure.

The demise of the *Post* was attended by considerable irony. The *Post* was at one time Cincinnati's dominant paper, flagship of the E.W. Scripps Co. which owned it and had its own headquarters there. Scripps actually bought the competing *Enquirer* in 1956. It overplayed its hand, however, by also buying the town's third newspaper two years later and folding it into the *Post*. That got the attention of the Department of Justice (DOJ), which took until 1964 to file an antitrust lawsuit that pointed to the obvious monopoly. Scripps finally agreed to settle the case by selling the *Enquirer* to local ownership in 1968.[2]

After the 1970 Newspaper Preservation Act blessed unions between newspapers if one daily could show that it was going out of business, the *Post* and *Enquirer* applied for a marriage licence in 1977. Scripps was a devotee of JOAs, having originated the concept in 1933 when its *Albuquerque Tribune* had taken up with the competing *Journal* in the depths of the Depression. While it was the first modern chain, the Scripps empire had been built on collusion and anti-competitive policies, according to journalism historians.[3] When the Newspaper Preservation Act went into effect, Scripps had a hand in no fewer than seven of the twenty-two existing newspaper partnerships. Subsequent JOAs had to get DOJ approval or else convince a judge that one newspaper would fold without a combination. When the DOJ balked at approving the Cincinnati JOA, hearings were held that required Scripps to prove its *Post* was "in probable danger of financial failure" unless it was allowed to go into business with its competition. Scripps produced figures to show that the *Post* had lost money since 1972, including $3.7 million in 1974, but some were skeptical. "A closer look at the Cincinnati story ... raises doubts about how these handsome losses were produced and how Justice goes about judging such a case," pointed out legal scholar Stephen Barnett, who noted that large overcharges by Scripps head office had reduced the *Post*'s profits substantially.[4] More objective measures showed that the *Post* was hardly failing, according to Barnett. It had fallen behind the *Enquirer* in circulation for the first time in 1977, but by March 1978 it had regained the lead. "In advertising linage, the *Post* had lost its lead over the daily *Enquirer* in 1973, and by 1977 was behind by about 10 percent," noted Barnett. "Ahead by a nose in circulation, behind by a neck in advertising, the *Post* was scarcely out of the race — assuming that it wanted to run."[5] The problem, according to Barnett, was that Scripps had long been intent on stifling newspaper competition in Cincinnati, and had been focused on a JOA ever since the DOJ forced it to sell the *Enquirer*.

> Having settled by that time on a joint operation, Scripps had every reason to shape its financial results to please the attorney general. The refusal to explore a Sunday edition was only one of several business decisions during this period that smelled of self-immolation. Another was the Post's failure in November 1977 to match a price increase by the Enquirer, even though the two papers had been raising their prices in lock step since at least 1957.[6]

The DOJ failed to call any expert witnesses at the hearings to counter the four that Scripps produced, noted Barnett, and the deal was approved. The owners of the *Post* had threatened to shutter it if a JOA was denied, flatly refusing to even consider a sale. "Told to take it or leave it," quipped Barnett, "Justice took it."[7] Gannett bought the *Enquirer* in 1979 and soon had the upper hand in Cincinnati as first readers and then advertisers fled afternoon dailies. Rust-belt Cincinnati deflated from a city of 500,000 in the 1960s to one of about 300,000. By 2004, the Enquirer was selling four copies for every one for the *Post*. Closure of the *Post* brought to twenty-three the number of U.S. cities with newspaper competition, but only eleven of those had separately owned and operated newspapers, with the rest being JOAs.[8]

The demise of newspaper competition in Cincinnati had the predictable effect on diversity of opinion there. According to a 2004 study, the Cincinnati JOA had provided some balance to the conservative voice of Gannett's *Enquirer*, as Scripps papers were traditionally liberal. The study of newspaper editorials published by both Cincinnati papers in January 2003 showed that the *Post* at least showed some skepticism during the run-up to the invasion of Iraq. "The *Post* published 14 editorials on Bush administration policies, and it opposed the president on five — a 64.3 percent rate of editorial support for the president's policies, compared to 100 percent for the *Enquirer*."[9] Scripps papers were "built on the foundation of working-class readers and editorial policies that promoted their concerns," noted John Nerone, a University of Illinois journalism professor and a Cincinnati native.[10] That soon changed to a more corporate orientation, according to Nerone. "By the time I was an adult, its identity had modified. It had become locked into its rivalry with the *Cincinnati Enquirer*, and appeared to pursue the same readers, the same advertisers, the same interests, and the same politics."[11] The closure of the *Post* was actually felt less in Cincinnati, according to a 2009 study, than across the Ohio River in Northern Kentucky, where it sold most of its copies as the *Kentucky Post*. The *Post* provided more than 80 percent of the local newspaper coverage in Northern Kentucky, according to a study by two economists, which found that a void resulted from its closure.

> Our findings suggest that even a small newspaper can make local politics more vibrant. Although competing publications or other media such as TV, radio and blogs may take up some slack when a newspaper closes, none of these appears so far to have fully filled the *Post*'s role in municipal politics in northern Kentucky.[12]

The economists found that politics changed drastically in the seven Kentucky counties where the *Post* had circulated. "The closing of the *Post* reduced the number of people voting in elections and the number of candidates for city council, city commission and school board in the Kentucky suburbs," it noted, "and raised incumbent council and commission members' chances of keeping their jobs."[13]

Halifax

Six weeks after the *Cincinnati Post* folded, staff members at the *Halifax Daily News* on Canada's east coast were called into a surprise Monday morning meeting. The mood was somber as terse executives from Transcontinental Media headquarters in Montreal announced that the *Daily News* was folding immediately after twenty-nine years of publication. Before the meeting ended, *Daily News* e-mail accounts had been cancelled and its logo replaced on its website with that of the free commuter tabloid *Metro*, which would begin distributing editions on the streets of Halifax three days hence — Valentine's Day. As a result, ninety-two people were suddenly unemployed. "There would be no goodbyes, no thank yous for nearly 30 years' service," griped Stephen Kimber, a former *Daily News* columnist who was also a journalism professor at the local University of King's College. "It was just over."[14]

The feisty tabloid had only a short history, being founded as a suburban weekly in 1974 before moving downtown five years later in competition with the entrenched *Chronicle-Herald* broadsheet. The *Daily News* had suffered through a succession of corporate owners since 1997, when it was bought by Conrad Black's Hollinger International, which sold its Canadian newspapers three years later to Canwest Global Communications, controlled by the Asper family. It was under Canwest that the *Daily News* endured its worst times, as the Aspers imposed their editorial views on their newly acquired dailies. Bill Turpin, who had been *Daily News* editor for sixteen years, and others resigned after a Kimber column that criticized Canwest was killed. Kimber blew the whistle in the *Globe and Mail*. "The Aspers support the federal Liberal Party," noted Kimber. "They're pro-Israel. They think rich people like themselves deserve tax breaks. They support privatizing health-care delivery. And they believe their newspapers, from Victoria to St. John's, should agree with them."[15]

Most *Daily News* staff members were thus elated when cash-strapped Canwest sold the paper in 2002 to Transcontinental, a printing company that also owned magazines and small newspapers. The *Daily News* foundered under its new ownership, however, with its circulation dwindling to just 20,000. "In 2006, Transcon laid off some of the paper's best journalists," noted the alternative weekly *The Coast*, "preferring to concentrate its efforts on a string of free weekly papers stuffed with soft 'stories' wedged between ads. As the *Daily News* coverage and morale slipped, circulation dropped."[16] Like all Metro tabloids, the Halifax edition was a barebones operation, which meant that almost none of the ninety-two *Daily News* staff members would be needed. "Six of its seven Canadian sheets are run out of Toronto," noted *The Coast* after *Metro* hit the streets later that week. "What the Transcon bean-counters did was close a real paper to make way for a cheaply produced but trendy advertising sheet."

> The news copy produced here is sent up the pipe, where Toronto editors lay out the local pages, add a few more stuffed with cheap wire copy and send them back to Halifax for printing. No analysis, no editorial cartoons, no investigative journalism.[17]

The Canadian Association of Journalists protested the conversion as part of a dangerous trend. "Halifax is left with an empty shell — a victim of publishers' current penchant for stripping news outlets of their content and delivering 'News Lite,'" said CAJ president Mary Agnes Welch in a statement. "Newspapers that rely mainly on wire reports ... offer the public all the local reporting skills of a photocopy machine."[18] Journalism professor John Miller of Ryerson University in Toronto told *The Coast* that Metro newspapers were designed to be read in twenty minutes, which he had learned from a former student who was editor of his city's edition. "They have a very specific demographic, which is younger, less affluent, but educated," said Miller. "They even have a name for their customer: Sarah — the only person in the world who gets younger every year. She started at 34 and now she's 22."[19] *Metro Halifax* would be published five days a week instead of the seven that the *Daily News* published, and would consist of only twenty to twenty-four pages per issue compared with fifty-six to sixty pages. Kimber told the *Ottawa Citizen* he doubted that a *Metro* would be successful in a city of only 300,000. "The paper they're starting seems to be just one more indication they don't really understand the business that well," he said. "They're starting a transit paper, but we don't have a subway system, and we don't have a very developed public transit system."[20]

Albuquerque

The Scripps chain considered closing its *Albuquerque Tribune* at a time when many were predicting that the combination of an economic downturn and competition from a new medium would kill newspapers. That was in the early 1930s during the Great Depression. No fewer than fifty U.S. dailies did in fact shut down between 1928 and 1933, as did almost 1,000 weeklies, according to journalism historian Edward Adams, as the new media miracle of radio steadily ate into newspaper advertising revenues. "From 1929 to 1939, newspaper advertising revenue fell 45 percent, while radio advertising revenue doubled," noted Adams. "In 1929 newspapers carried 54 percent of the national advertising available, whereas radio received 4 percent. By 1939, newspapers had only 38 percent while radio had increased its share to 27 percent."[21] In Albuquerque, the evening *Tribune* that Scripps had bought in 1923 came under attack when the morning *Journal* started an evening edition that threatened to wipe it out. While the *Tribune* had boasted more than twice the *Journal*'s circulation in 1926, seven years later the combined editions of the *Journal* had a comfortable lead. In a breathtaking downturn, the *Tribune* lost 26.6 percent of its advertising revenue between October 1931 and October 1932, noted Adams, compared to a loss of 15.3 percent for the *Journal*. Executives of the Scripps chain, then known as Scripps Howard, considered drastic action if the situation didn't improve. "Keeping a close eye on the bottom line, [general manager] Roy Howard slated the *Albuquerque Tribune* for closure if the downward trend continued," wrote Adams.[22] Instead, Scripps Howard executives began working on a plan to preserve the *Tribune* and some of their other flagging newspaper properties. They met the *Journal*'s owner in Chicago to pitch their plan for combined operations in late 1932, according to Adams.

> The key to the plan called for the elimination of the afternoon Journal, leaving the Journal as the only morning paper and the Tribune as the only evening paper. Scripps Howard management and [Journal owner Thomas] Pepperday met at the Scripps Ranch in Miramar, California, on February 14, 1933 and finalized an agreement.[23]

A key component of the partnership was designed to head off complaints from those who pointed to a business partnership possibly stifling editorial competition. "It seems to me inevitable that the community will suspect that there is some element of a frame-up in this proposition," Howard wrote to Pepperday. "With this in mind, I think it is especially important that both papers pursue divergent editorial courses and be sure that they do not, consciously or unconsciously, justify the public in any belief that they are indulging in mutual back scratching."[24] The "Albuquerque plan," which included separate newsrooms, became the template for subsequent agreements over the next five years between Scripps newspapers and competitors in El Paso, Texas, and Evansville, Illinois. In all three markets, Scripps papers were in second place and thus in danger of extinction under the circulation spiral. "During the 1950s Scripps Howard was involved in JOAs in Birmingham, Alabama; Knoxville, Tennessee; and Columbus, Ohio," noted Adams. "In the 1960s Scripps Howard established a joint operating agreement in Pittsburgh."[25] Scripps was a major lobbyist for the 1970 Newspaper Preservation Act, and negotiated its JOA in Cincinnati shortly after its passage. "By 1980," noted Adams, "out of the ten major dailies owned by Scripps Howard, only two were not involved in a JOA — the *Rocky Mountain News* and the *Memphis Commercial Appeal*."[26]

Joint operating agreements weren't a permanent solution to newspaper preservation, however, and in most cases provided only a temporary fix to a long-term problem. "In the late 1970s, 28 cities had two papers joined at their wallets via JOAs," noted Paul Farhi in 1999 after JOA dailies died in St. Louis, Miami, El Paso, Nashville, Pittsburgh, and elsewhere. "Today, only 13 do — and the vital signs of papers in many of those towns are weakening by the month."[27] The cause of death in many cases was ruthless business, as the dominant morning paper often bought out its afternoon partner while the DOJ looked the other way, or simply refused to renew the agreement after it expired. "The cause of death for many JOA papers over the past 15 years seems more closely akin to homicide than advanced age," Farhi wrote. "The suspension of solvent

JOA newspapers does seem to raise a question: Exactly what is the Newspaper Preservation Act preserving?"[28] The simple fact was that one newspaper could often make more money than two because its costs were much lower. As the JOA parties usually split the profits whether one paper published or two, it could be more profitable to close one. In Miami, Knight Ridder actually extended its JOA with Cox Newspapers for twenty-five years just before Cox folded its evening *News*, noted Farhi, guaranteeing Cox a share of the surviving *Herald*'s profits until 2021. "Critics say such pay-for-not-playing deals — repeated with variations in Knoxville, Tulsa, Pittsburgh and other cities — pervert the spirit and intent of the Newspaper Preservation Act."[29]

In Albuquerque, the *Tribune* suffered from the same wasting disease that afflicted every afternoon daily that did not enjoy a local monopoly. By 1988 its circulation was down to a barely sustainable 42,000. Two decades later it was reduced to 10,000 while the morning *Journal* sold more than ten times that number. For the second time in two months, the Scripps chain decided to remove a money-loser from its books. When it pulled the plug, the journalism world finally started to take note of a trend. The *American Journalism Review* published a paean to the deceased daily penned by a *Tribune* reporter. "The *Trib* was one of the last of its kind, where writers spent as much time plotting crusades as they did pondering leads," Tony Davis waxed nostalgically. Its smaller staff prevented it from even pretending to be a newspaper of record, noted Davis, so it left routine news to the *Journal* while it focused on enterprise reporting. "The *Trib*'s decline was the stuff of Greek tragedy," he wrote, "a paper that basked in the limelight of well over a dozen big national awards while circulation plummeted."[30] It took until 2014 for the *Columbia Journalism Review* to offer a more clear-eyed assessment. "Though known for its solid reporting and stalwart voice — it had won a Pulitzer in 1994 — the small afternoon daily in New Mexico's largest city never really stood a chance," it noted.

> Most Albuquerqueans (or Burqueños, as the locals call themselves) would have agreed that the Tribune was superior to the city's other daily newspaper, the Albuquerque Journal. The Trib boasted stronger

reporting, better photography, and cleaner design. But it was stuck, bound by an operating agreement that forced it to stay an afternoon paper.[31]

Madison

America's entry into World War I in 1917 divided journalists. Seeing it as their country's chance to take its place on the world stage, many leading Progressive journalists, including the legendary Walter Lippmann, signed on to the government's propaganda effort.[32] Others, such as William Evjue, saw the war as a foreign entanglement designed to enrich arms merchants. Evjue was managing editor of the *Wisconsin State Journal* when the war began, but when the newspaper turned on local senator Robert La Follette, who opposed the war, Evjue quit and started his own daily. His *Madison Capital Times* supported La Follette and opposed the war, but it had to endure an advertising boycott that at one point reduced it to only one display ad. "This was not a popular position," noted longtime *Capital Times* editorial pages editor John Nichols. "The first copies of *The Capital Times* were put to use as kindling for the fires that burned the senator in effigy. The administrators of the University of Wisconsin's Department of Journalism refused to allow students to intern on the paper because of its anti-war position."[33] But Evjue sold shares in the Capital Times Co. for $1 each and the newspaper survived, in part because of its support for labor unions. His upstart daily provided such vigorous competition for the *State Journal* that it took the circulation lead in the 1940s. Exasperated, the *State Journal*'s Iowa-based owner, Lee Enterprises, agreed to a joint operating agreement in 1949 and moved to morning publication. For taking the then less-favored time slot, the *State Journal* got to publish on Sundays while the *Capital Times* put out a Saturday paper. The *Capital Times* provided a rare liberal voice, opposing Senator Joseph McCarthy and his Communist witch hunts in the 1950s, and the Vietnam War in the 1960s, before it became fashionable. It was among the first to champion civil rights, environmentalism, and gay rights. Evjue died in 1970.

By 2008, *Capital Times* circulation had dropped below 17,000, while the *State Journal* sold almost 90,000 copies in the increasingly more popular morning slot and also reaped the benefits of the lucrative Sunday paper. Under their joint operating agreement, profits of both papers were split equally between Lee Enterprises and Capital Times shareholders. The Madison agreement was different from other JOAs, however. "You have what looks like a JOA, walks like a JOA, and quacks like a JOA, but isn't a JOA," John Morton told the Madison alt-weekly *The Isthmus* for a cover story in late 2007 marking the newspaper's ninetieth birthday.[34] The key distinction was that most other JOA papers owned a third company that performed joint functions like printing and distribution, while in Madison the company that performed the joint functions also owned both papers. Capital Newspapers Inc. was in turn owned equally by Capital Times shareholders and Lee Enterprises. This arrangement meant that, unlike other JOAs that had a finite term, the Madison partnership was ongoing, with no end date. It was also a mysterious agreement. "We're governed by a contract that was negotiated in 1948 that very few of us know the contents of," *State Journal* editor Ellen Foley told *The Isthmus*. One thing that was obvious to the numerous Capital Times shareholders, however, was that it was a very profitable partnership. "Last year, the company paid about $7.3 million in dividends," noted *Isthmus* writer Jason Shepard. "Since the Capital Times Co. is half-owner of Capital Newspapers, profits for the overall operation likely topped $14.5 million." When Shepard interviewed *Capital Times* executive editor Paul Fanlund for his feature, however, he was curiously evasive on some topics. "There's his odd refusal to talk about the future of the newspaper," noted Shepard, "awkwardly sticking to a 'no comment' mantra in an otherwise cordial interview."

> "I'm just not willing to look forward." He measures his words carefully, at one point leaving a full 60 seconds of silence between question and answer. "There are two things I've decided just not to comment on: the future of *The Capital Times*, and the future of its journalistic focus and emphasis."[35]

The reason for Fanlund's reticence became clear two months later, when the *Capital Times* announced it would cease print publication that April, focusing its efforts on the Internet and also producing two weekly insert sections for the *State Journal*. The decision outraged some, who pointed to the profits the newspapers were making. "The corporate decision to transform the *Cap Times* into an online daily ... was driven by cool calculation and raw greed," railed Bill Lueders, a columnist for *The Isthmus*. "In the end, the corporate desire to make a few more dollars by killing the paper won out." Lueders pointed for evidence of rapaciousness to a radio interview that Nichols gave. "We could have kept publishing a daily newspaper for as long as we wanted," Nichols admitted. "This isn't a situation where we had to shut down."[36] One week later, Lueders hadn't calmed down. "It's sad for subscribers who are not web-connected, and thus can't 'access' the publication's 'content' online," he wrote. "It's sad for those to whom reading a daily newspaper means, curiously enough, reading a newspaper — not snacking on news bytes in-between watching videos on YouTube and checking for new friends on Facebook."[37]

Capital Times management swung into damage control mode. "It's been no fun dying on the vine," news editor Ron McCrea told *The Isthmus*. "I can't tell you how many times I've had the experience of talking to people about a great story we've had, and nobody has a clue that we published it." A turning point came, he said, when the paper failed to win new subscribers in working class neighborhoods with a promotion that offered free copies. "We thought this would be a rich target for us to fill out our circulation, but people just weren't buying," said McCrea. "Some people even complained that we were littering! They asked that we take the papers away." By becoming the first U.S. daily to convert to digital publication, the *Capital Times* hoped to reach more readers than it could in print, he added. "You can only do so much before you finally have to face reality," said McCrea. "Online is clearly the future of journalism."[38]

Part of the reasoning behind the move was also to spread their founder's brand of Progressive journalism farther and wider on the Internet, *Capital Times* editor Dave Zweifel told the *State Journal*. "If we wanted to keep Evjue's voice and vision alive, [moving to the Internet] was a necessary step and one he probably would have taken," said Zweifel. "We could continue to do this for a long time to come, but what's the point if we're only going to be talking to a select few people?"[39] Another factor was the financial plight of Lee Enterprises, which was suffering worse than most newspaper companies with the recession because it had taken on so much debt in buying the Pulitzer chain a few years earlier. While the Madison partnership was profitable, the *Capital Times* was no doubt a money loser and thus a drag on Lee. By the time the last daily edition of the *Capital Times* rolled off the presses, even the *New York Times* had taken notice. "We felt our audience was shrinking so that we were not relevant," publisher Clayton Frink told the *Times*. "We are going a little farther, a little faster, but the general trend is happening everywhere."[40]

The Christian Science Monitor

While print advertising revenues began to slow at most newspapers in a serious way in 2007, online ad revenues had more than doubled between 2004 and 2006. For many beleaguered publishers, that pointed to the Internet as the way of the future. At the rate digital ad revenues were increasing, the reasoning went, it would take only a few years for them to make up what newspapers were losing in print advertising. The lure of digital-only publication was strong, noted Thomas Kunkel, because it fulfilled not only the vision of convergence, but a longer-standing vision of a "paperless" society. "When that day arrives, some of the happiest people on earth are apt to be newspaper publishers," said Kunkel, who was dean of the University of Maryland's College of Journalism.

> For that day will mark the culmination of a technological march that began nearly half a century ago. I mean, think about what a paperless world will actually mean to publishers:"
> • No more newsprint to buy — and other than the annoying cost of human beings, this is the single largest expense newspaper companies have.

- No more presses — as long and as heavy as oceangoing ships, and about as expensive — to buy.
- No more people to run those presses.
- No more circulation departments to run.
- No more circulation trucks to buy, gas up and maintain.
- No more delivery people to hire.[41]

The paperless society had been predicted for decades and was a concept that grew out of the "paperless office," which was first bruited by *BusinessWeek* magazine in 1975. The expansion of computer technology from data processing to word processing, it predicted, would mean that by 1990 little if any paper would be used in modern offices.[42] A few years later, librarians were told that their stacks of books and journals would soon be replaced by digital documents. "The paperless society is rapidly approaching, whether we like it or not," predicted F.W. Lancaster in a 1978 book.[43] But the predictions of paperlessness proved at least premature. Paper stubbornly endured, noted the 2003 book *The Myth of the Paperless Office*, because it had some definite advantages over words displayed on computer screens. "Paper tends to find its natural place in . . . the kinds of activities we normally think of as key to knowledge work," wrote authors Abigail Sellen and Richard Harper, "activities that involve making judgments, solving problems, making sense of information, making plans, or forming mental pictures of information."[44] As for the paperless society, the proliferation of computers seemed to have the opposite effect, noted one librarian the following year. "We live not so much in a post-Gutenberg society, as in a Gutenberg society on digital steroids," wrote David Kohl, who pointed out that computers had only accelerated the use of paper and that book sales had risen dramatically.[45] By 2012, noted Nicholas Basbanes, author of the book *On Paper*, computer printers were churning out about three trillion pages a year, enough to cover New York City 237 times over, and the average American was using about 750 pounds of paper a year. "The 21st century may well prove to be the digital century," quipped Basbane, "but it seems misguided to set the obituary of paper down in cold type."[46]

Yet some newspaper publishers were seduced by the savings

they could make from ditching their print editions, as the *Capital Times* had done. "The road to e-profitability is a lot easier if you can shed well over half your existing costs," noted Kunkel.[47] Such a drastic measure was called for by the drastic times at the *Christian Science Monitor*, a Boston-based daily that was founded in 1908 by the Church of Christ, Scientist and was once considered one of the world's top newspapers. It circulated mostly by mail and had won a string of Pulitzer Prizes and other awards, mostly for its lavish international coverage. The *Monitor* last made a profit in 1956, however, and had subsequently lost hundreds of millions of dollars for the church.[48] Circulation peaked at 240,000 in the early 1970s and had fallen to around 186,000 by the late 1980s when a colourful redesign saw it dubbed "USA Yesterday."[49] Circulation plunged to 78,000 by 1997, when another redesign sent the *Monitor* downmarket in search of readers. "The idea that the Monitor redesign may be aimed at 'soccer moms' has generated some concern that the paper is headed down the slippery slope of news lite," noted the *Boston Globe*.[50] By 2008, circulation was down to 56,000 and the *Monitor* was losing $18.9 million a year while bringing in only $12.5 million a year in revenue. As the newspaper passed its hundredth birthday, the announcement was made that it would cut back to weekly publication and focus on its website. "We have the luxury — the opportunity — of making a leap that most newspapers will have to make in the next five years," *Monitor* editor John Yemma told the *New York Times*.[51] With this news, along with that of layoffs at Time Inc., Gannett, Tribune, and the *Newark Star-Ledger*, the *New York Times* locked on to the Death of Newspapers meme. "Clearly, the sky is falling," wrote media columnist David Carr. "The question now is how many people will be left to cover it."[52]

On the Death Watch

The Internet enabled just about anyone to publish just about anything online, and the prospect of newspaper closures led technology journalist Paul Gillin to start a blog in 2007 called Newspaper Death Watch. Gillin had predicted in a 2006 essay posted on his website that the ability of bloggers and citizen journalists to post content online would soon lead to the demise of most daily newspapers. "In 10 years, probably a third of metropolitan daily print newspapers will be gone," he wrote. "Instead of 1,500 print newspapers, there will be perhaps five to 10 national 'super-papers' and many thousands of regional and special interest community news sites."[53] Gillin listed each new casualty on Newspaper Death Watch under the heading R.I.P., but he seemed to be reaching sometimes. For example, he added the *Cincinnati Post* and the *Kentucky Post* as separate entries when they were the same newspaper. When Lee Enterprises merged its 104-year-old *South Idaho Press* with the nearby *Twin Falls Times-News* in August 2008, Gillen added the *Press* to the list, despite the *Press* having had a circulation of less than 4,000. And when the *San Juan Star* just happened to fold while Gillin was vacationing in Puerto Rico, its name also went up under R.I.P.

Gillin was soon joined in newspaper death blogging by Martin Langeveld, who started News After Newspapers in September 2008. Langeveld was newly retired from a thirty-year newspaper career that saw him serve for thirteen years as a publisher and group vice-president for the MediaNews chain in New England. He saw continual cost-cutting as dooming newspapers. "The problem is that many newspapers may be damaged so severely by these cuts that readers will abandon them in droves, followed by some of the remaining advertisers, setting up a death spiral from which they cannot recover."[54] He also made the single best argument that newspaper doomsayers could muster, which was that their readership was growing older because young people were not taking up the reading habit. "Within a few years, the average newspaper reader will be of retirement age, and only the 65-and-up age cohort will still have a majority (but barely) that reads a daily newspaper. That's not a sustainable business model."[55] In early 2009, just as the panic over newspaper closures was picking up steam, Langeveld struck blogger gold when the Nieman Foundation at Harvard added his blog to its compendious website. Nieman Journalism Lab, which focused on the future of news media, also began to run regular contributions from Ken Doctor under the banner of

"Newsonomics" in early 2010. Doctor, a former managing editor of the *St. Paul Pioneer Press* who had gone into media analytics with marketing consultants Outsell Inc., had just published his book *Newsonomics: Twelve New Trends That Will Shape the News You Get.*

On the west coast, another former newspaper journalist with even more impressive industry credentials than Langeveld or Doctor was already a veteran blogger. Alan Mutter had been city editor of the *Chicago Sun-Times* and a senior editor at the *San Francisco Chronicle* before bolting in 1996 to Silicon Valley, where he was CEO of three start-ups. He started his blog Reflections of a Newsosaur in 2004, and tracked the falling fortunes of his former industry with equal parts insight and alarm. As a former CEO, he focused on data that showed newspaper circulation, stock prices, and especially advertising revenue were all plummeting. As 2008 ended, he calculated that their annus horribilis had seen 83.3 percent of newspaper stock value wiped out in twelve months, vaporizing $64.5 billion in equity. "Investors have not seen any plausible strategies from publishers to reverse the accelerating declines in readership, advertising and profitability that have been under way since 2006," he noted.[56] In early 2010, with the newspaper death meme in full bloom, Mutter was given a column in the monthly magazine *Editor & Publisher*, which had been covering the newspaper industry since 1884.

Baltimore

If 2008 was a bad year for newspapers, the New Year ushered in a full-on disaster. The downturn in advertising revenues hit giveaway newspapers hardest because they were usually second choice of advertisers and had no circulation revenue to fall back on. Of the 320 free dailies that had launched worldwide, a quarter had closed by mid-2008 and an estimated 70 percent of the rest were losing money. Denmark, which had eleven freesheets in 2006, was reduced to four.[57] Of Metro International's twenty commuter tabloids, only nine were profitable in 2008, according to the company's annual report.[58] In Baltimore, the *Examiner* cut back home delivery from six days a week to two in mid-2008. "When it first hit the ground in Baltimore, we found it lacking," noted the alt-weekly *Baltimore City Paper*. "The paper had a lot of stuff in it, but it had little depth or dimension. Over the past couple of years, though, the paper has improved significantly." The *City Paper* even selected the *Examiner* as "Best Local Newspaper" in 2008 over the long-publishing *Baltimore Sun*, whose journalism had suffered with cutbacks like all dailies owned by Tribune, which went into bankruptcy that December.[59] With the recession, however, ad sales collapsed. Clarity Media announced in January 2009 that it would cease publishing its Baltimore edition of the *Examiner* and focus on its editions in Washington and San Francisco. "It is not possible to maintain two major daily newspapers within a 50-mile distance and do justice to both publications," said Clarity CEO Ryan McKibben.[60]

The company was already going in another direction. In February, Clarity began a recruitment drive for writers to provide content for its proliferating websites. Since its launch in April 2008, Examiner.com had been growing exponentially, with 2,000 writers in sixty major U.S. markets. It would be named the fastest-growing Top 30 news site by Nielsen Online in 2009, with 7.5 million unique users by August of that year, up 342 percent from a year earlier. Its writers weren't exactly journalists, however. They were called "examiners" by Clarity and were paid according to the number of people who clicked on the stories they wrote. "I hesitate to call them journalists," Clarity Digital Group CEO Rick Blair told *Advertising Age*. "We're not trying to act like we're taking the place of newspapers." Edmund Lee of *Advertising Age* deconstructed the formula.

> "Examiners" are paid anywhere from $1.00 to $7.50 for every thousand page views, based on a black-box formula. . . . Writers associated with a sponsored area are paid only slightly more, but Mr. Blair declined to elaborate. "I tell our examiners not to quit their day jobs," he said. "No one's doing it for the money. They want credibility."[61]

Blair bristled at suggestions by PBS, however, that because Examiner.com allowed advertisers to "sponsor" content, its writers would be pushing their goods or products. "We don't allow our Examiners to shill for advertising," he told PBS's *MediaShift*. "They can have their ad adjacent to relevant content."[62] Clarity set a target of recruiting 12,000 examiners to write on more than twenty topics in each of its local markets. "Examiner.com recruits Examiners who are knowledgeable about their chosen topics and willing to write three or four articles a week related to the subject," the company said in a news release. "All Examiners go through a detailed selection process including background checks, which differentiates them from bloggers or citizen journalists. The Examiner population includes current and former journalists, students, educators, professionals, and a variety of informed and insightful contributors."[63] By 2010, Examiner.com had expanded into 240 U.S. markets and five in Canada and boasted more than 24,000 examiners. "While it doesn't disclose specific payouts, news sources and online discussions by current contributors put the rate at one cent per page view," reported the *Montreal Gazette*. "An informal survey by WritersWeekly, an online magazine for freelance writers, showed the average pay for nine Examiner writers was $1.46 U.S. per article."[64] Examiners were encouraged to write stories on trending topics that would show up on search engines and they were even tutored in the new science of "search engine optimization" (SEO). As such, Examiner.com tended to get lumped in with "content farms" like Demand Media and Associated Content, which produced online "clickbait" designed to drive web traffic and thus increase advertising revenues. *Advertising Age* found one examiner, however, who claimed she made almost $100,000 a year writing about celebrities like Taylor Swift and Justin Bieber.

> She posts anywhere from 100 to 130 articles in a week, and ... given that her beat — entertainment — is a semivaluable category, she's booking close to $1,800 for every 120 articles, or about $15 per article, which is a handsome though not unheard of rate in the blogging world.[65]

Denver

The turn of the twenty-first century saw something unusual in Denver — a good old-fashioned newspaper war. It was one of the few cities where a Scripps newspaper competed rather than cohabited with another daily, and its *Rocky Mountain News* competed hard. It was Colorado's first newspaper, being founded in 1859, a full seventeen years before statehood. The scrappy tabloid was much loved by Coloradans, who called it by its first name. The *Rocky* battled the broadsheet *Denver Post* toe-to-toe. The *Post* was founded in 1895 and had been acquired in 1980 by Times Mirror, which got tired of battling the *Rocky* and sold it in 1987 to the upstart MediaNews chain. Its CEO Dean Singleton had backed doomed dailies in Houston and Dallas and was determined not to lose in Denver. Singleton moved MediaNews headquarters there and took over as publisher of the *Post* to personally fight its battle with the *Rocky*. "Singleton proved to be one tough Texan," noted former *Rocky* reporter Bob Diddlebock. "He won union concessions, slashed costs, marketed his product as 'Denver's paper,' stepped up local coverage and, lore has it, told the *Rocky* to drop dead when it inquired about a merger."[66]

The *Post* took the circulation lead in 1997, but lost it again in 1999 after the *Rocky* started selling subscriptions for a penny a day. The circulation gains were not followed by enough advertising to pay the cost of the extra newsprint the *Rocky* needed to print all those copies, however, of which its journalists were blissfully ignorant. "The staff of the Denver *Rocky Mountain News* had no clue that they were working for a failing enterprise," noted the *Columbia Journalism Review*. "In fact, by the usual indicators reporters use to keep score on such matters, they were clearly winning their battle with *The Denver Post*."

> Almost every week, it seemed, there was another party in the office to celebrate some circulation milestone or editorial coup. The sheetcakes kept coming. But while the troops savored the well-frosted spoils of victory, their corporate generals at Scripps were secretly suing for peace.[67]

The surprise announcement came just after the turn of the millennium. Scripps had been bleeding red ink from the battle, according to its Cincinnati head office. "Reporters were stunned to learn that the News had suffered $123 million in operating losses over the past ten years while the Post claimed $200 million in profits," noted the Columbia Journalism Review.[68] Scripps agreed to pay MediaNews $60 million in exchange for an equal partnership, and the Post also got to publish the lucrative Sunday paper. In the application for a JOA, the Rocky was cast as a failing daily. This bucked the trend in JOAs, which had just seen another partnership fail, this time in Honolulu. "The Post gets the Sunday paper and $60 million, and you don't have to ask who the winner is," observed F. Gilman Spencer, a former Post editor.[69]

The loser was not so much Scripps, which got to share in Post profits for the next fifty years, as it was readers and advertisers in Denver. "From what we've seen based on San Francisco, you are going to see declining circulation and quality of journalism," predicted Tim Redmond, a reporter for the alt-weekly Bay Guardian. "The advertisers really get screwed."[70] Sure enough, after the deal gained DOJ approval, advertising rates went up fourfold, according to a furniture store owner who filed a lawsuit in an abortive bid to fight the merger.[71] Given the rate at which JOAs had failed in other cities, however, some predicted the partnership would only buy time for the Rocky. "I don't think citizens of Denver should count on it lasting," said Stephen Barnett, who tracked JOAs as a law professor at the University of California at Berkeley. "I would give it perhaps 10 years."[72] He was off by only a couple of years.

After the October 2008 stock market crash deepened the recession into the worst since the Great Depression, the Rocky began gasping for air. Scripps offered the newspaper for sale, in vain. When no buyer emerged, and with the paper having lost $15 million in the previous year, Scripps closed the Rocky down in February, throwing 215 people out of work. MediaNews was also in dire straits, having taken on $350 million in debt to buy four dailies from McClatchy in 2006 after its takeover of Knight Ridder. Letting the *Rocky* go was likely in the best interests of both Scripps and MediaNews, noted the Denver alt-weekly *Westword*.

> It's hard to imagine Singleton promising to hand over 50 percent of his revenues for the next four decades-plus in exchange for Scripps's desertion of the market unless he believes the print-journalism industry as a whole will be little more than a memory a lot sooner than mid-century.[73]

Singleton washed his hands of any blame. "The economic model changed on us," he told *Westword*. "The bottom line is, to continue with two newspapers would mean the death of both."[74] Others were pretty sure they knew where the blame lay. "The black hats in this sad Western tale are the suits," concluded Diddlebock. "The Scripps' newspaper executives whose ineptitude over the past 25 years fumbled away a prime market to a competitor they should have killed off two decades ago."[75]

Seattle

Perhaps the ugliest JOA breakup of all was in Seattle. "Most JOAs are shotgun marriages," said *Editor & Publisher* in a 2003 editorial. "In Seattle, the newspaper industry is witnessing its first shotgun divorce."[76] The relationship began in 1983, when the long-publishing *Times* walked down the aisle with the even longer-publishing *Post-Intelligencer* in a fifty-year JOA. "Over the next 17 years, the arrangement worked well," noted *Mediaweek* in 2000.[77] Then, just as the millennium loomed, all hell broke loose. The family-controlled *Times* had been doing better than most afternoon newspapers and actually dominated the Seattle market by offering superior journalism, but Seattle's worsening rush hour traffic was hampering its distribution. It demanded costly new suburban presses and used this as leverage to persuade the *Post-Intelligencer* to renegotiate the JOA in 1999. The revised deal allowed the *Times* to also publish in the morning, extended the JOA by another fifty years, and boosted the *P-I*'s share of the profits from 32 percent to 40 percent. Then in late 2000 both newspapers were hit by a seven-week strike that began at the height of the Christmas advertising season. Then the economy went into recession, which was worsened in aero-space-sensitive Seattle by layoffs at Boeing. Then came the 9/11 terrorist attacks, which deepened the recession. The effect on the *Seattle Times* was worsened by the high level of debt it carried from acquiring newspapers in Maine and Washington.

An unusual clause in their renegotiated JOA stated that if either newspaper lost money for three straight years, it could ask that one of them agree to fold, and collect its share of the profits until 2083. If there was no agreement within eighteen months, the JOA — and the profit sharing — would automatically end. The *Times* made such a request in 2003, claiming it had incurred three straight years of losses. The *P-I*, which was owned by the Hearst Corporation, sued to stop the dissolution and also claimed damages from the *Times*, arguing that its mismanagement of the JOA had depressed *P-I* circulation. It also argued that the losses the *Times* incurred in 2000 and 2001 due to the strike and in 2001 due to 9/11 should not be counted because they were extraordinary events. It pointed to the hiring of seventy-one additional journalists by the *Times* in 2002 and argued it was designed to create a third year of losses so the *Times* could get out of the JOA. "After the strike years, the *Times* spent money like a drunken sailor to manufacture that magical third year of loss," Hearst lawyer Kelly Corr argued in court.[78]

The Blethen family, which had owned the *Times* since 1896, claimed that Hearst planned to take it over as it had done with for-mer JOA partners in San Francisco and San Antonio. The Blethens were actually in bed with and battling not just one but two of the world's largest media corporations. In addition to Hearst, it was also in partnership with Knight Ridder, because it had sold a 49.5 percent ownership of the Seattle Times Co. to the Ridder family in 1929. As the Hearst lawsuit approached trial, Knight Ridder even admitted that it was also hoping to take over the market-leading *Times*. "We want to end up with the *Seattle Times*," CEO Tony Ridder told the *Wall Street Journal*, adding that Knight Ridder had made offers to buy the *Times* in 1993 and 2000. "The Blethen family says they don't want to sell."[79]

When Hearst's lawsuit came to trial in 2003, it argued it could not survive without the JOA because the *Times* did its printing and distribution. The *Times* argued that the money-losing *P-I* was bleeding it dry while the deep-pocketed Hearst Corp. waited out a war of attrition. A Superior Court judge ruled against the *Times*, which launched an appeal. The ruling was reversed on appeal, which prompted an appeal by Hearst. The litigation dragged on until 2007, when both parties agreed to take their dispute to arbitration. On the eve of the arbitration hearing, however, they settled the case with the *Times* agreeing to pay Hearst $49 million to settle its claims of mismanagement and also to buy out its right to receive a share of future profits if the *P-I* folded. Hearst agreed to pay the *Times* $25 million for a promise to keep the JOA going for at least another decade. That created jubilation at the *P-I*, but the celebrations were premature. After losing $14 million in 2008, Hearst finally cried uncle and stopped printing the *P-I* on March 17, 2009. It would not disappear completely, Hearst announced, but would live on as a news website. Of its 165 staff members, however, all but 20 lost their jobs.

From a Trickle to a Wave

Closure of the print *P-I*, coming hard on the heels of the folding of the *Rocky*, led to a cacophony of voices predicting that the world would soon be newspaper-free. In the U.S. and Canada, however, the pandemic was quickly contained and only a couple of more dying dailies fell by the wayside. In May of 2009, Gannett closed its *Tucson Citizen*, which had been in a JOA with the *Arizona Daily Star* since 1940. Gannett would continue to collect half of the *Star*'s profits for six more years, until the JOA expired in 2015, so there was little incentive for either to subsidize a money-losing daily. As an afternoon newspaper, the *Citizen*'s circulation had slipped to 17,000 from about 60,000, compared with almost 100,000 with the *Star*, which was owned by Lee Enterprises. While Gannett was one of the strongest newspaper chains, Lee was struggling with a heavy debt load incurred in its 2005 purchase of the Pulitzer chain and had flirted with bankruptcy. In mid-2010, the *Honolulu Star-Bulletin* merged with its JOA partner of forty-eight years, the *Advertiser*, to form the *Star-Advertiser*. The *Star-Bulletin*, which had published since 1882, had languished like most afternoon dailies, and had been threatened with closure in 1999 until a lawsuit filed by a citizen's group forced a sale. It was bought the following year by Black Press, a rapidly-expanding Canadian chain, which converted it to tabloid format in 2009. Black Press (which has no connection with Conrad Black) bought the larger *Advertiser* the following year and merged the papers.

Since 2009, however, the R.I.P. list at Newspaper Death Watch has stubbornly refused to grow as newspapers hunkered down, cut costs, and rode out the recession. As predicted by many, advertising never did return to its previous levels even after the economy improved. In fact, it kept going down. Most advertisers had discovered the Internet and many would never again patronize newspapers. Classified advertising in particular had vaporized with Craigslist and other online ad databases. But enough core advertising remained to sustain monopoly newspapers, as most local merchants found that print on paper was still the most effective way to reach their customers. Newspapers also turned to their readers for increased revenues, both from print sales and for online access. Affluent readers who tended to pay closer attention to their communities were the ones that advertisers sought most, and they were also more likely to pay a little bit extra for their daily newspaper.

It turned out that the business model for newspapers wasn't broken after all, and was instead quite robust, if somewhat arcane. Yet predictions of the imminent demise of newspapers persisted, even from some who should have known better. The doomsayers continued to point out that many of the largest newspaper chains had been forced into bankruptcy. They certainly had, and therein lies a tale or twelve.

SEVEN

The Chapter 11 Club

Chapter 11 is a section of the U.S. Bankruptcy Code that acts as a lifeline for business owners who have gone "underwater," like hapless homeowners who took mega-mortgages at the top of the housing bubble and soon owed more than their houses were worth. Unlike a Chapter 7 bankruptcy, which requires the liquidation of a business and the sale of its assets, the advantage of a Chapter 11 bankruptcy is that it allows a business to continue operating while it "reorganizes" its financial obligations. It provides court-ordered protection from lawsuits to prevent creditors from shutting down the business by seizing its assets to satisfy their claims. That's because the business is still making money and is thus worth something as a going concern, so it can be sold off to pay at least some of the debts racked up by the owner. Plus everyone gets to keep their jobs, at least until the new owner takes over and looks for ways to cut costs and boost return on investment.

Chapter 11 was a perfect haven for distressed newspaper companies. They were invariably still making money, just not as much as before they went so deeply into debt. Their lenders would take a haircut and walk away with pennies on the dollar and maybe a share of ownership. Most of the employees would stay on the payroll, perhaps with their wages or benefits reduced, and a new owner would take over.

The lenders first in line to recover their money gave loans that were backed with hard assets as collateral, such as shares of ownership. They could thus take those in lieu of payment. The old shareholders would usually be cut out of the picture, but could keep part of the company if they had any equity left after all the secured lenders had been paid. In any event, the business continued. Sometimes the lenders would take over and run the business themselves if they couldn't quickly sell it. Increasingly during the economic hard times that attended the financial crisis and recession, however, a new kind of "vulture" capitalist swooped in to buy up the debt of failing companies at bargain prices and run them until they could be "flipped" once things improved. There was only one problem with that plan. With the recession, things only got worse for newspaper companies, but that didn't stop private equity firms with little interest in journalism from picking off the ones that fell back from the herd.

Membership in the Chapter 11 Club grew to include some of the largest newspaper companies in North America. (See Table 1 on next page.) Some were sold or went bankrupt more than once during the shakeout. Declaring bankruptcy and resorting to court protection under Chapter 11 was a real comedown for newspaper owners, whose businesses had historically been among the healthiest and most profitable. While the newspaper industry had always suffered its ups and downs in lockstep with the economy, this downturn seemed like the ultimate bad news, as industry magazine *Editor & Publisher* pointed out in 2009.

> For all the reversal of fortune newspapers have endured over the past half-century — the disappearance of afternoon papers from big cities, diminished household penetration and accelerated loss of young readers with each new generation — bankruptcy remained something that was merely covered in their business pages. It was something that happened to someone else.[1]

THE CHAPTER 11 CLUB

Company	Year	Dailies	M-F Circulation	Debt (m)
Tribune Co.	2008	9	1,216,720	13,000
Star Tribune Holdings	2009	1	298,147	661
Journal Register Co.	2009	24	652,866	692
Philadelphia Newspapers	2009	2	435,291	390
Sun-Times Media Group	2009	8	592,671	801
Heartland Publications	2009	17	133,154	166
Canwest Publications	2009	10	1,141,616	3,700
Freedom Communications	2010	28	1,200,000*	770
MediaNews	2010	63	3,098,580	930
Morris Publications	2010	13	375,232	415
Lee Enterprises	2011	52	1,343,650	1,300
Journal Register Co.	2012	20	433,133	165

*estimated

The flight of newspaper chains into Chapter 11 bankruptcy protection contributed to the perception that the newspapers themselves were going out of business. It was just their over-extended owners who were taking a fall. As money-making businesses, the newspapers themselves were still worth something, and if their owners were in over their heads, then they would get new ones. Sometimes the process was quick and agreeable, with "pre-packaged" bankruptcies sailing through court if they got enough lenders and creditors onside in advance. Other Chapter 11 bankruptcies dragged on for years. The acrimonious carve-up of the multimedia Tribune Company, for example, took four years and cost an estimated $500 million in legal fees alone. The ownership merry-go-round at the *Philadelphia Inquirer* and its *Daily News* tabloid twin similarly spun into a long-running soap opera.

Tribune tribulations

The painful bankruptcy of the Tribune Company, which began in late 2008, exposed the seamy underbelly of not just media mismanagement but of the Chapter 11 bankruptcy process itself. Tribune had been bought just the previous year by colorful real estate mogul Sam Zell in a controversial acquisition totaling $8.3 billion. Zell came up with a scheme that involved the company's Employee Stock Ownership Plan (ESOP). The complex arrangement had tax advantages, such as eliminating corporate income tax and capital gains tax on asset sales, as the *Columbia Journalism Review* explained.

> Zell used an ESOP because the employee-owned structure elimi-
> nates federal income tax, which cost Tribune an average $332 million
> a year from 2004 to 2006. Tribune will also no longer pay a dividend,
> which saves $201 million a year. And by paying employees with stock
> instead of cash, it will save tens of millions of dollars more annually.[2]

Zell planned to sell some Tribune assets to pay down the $8 bil-lion in debt taken on in the purchase. No sooner had the ink dried on the paperwork, however, than plunging advertising revenues and a tanking economy made that unrealistic. Chief among the assets that Zell wanted to flip were the Chicago Cubs baseball team, which Tribune had bought in 1981 for $20.5 million. With the value of sports franchises skyrocketing ever since, the Cubs were expected to fetch a handsome price, especially after *Forbes* valued the team at $592 million in 2007. But the deflating economy soon burst that bubble and the sale was put on hold. Then there were the twenty-two television stations that Tribune owned, several of which it had acquired in its $8-billion takeover of Times Mir-ror in 2000. That purchase was made at the height of the previous economic cycle, which nosedived with the bursting of the bubble in technology stocks. It created a multimedia behemoth by com-bining two of the country's top ten newspaper companies into the third-largest chain behind only Gannett and Knight Ridder. Tribune also became the country's second-largest holder of TV licences in the deal, and that caused problems with the federal broadcasting regulator. Tribune had been a multimedia pioneer, founding WGN radio in 1924 and WGN-TV in 1948. It was "grand-fathered" and allowed to keep both after the FCC banned newspa-per owners from holding licences for television stations in 1975. Tribune also bought TV stations such as WPIX in New York City and WTLA in Los Angeles and started the all-news ChicagoLand TV (CLTV) cable channel in 1993. It even threw in with Warner Brothers for 25 percent of its startup WB Television Network in 1995.

Tribune also became a pioneer on the Internet. It was an early investor in America Online, putting $5 million into it in 1991, and together they started Chicago Online. It started Cars.com with the Washington Post Co. and Times Mirror, and CareerPath with seven other publishers. In the cities where it owned both a television station and a newspaper, Tribune dominated the market with multimedia combinations including extensive online operations. There was only one small problem with its Internet businesses, noted the *American Journalism Review* in 2000 — they were losing $30 million a year.[3] That was easy to swallow when the company was making annual profits north of $600 million, as it did in 1998, but not in an economic downturn. To prop up its investments in both broadcasting and the Internet, Tribune cut back on its newspaper operations, reducing its bureaus both domestically and overseas. Layoffs soon followed, and the lavish operations at its *Los Angeles Times* bore the brunt of the cost cutting, with staff cut from 5,300 to 3,400. The newspaper's editor and publisher both resigned in protest, so Tribune sent one of its own to wield the hatchet, but he didn't last long. James O'Shea resigned after little more than a year on the job in protest of cutbacks he was ordered to make. He would write a 2011 book about Tribune's takeover of Times Mirror called *The Deal From Hell*, in which he blamed corporate greed for the "hollowing out" of American journalism.[4]

The cutbacks continued under Zell. To *Washington Post* columnist Harold Meyerson, he was "destroying" the *Times*. "Zell has taken bean counting to a whole new level," wrote Meyerson, a Los Angeles native, after he ordered Tribune's dozen dailies to reduce editorial content. "In Zell, what Los Angeles has is a visiting Visigoth, whose civic influence is about as positive as that of the Crips, the Bloods and the Mexican mafia."[5] The cost cutting couldn't save Tribune from Chapter 11, however. Then the lawyers got involved. Before the company emerged with a clean slate and a new board of directors on the last day of 2012, more than half a billion dollars in legal fees had been racked up. The vultures started circling even before the official bankruptcy filing, according to an investigation by *Chicago Tribune* reporters. Their 2013 series untangling the bankruptcy found it "a messy product of the unchecked Wall Street deal-making and aggressive financial engineering that soon would threaten the American economy."[6] Just as Zell's takeover of the company helped pull back the curtain on some of the excesses of high finance, the series noted, the ensuing bankruptcy "exposed a powerful but little-known industry thriving in the midst of the American bankruptcy court system."[7]

> The only ones who truly may have something to smile about are the members of a powerful industry set up to profit from the inevitable boom-and-bust cycles on Wall Street. They include the massive investment funds that buy and sell the debt of troubled companies like Tribune Co. and the army of lawyers and other bankruptcy professionals who follow them around, charging as much as $1,000 an hour.[8]

At the first sign of blood in the water, private equity firms Oaktree and Angelo Gordon began buying up the distressed company's debt from nervous lenders at deep discounts. The vulture capitalists were part of "a clubby group of specialist investors," noted the *Tribune*, who would buy up the debt of troubled companies and then "match wits at the negotiating table or in court to see who can walk away with the biggest pieces." The bottom feeders bought enough secured debt, noted the *Tribune*, to engineer a "bargain-priced backdoor takeover."[9]

Strib redemption

The story of the *Strib*, as the *Minneapolis Star Tribune* was affectionately known in the Twin Cities, was the story of American newspapers in microcosm, except for the surprise ending. Long-standing family owners sold it to a large corporation, which wound up selling it for a huge loss to a new owner who put it into bankruptcy. Finally, it emerged from bankruptcy to a brighter future. If only such a happy ending could visit all daily newspapers.

The Cowles family, which owned a small empire of newspapers, magazines, and TV stations, sold the *Strib* to the McClatchy chain for $1.2 billion in 1998. The purchase put McClatchy, a growing chain from California, into a major market for the first time, but a bidding war with the New York Times Co., the Tribune Co., and the Washington Post Co. had inflated the price by an estimated $200 million.[10] Still, newspaper stock analyst John Morton saw it as a good deal for McClatchy. The *Strib*, he pointed out, was "a newspaper that does not need fixing."

> The *Star Tribune* has a well-deserved reputation for journalistic qual-
> ity and a state-of-the-art printing plant, and it operates in a rapidly
> growing, prosperous market. Newspapers of this size and quality in
> an attractive market rarely become available, and when they do they
> command a high price.[11]

The *Strib*'s operating profits, according to Morton, were about 20 percent, compared to 12.3 percent for the publicly-traded McClatchy. "McClatchy ... paid a high price, but in the long run it will prove to have been well worth it."[12] Wall Street disagreed, sending McClatchy's stock price down almost 17 percent over the next two days. McClatchy quickly set about doing what Wall Street likes best, which is cutting costs. It eliminated corporate staff and offered buyouts to unionized workers. But it could not have foreseen the depth of the 2001–02 economic downturn, which was deepened by the 9/11 terrorist attacks. It was unprepared for the fact that the Internet would soon skim off most of its lucrative classified advertising, which according to one former editor had grown by 400 percent from 1991 to 1998.[13] Yet when McClatchy sold the *Strib* in late 2006 to a private equity firm, it was still nicely profitable, just not as profitable as the rest of McClatchy's newspapers. It was a drag on the chain's profit margin, which was by then north of 25 percent, noted Morton. "McClatchy has demonstrated that its devotion to profit-and-loss statements that appeal to Wall Street trumps any presumed role as the publisher of quality newspapers."[14]

McClatchy took a bath on the deal, getting back only $530 million for the Strib, or less than half of what it had paid for it eight years earlier. New owner Avista Capital set about downsizing the Strib even more. Two rounds of buyouts eliminated sixty-eight staff, but the cost cuts couldn't keep the Strib's earnings high enough to service the enormous debt its new owners took on in the purchase. Two years later, in the depths of the financial meltdown, Avista filed for Chapter 11 bankruptcy protection, citing assets of $493 million and liabilities of $661 million. Its earnings in 2008 were about $26 million, or less than a quarter of the $115 million the Strib had made in 2004. Its value, which was then estimated at between $118 million and $144 million, had fallen by about 90 percent from what McClatchy paid for it a decade earlier. When it emerged from bankruptcy in 2009, the Strib was 95 percent owned by its lenders, including several opportunistic investment funds, and had reduced its debt from $480 million to $100 million.[15]

Thus unburdened, and with its newsroom staff reduced to about 250, down almost 40 percent from its height of 400, the Strib set out on the road to recovery. Surprisingly to some, given all the doom and gloom surrounding the newspaper industry, it began to pull itself out of the mire. Private equity ownership worried many Minnesotans after the Avista experience, but local fund Wayzata Investment Partners bought out other lenders in 2012 to take a controlling 58 percent interest. The course its new owners set the Strib on turned out to be as successful as it was basic. Mark Lisheron, who had profiled the Strib for *AJR* five years earlier, returned to Minneapolis in 2012 and noted a sharp turn away from the newspaper's previous corporate strangulation. "The plan is so simple, so logical and for so long so widely discounted that it almost seems counterintuitive," Lisheron wrote. "It is based on principles followed by every industry in America that isn't a monopoly — that you succeed by giving the customer more not less; better not worse — and you don't give your product away." A new era of fiscal prudence thus visited the Strib, brought on by a sharp increase in revenue from readers. It raised subscription rates and single-copy prices, yet circulation increased. It introduced a paywall for digital readers, yet more than 18,000 customers ponied up. That brought reader revenue to about 45 percent of total revenues, with a goal of 50–50. The reason readers got on board and paid their fare was simple, according to Lisheron. "The *Star Tribune* is a newspaper worth paying for."

> Day in and day out, customers in Minnesota get what remains one of the fine regional newspapers in the country. From the front page through all of the section fronts, the paper captures a true sense of living in a smart, connected city in one of the northernmost and mostly rural parts of America. Big ticket investigations read like answers to real community problems rather than responses to a call for prize-contending ideas in an editorial meeting. Eight- and 12-inch stories show an attention to detail.[16]

Even the competition noticed the improvement. "Readers of the *Star Tribune* should realize that they're getting one of the nation's best, deepest and most enterprising local news reports," noted MinnPost, a digital startup founded in 2007 by a former *Strib* publisher.[17] As a result of its reinvigoration, the *Strib* was able to pay down its debt to $70 million and its staff members, who had taken pay cuts of 8–14 percent as part of the austerity measures, began receiving annual profit sharing payments. A staff meeting was called in early 2011, noted *New York Times* media columnist David Carr, "not to tell employees about layoffs or cuts, but to hand each of them $1,163 in profit-sharing gains for 2010."[18] In mid-2014, the *Star Tribune* was purchased for $100 million by local billionaire Glen Taylor.[19]

Journal Register, Going Once . . .

Bankruptcy has been a recurring theme for the Journal Register Company, which made the company's often stratospheric profits puzzling. The company was even created out of bankruptcy, formed from the ashes of the Ingersoll family newspaper empire in 1990. Ingersoll Publications consisted of sixty-two weeklies and a dozen or so minor dailies headlined by the *New Haven Register* when it all came crashing down in a pile of junk bonds during the stock market crash of 1987. The chain passed to its biggest lender, the investment firm Warburg Pincus, and was renamed the Journal Register Company. Headquartered in suburban Philadelphia, it quickly became one of the worst examples of bottom-line corporate newspapering. Strict cost controls squeezed out profit margins in the mid-30 percent range throughout the 1990s, much of which was reinvested in acquisitions to avoid paying income tax as the chain grew to eighteen dailies and 118 non-dailies.[20] The company went public in 1997 and sold stock to raise capital for further expansion. By 1999, it owned twenty-four dailies. The debt it took on in financing its purchases, however, grew to $765 million.[21]

Journal Register threw off so much in earnings every year, however, that it was able to keep its high-wire act aloft until the effects of the 2007–09 financial crisis and the Internet precipitously reduced newspaper revenues. Its brand of lean-and-mean "cheapskate" journalism, as *Forbes* dubbed it, enabled the company to weather even the recession of 2000–01 with a profit margin of 35 percent.[22] Perhaps that made Journal Register management think the company was recession-proof. It wasn't. The purchase of a chain of four Michigan dailies and eighty-seven non-dailies in 2004 was ill-timed, as it resulted in Journal Register taking on another $415 million in debt. Its once-lofty profit margins soon began to slide into the teens, which would be enviable for most companies but was unsustainable for one as highly leveraged as Journal Register. (See table on next page.) Worse, the drop in its annual earnings threatened to put Journal Register in default of its loan agreements, as *Editor & Publisher* magazine explained in 2008.

> Journal Register's covenants, which were renegotiated as recently as May, limit its debt ratio to 6.5 times [earnings] for the remainder of this year, and sets 7 times as the 2009 limit. It's not clear if that might be too high to justify a waiver.[23]

Its earnings were still more than enough to pay the $40 million or so in annual interest owing on its debt, but in mid-2008 Journal Register drifted into default because its falling earnings boosted its debt-to-earnings ratio. "Theoretically, its creditors could then

JOURNAL REGISTER CO. EARNINGS (US$) 2003-07

REVENUE	2003	2004	2005	2006	2007
Advertising	268,723	329,205	403,566	393,214	352,994
Circulation	73,055	80,507	94,405	93,581	91,650
Other	16,864	17,032	18,617	19,270	18,571
Total	358,642	426,744	516,588	506,065	463,215
Expenses	258,721	314,766	390,204	397,443	380,704
Earnings	99,921	111,978	126,384	108,622	82,511
Profit margin	27.8%	26.2%	24.4%	21.4%	17.8%

Source: Journal Register Co. 2007 annual report

demand repayment of the entire amount," warned *Editor & Publisher* as the date for calculating Journal Register's debt-to-earnings ratio loomed.[24] The company scrambled to sell or close about half of its more than 300 newspapers. Journal Register shares, which once traded above $20, fell below a dollar, making it a penny stock. Under the rules of the New York Stock Exchange, the company's shares were de-listed. Then the market crashed in October of 2008 and Journal Register shares fell along with it, bottoming out at a half cent. That put the total value of the company's stock at less than $200,000, well below its estimated $77 million in assets. Even that figure was dwarfed by its $692 million in debt, however, putting Journal Register well underwater.[25]

Before long, the company was owned by its bankers and bondholders following a Chapter 11 bankruptcy filing that reduced its debt to $225 million, but not before a couple of fast moves in court. First, company executives claimed $1.3 million in bonuses that had been promised to them for closing newspapers and terminating employees in the company's Hail Mary drive for cutbacks. The attorney general for Connecticut objected, calling it "rewarding failure," as did the Newspaper Guild, which represented some of the terminated employees. Even dodgier was how the company's "critical" suppliers, such as ink and newsprint providers, got paid off in full to the tune of $6.6 million, while the rest of the chain's unsecured creditors received only 9 cents on the dollar.[26] After all, if Journal Register's paper and ink suppliers didn't get paid, there was little likelihood that its newspapers would be able to continue publishing.[27]

The Philadelphia Story

The soap opera that attended ownership of Philadelphia's jointly-owned dailies in the early 20th century could be made into a movie, complete with villainous hedge funds and a local hero or two. The drama saw the dominant *Inquirer* and its *Daily News* tabloid twin change hands no fewer than three times between 2006 and 2012, with the selling price plummeting each time, from $562 million in 2006 to $139 million to $55 million in 2012. In the space of 53 years, the *Inquirer* and *Daily News* went from local ownership to corporate ownership, back to local ownership, to ownership by a pair of feuding hedge funds, and back to local ownership again. The dailies operated jointly but shared the same owner, so this was not a JOA. Walter Annenberg inherited the *Inquirer* in 1942 after his father died in prison, where he was serving a sentence for tax evasion. He bought the *Daily News* in 1957 and combined its operations with the *Inquirer*'s, selling both to Knight Newspapers twelve years later. Knight merged with Ridder Publications in 1974 to form Knight Ridder, which was briefly the country's largest newspaper chain before being surpassed by Gannett. Under legendary editor Gene Roberts, the *Inquirer* became renowned for investigative reporting, winning seventeen Pulitzer prizes between 1972 and 1990. Knight Ridder was sold in 2006 to McClatchy, which immediately put the Philadelphia dailies up for sale. The winning bid of $562 million for the *Inquirer* and *Daily News* came from an investment group called Philadelphia Media Holdings (PMH), which was led by advertising and public relations executive Brian Tierney. *Editor & Publisher* ventured that the price tag "almost represents a fire sale compared to past newspaper transactions involving metro papers."

> To put this deal into perspective, McClatchy paid twice that much — roughly $1.2 billion — when it bought the Star Tribune in Minneapolis in 1997. The New York Times Co. spent about $1.1 billion for The Boston Globe in 1993.[28]

Tierney promised to reverse the years of job cuts at the newspapers by investing in journalism. "We want to grow the business," he said, "not manage for decline."[29] But with the economy turning to recession, it was barely two years before the dailies were in financial trouble. With advertising revenue falling off a cliff, the company's debt-to-earnings ratio dipped below the threshold level allowed for in its loan agreements and things started getting nasty. That set the sharks to circling as the price of the company's distressed debt fell. "The market is shying away from a media ship that looks increasingly like the *Titanic*," quipped *Philadelphia* magazine. "PMH's loan was trading at 70 cents a dollar in early June, but is now trading in the mid 40s."[30]

That fall the stock market crashed. As soon as PMH breached its loan covenants, the interest rate on its loans automatically increased by a full percentage point. When the lawyers for its bankers got involved, under the terms of its loan agreement the company was also on the hook for paying their fees. That soaked up more than $2 million a month. The company filed for Chapter 11 in early 2009 and proposed a reorganization plan that would have kept Tierney in charge. It offered to settle the $318 million remaining in debt for $66 million in cash and real estate (including the newspapers' historic downtown tower) which worked out to about 21 cents on the dollar.[31] The debtholders, who by now consisted mostly of hedge funds Alden Global Capital and Angelo Gordon, insisted the newspapers go up for auction. Lawsuits and appeals followed, while legal fees mounted. After the first year, they totaled $26.6 million, which more than ate up the company's $15 million profit for 2010.[32] The hedge funds outbid a group of local investors put together by Tierney and won the auction in April 2010 with a final offer of $139 million.[33]

Before long, however, the hedge funds began to quarrel about what to do with the Philadelphia dailies. Alden wanted to fold them into its Journal Register Company, according to the *New York Post*, which it had also acquired out of bankruptcy. Angelo Gordon balked at that idea and the hedge funds, which both owned about 30 percent of the Philadelphia newspapers, sold them instead to a group of local investors in April 2012 for $55 million. Mercifully, and unusually, the deal was for cash, with no debt.[34] In mid-2014, minority owners of the newspapers forced a court-ordered auction of the dailies after disagreements arose over their management. This time the selling price went up 60 percent, as the dissidents won the auction with a bid of $88 million.[35] Documents subsequently emerged that showed advertising revenues of the dailies had fallen by more than 75 percent from 2000 to 2012. Despite cutting labor expenses from $243 million in 2000 to $135 million, the papers went from a $145.8 million profit in 2000 to losing more than $5 million in 2012.[36] New ownership of the privately-held dailies, however, insisted that their profit picture had improved since 2012.

Crimes at the Sun-Times

The *Chicago Sun-Times* was jinxed, insisted Alan Mutter, a former city editor at the scrappy tabloid. He pinpointed the curse to the day in 1984 that it was bought by Australian media magnate Rupert Murdoch. "If newspapers were characters in comic strips," wrote Mutter, "the *Chicago Sun-Times* would be Joe Bft'splk, the perpetually jinxed guy in the old Al Capp panels who walked around with a black cloud over his head." Mutter, who after retirement cast a keen eye on the newspaper business in his blog Reflections of a Newsosaur, could find no other explanation for twenty-five straight years of "colorful, sometimes criminal and almost always dysfunctional corporate governance."[37] But whatever his other sins against journalism, Murdoch can hardly be blamed for the fiasco that befell the *Sun-Times*, which he owned for only two years. A pair of crooked Canadians was almost entirely responsible for that. When it all came crashing down in early 2009 and the Sun-Times Media Group filed for bankruptcy, a local blogger excoriated them. "May Conrad Black and David Radler Rot in Hell," journalist Allison Hantschel wrote. "And there be forced to make night cop calls on Saturdays, in search of a crucial piece of information for an A-1 story, and may no one ever, ever, ever agree to comment." Hantschel expressed the disgust felt by many Chicagoans over what they saw as nothing less than Black and Radler pillaging the second city's second newspaper.

> Increasingly and to my immense satisfaction people are no longer buying their bullshit. The evidence of criminal neglect and dereliction of even a semblance of duty is finally stinking up the doorstep of society enough that ordinary people can't ignore the smell.[38]

While some corporate newspaper machinations have been questionable ethically, most at least stayed within the law. What happened to the Sun-Times Media Group, however, was literally a crime, for which Black and Radler went to prison. Radler went quietly after turning state's evidence and testifying at a 2006 fraud trial. He received a twenty-nine-month prison sentence, of which he served about a year in a minimum-security "country club" institution in Canada, and repaid the company $61 million. Black, who never does anything quietly, went to trial in Chicago and then to prison in Florida loudly proclaiming his innocence. Baron Black of Crossharbour, as he was known in the British House of Lords, appealed his conviction and had his six-and-a-half-year sentence reduced to five years.

It was the culmination of corporate acrimony that began in 2003 when shareholders of what was then called Hollinger International began to smell a rat.[39] They questioned why tens of million of dollars in "non-compete" payments negotiated in the sale of Hollinger newspapers were going to company executives personally and not to Hollinger. They also questioned why Hollinger was footing the bill for Black's lavish lifestyle, including a trip to Bora Bora on the company jet with his wife, Canadian columnist Barbara Amiel, and $3 million to subsidize the purchase of their condominium on New York's Upper East Side. The company also spent $8 million on a collection of personal papers of former U.S. president Franklin Delano Roosevelt, on whom Black was writing a biography. An investigation found that some payments were not properly authorized, so Black and Radler both promised to repay $7.2 million. Radler did, but Black balked. He also refused to testify at hearings convened by the U.S. Securities and Exchange Commission (SEC).

In early 2004, Hollinger International filed a lawsuit against Black, Radler, three other executives, and companies they controlled, claiming $200 million in damages. A 513-page report to the SEC described Hollinger International under the management of Black and Radler as a "corporate kleptocracy." It detailed a "self-righteous and aggressive looting" of the company by its controlling shareholders. It counted more than $400 million it claimed Black and others had appropriated for their own use between 1997 and 2003, or more than 95 percent of Hollinger International's adjusted net income during that period.[40] Even fishier was the sale of numerous Hollinger newspapers to companies secretly controlled by Black and Radler for bargain prices as low as $1. In the non-compete agreements in those sales, Black and Radler paradoxically agreed not to compete with themselves.

Under new management, Hollinger International's newspapers were sold off until only the *Sun-Times* and a chain of fifty-eight other Chicagoland titles remained, so it was renamed the Sun-Times Media Group in 2006. As usual with directors, the company was on the hook for their legal expenses in both the criminal and civil proceedings, even when the company was suing them. Between 2003 and 2008, the company spent more than $215 million on legal fees incurred by its former management. It recovered about $163 million from them, for a net loss of more than $52 million.[41] That put a dent in its profits, which disappeared in red ink as revenues fell with the recession, from $420 million in 2006 to $323 million in 2008. Operating losses grew from $39 million in 2006 to $140 million in 2007, to $381 million in 2008, with the latter including a paper loss of $281 million for impairment of asset value.[42]

Then there was the 2004 circulation scandal that saw sales figures inflated, which resulted in the *Sun-Times* having to refund $27 million to advertisers. Even worse was the $699 million tax bill the IRS stuck the company with. That forced the Sun-Times Media Group into Chapter 11 bankruptcy in 2009. The only bidder at auction was a local group that offered to pay just $5 million for the company and to assume $21.5 million of its liabilities, conditional on its unions agreeing to a permanent 15 percent wage cut. The liabilities the new owners assumed did not include the tax bill or another $37.4 million in pension obligations. With revenues still above $200 million a year and a cost-cutting program having eliminated about 400 of the company's 2,200 or so employees, the new owners hoped to soon restore the company to 10-percent profitability. At that rate, the buyers would recoup their full purchase price in little over a year.[43]

From his perch in a Florida prison, Conrad Black had a different perspective on how his former company came to ruin. The blustering Black didn't need a blog to give his side of the story. It appeared in the *National Post*, a conservative Canadian daily he had founded in 1998. Black blamed the sorry mess on "the corporate-governance suicide bombing of what had been a great and distinguished Canadian international media company."

> Those who usurped the management of our company took four years to squander the $2-billion of shareholder value while personally taking $300-million for themselves. ... The long-great Hollinger, an authentic Canadian institution, was killed and plundered at the behest of the lowest mutation of the Ugly American, the allegory of extraterritorial arrogance. . . . . trampled by this hippopotamus of trans-border injustice.[44]

Canwest and the Aspers

The second generation of the Asper family tried to build the kind of global media empire their father envisioned, but their reach exceeded their grasp and they ended up losing the firm. When Canwest Global Communications founder Izzy Asper bought the Southam newspaper chain from Black in 2000, he appointed his son Leonard to head the multimedia conglomerate he had created. Canwest, which had built Canada's third television network, Global Television, suddenly became a major convergence player with the addition of most of the country's major daily newspapers. Leonard Asper, then just thirty-six, was a leading proponent of convergence, but his mismanagement of Canwest contributed to the multimedia model of media ownership ending up in flames within

CANWEST PUBLICATIONS/POSTMEDIA NETWORK

	Revenue	Earnings	Profits
2006	1,261	248	19.7%
2007	1,285	269	20.9%
2008	1,298	293	22.5%
2009	1,099	172	15.6%
2010	1,052	191	18.1%
2011	899	189	21.0%
2012	832	144	17.3%
2013	751	130	17.3%
2014	674	109	16.2%

*as of year end August 31

a decade in Canada. He took on even more debt to buy a stable of cable channels in 2007. Profits for Canwest's newspapers had been 20 percent or higher until 2009, when revenue dropped sharply and earnings fell even more. Its profit margin was still above 15 percent, but its earnings weren't enough to cover its loan payments. Canwest was forced to declare bankruptcy and was de-converged in 2010 when its newspapers were sold off separately from its Global Television network. Its secured debt had been bought up by speculators, including hedge fund Angelo Gordon, which paid as little as 15 cents on the dollar.[45] The company's creditors bid for its newspaper division at auction with financial backing from the U.S. private-equity firm Golden Tree Asset Management and bought them for $1.1 billion. They renamed the newspaper chain Postmedia Network after its flagship National Post and took the company public with a 2011 IPO. (See table on this page.)

Freedom Isn't (Debt) Free

As a libertarian, R.C. Hoiles was opposed to public education, labor unions, and the U.N. He thought that paying taxes should be voluntary. His vision of limited government was more like no government. He called his company Freedom Newspapers after these values, which he promoted relentlessly. He moved to California in 1935, bought the *Santa Ana Register*, and soon began scooping up newspapers from Colorado to Texas. After his death in 1970, Freedom Newspapers passed to a second generation of Hoileses. Its flagship was renamed the *Orange County Register* in 1985, and Freedom diversified into the magazine and television businesses in the 1990s. Soon sibling differences tore Freedom apart, however. Harry Hoiles, who was publisher of its *Colorado Springs Gazette-Telegraph*, felt the company's newspapers had strayed too far from their libertarian roots. His brother and sister didn't feel as strongly about promoting their father's views. Harry lost the power struggle, but his heirs would win the war and the other two branches of the family would eventually be left with nothing.

Harry launched a takeover bid for Freedom in 1985 that topped $1 billion. When that was rejected, he went to court in an effort to break up the company. That failed, too. After Harry's death in 1998, his son Tim continued to push for liquidity. Other members of the seventy-five or so third-generation Hoileses also wanted out. When their numbers grew too big to be ignored, Freedom bought them out in 2004. In doing so, however, it took on $770 million in debt. With twenty-eight dailies and more than seventy non-dailies, Freedom was by then the thirteenth-largest newspaper company in the U.S., and the third-largest privately-owned chain. It also owned eight television stations scattered from Oregon to Massachusetts. When the Great Recession rolled in a few years later, the debt that Freedom had taken on proved a millstone around its neck. Revenue fell by 13 percent in 2008, dropping earnings from $150 million to $34 million. Things got even worse in 2009. Revenue fell another 23 percent in the first nine months of the year, with earnings of only $13 million, which was nowhere near enough to service the company's debt. The final straw came in a $28.9 million judgment against the company in a class action lawsuit brought by 5,000 former *Orange County Register* paper carriers. They claimed they should have been considered employees instead of contractors and been paid wages, including overtime. The only option for Freedom was Chapter 11.[46] The remaining Hoiles family members fought to keep a slice of the company their opinionated ancestor had founded, but they were cut out of the deal. J.P. Morgan and the other debt holders, including hedge funds Alden Global Capital and Angelo Gordon, not only wound up with the business, but it still owed them $325 million.[47]

MediaNews Implodes

Dean Singleton kept expanding his MediaNews empire after the turn of the millennium, and that proved his undoing. He bought into JOAs when he acquired the *Salt Lake Tribune* in 2000 and the *Detroit News* in 2005. Singleton scooped up the *San Jose Mercury News* and the *Contra Costa Times* for $1 billion in the 2006 Knight Ridder carve-up. The deal made MediaNews the fourth-largest newspaper chain in the U.S., with fifty-one dailies in thirteen states, but it outraged some Bay area residents with the ownership consolidation it brought. Singleton made the purchase with a little help from *San Francisco Chronicle* owner Hearst, which contributed $263 million of the purchase price in exchange for 31-percent ownership of Media-News. "It gives Singleton and Hearst an extraordinary monopoly on the entire Bay area," complained Ben Bagdikian, dean emeritus of journalism at the University of California at Berkeley. "It gives them, and especially Singleton, great control over advertising and subscription rates in the area."[48] A half dozen Bay area congress-men demanded an investigation by the Department of Justice, which found the deal was "not likely to reduce competition sub-stantially."[49] A lawsuit by a local real estate developer blocked joint advertising sales, however, and was settled in exchange for citizen representation and notice of any planned collaboration.[50]

Even Singleton couldn't hold back the rising tide of the Great Recession, and its $950 million in debt dragged MediaNews under-water in early 2010. All but one of its newspapers were profitable, Singleton pointed out as MediaNews entered Chapter 11.[51] The only money loser would have been the *Los Angeles Daily News*, which recorded an operating loss of $2.1 million for 2009.[52] Despite their profitability, the reduced earnings of MediaNews publications came nowhere near paying the interest on the company's debt. Singleton's right-hand man Jody Lodovic engineered a "pre-packaged" bankruptcy that not only sailed through court but also left them in control of the company's board, albeit with only 11 percent owner-ship. Secured lenders took 89 percent ownership in the company, which still owed them $164 million.[53] Singleton and Lodovic made out like bandits in the bankruptcy. Lodovic picked up a $500,000 bonus for engineering the agreements, while both he and Single-ton collected annual bonuses of another $500,000 in addition to their approximately $1 million salaries.[54] In early 2011, however, Singleton's luck ran out as Alden Global Capital, which had taken control of the reorganized company, elevated him to chairman of the board and ousted Lodovic. "Without Lodovic he lacks the necessary financial engineering savvy," noted former MediaNews publisher Martin Langeveld, "and without control of the board, he can't make anything happen. The new title for Singleton looks and feels like a face-saving ambassadorial position."[55]

Morris Less

Unlike most newspaper companies, Georgia-based Morris Pub-lishing Group was founded by an accountant rather than a journal-ist. Perhaps that was why the company was able to reorganize its finances so effectively that its 2010 pre-packaged bankruptcy plan gained the overwhelming approval of its debt holders and sped through court. NewsInc. called it "one of the first good news stories in the world of over-leveraged newspapers."[56] The company had been founded in 1940 by William Morris, Jr. when he bought the Topeka State Journal in Kansas and then the Augusta Chronicle, where he had been a bookkeeper in 1929. His son Billy Morris III expanded the company rapidly starting in the 1970s after his father's death, buying newspapers in Texas, Florida, Alaska, and Minnesota. By 2009, the company owned thirteen dailies, headed by the 100,000-circulation Florida Times-Union in Jacksonville, and almost fifties non-dailies in eight states. It also had $419 million in debt from all those purchases, and with the recession it suddenly didn't have enough income to make its loan payments. Its newspapers were still making money, with positive cash flow of $35.2 million in 2008 and $22 million through the first nine months of 2009. It was just not enough to pay its loans. The Morris family made a deal with its creditors, however, that allowed it to keep control of the privately held company. It put up $110 million of family money to settle $136 million in secured bank debt and offered unsecured bond holders 36 cents on the dollar. It needed 99 percent approval from its creditors to avoid going to court and almost got it, but with 93 percent the application took less than twenty minutes. "You made it easy for me," Judge John S. Dalis told Morris lawyer Mark Berkoff in approving the deal.[57] By mid-2012, after a round of cost cutting as the economy began to improve, the company was able to pay off almost half of its debt two years early, reducing it to only $57 million.[58]

Lee Teeters

With the economy improving, the year-long spate of newspaper bankruptcies abated for almost two years. Two debt-laden chains, however, continued to flirt with Chapter 11. Ironically, they were also the most profitable. Both the McClatchy Co. and Lee Enterprises recorded profit margins in the mid 20-percent range before the recession, and the economic downturn hardly slowed them down. Lee dipped to 20.1 percent in 2008 and 19.8 percent in 2009 before recovering to 21.9 percent in 2010. McClatchy dipped only in 2008, to 19.1 percent, then bounced back to 23 percent in 2009 and 27 percent in 2010. So how could such profitable companies teeter on the edge of bankruptcy? Both had taken on massive amounts of debt — Lee to buy Howard Publications for $694 million in 2002 and the Pulitzer chain for $1.46 billion in 2005, and McClatchy to buy most of Knight Ridder for $6.5 billion in 2006. While their profit margins remained robust, their revenues took a plunge during the recession, dropping about 40 percent. That meant they had to squeeze out every nickel they could just to keep their heads above water. McClatchy did, but Lee couldn't quite make it. Thanks to a nicely packaged bankruptcy deal, however, Lee safely swam to shore.

Iowa-based Lee began struggling with its $1.24 billion in debt, most of which it had taken on in buying the larger Pulitzer chain and its fourteen dailies, including the St. Louis Post-Dispatch. Its shares, which had traded as high as $42 in 2004, fell to a low of 28 cents in mid-2009. That's when the vultures moved in, buying up the company's debt at steep discounts. Yet Lee managed to tread water. It had fought off takeovers before. It first offered to sell "junk" bonds in 2011 to thwart the vulture capitalists, who were furious at the prospect, according to the Wall Street Journal. "Lee's demise looked so inevitable that some of the investors even conferred two months ago to discuss the most favorable ways to restructure the company, according to people familiar with the matter."

> The prospect that Lee might benefit from the junk-bond boom was too much to bear for fund managers at Alden Global. One manager there was so frustrated that he called Lee's bankers at Credit Suisse AG last month to berate them for sabotaging his plans, according to a person familiar with the matter.[59]

The bond offering failed to gain enough interest, so Lee turned to Plan B, which similarly thwarted the bottom feeders. "The group had been betting the company would default, and that they could turn their holdings into an ownership stake, giving them access to the company's assets," noted the Wall Street Journal. "Instead, they will get repaid, but miss out on the chance to make even bigger profits as owners."[60] Plan B involved Lee renegotiating its loans, which it did by offering its lenders a higher interest rate and also giving some of them 13 percent ownership of the company. All but 6 percent of the lenders agreed, so Lee had to get court approval. "I've covered many bankruptcies over the years, and last week was the first time I can remember a CEO calling the filing a 'welcome event,'" noted Post-Dispatch columnist David Nicklaus. "Unlike many bankrupt companies, Lee plans to pay all its bills, and shareholders' ownership will be diluted but not wiped out."[61] By this time, it was starting to dawn on some people that the plight of newspapers was nowhere near as bad as others were claiming. Advertising Age hit the nail on the head in reporting Lee's $889 million net loss in 2009.

"Its loss primarily reflected a huge accounting write-down as the company adjusted its estimated value," noted Nat Ives. "It's not that $889 million of cash flowed from the coffers just to make payroll and keep the presses running. Strip out the accounting charge to look at the real dollars Lee papers collected and spent. Its operating profit for those 12 months topped 20%."[62]

Lee was actually faring better than most chains because its newspapers were mostly in smaller markets that weren't as badly affected by the recession or by online sites such as Craigslist. After a judge approved Lee's bankruptcy plan and the company emerged from Chapter 11 in early 2012, the company announced plans to erect paywalls around its newspaper websites. It also began to attract the interest of a very savvy investor. In April, Warren Buffett bought $85 million of the company's debt at 65 cents on the dollar.[63] Buffett was a longtime investor in newspapers, having owned the *Buffalo News* since 1977, and he had long been bullish on their profitability. "The newspaper business was as easy a way to make huge returns as existed in America," he once said. "No paper in a one-paper city, however bad the product or however inept the management, could avoid gushing profits."[64] He had warned against buying them, however, during the 2007–09 financial crisis. "For most newspapers in the United States, we would not buy them at any price," he said in 2009. "They have the possibility of going to just unending losses."[65] With the recovery under way and prices at a bargain, however, he became a buyer in 2012. He bought his hometown newspaper, the *Omaha World-Herald* for $150 million, then added the Media General chain for a bargain $142 million. He also began buying up shares in Lee, and by August his Berkshire Hathaway empire owned 6 percent of the company. When news of Buffett's purchase got out, it sent Lee shares up 20 percent in one day, to $1.59.[66] "Buffett sees value," a stock analyst told the *St. Louis Business Journal*. "It's a cheap, cheap stock relative to its potential asset values."[67] Buffett also refinanced $94 million of Lee's debt at a lower interest rate in early 2013. "Lee fits our definition of locally focused newspapers serving indispensable information in markets with a deep sense of community," he said.[68] That helped Lee pay off its debt by almost $100 million in 2013, and its growing health boosted its share price to $2.72.[69] Lee refinanced another $175 million of its high-interest debt in early 2014 to reduce the interest rate from 15 percent to 12 percent, which sent its stock up more than 20 percent in a week, to $4.90. The company had cut costs by 36 percent since 2007, including almost 40 percent of its compensation costs.[70] From 8,300 employees in 2007, it was down to 4,600 by 2013. For her efforts, Lee CEO Mary Junck received a bonus of $700,000 in 2013 after getting bonuses of $500,000 in 2011 and 2012, when she also received $655,000 in stock on top of her $900,000 salary. That outraged some Lee journalists, whose ranks had been thinned drastically by layoffs. "At the same time the workers are stressed, the big bosses are making more and more," noted *Post-Dispatch* columnist Bill McClellan in 2012. "In fact, it seems there is a certain correlation between layoffs and bonuses."[71] Her defenders, noted the *Columbia Journalism Review*, pointed to Junck's work in reorganizing the company and reducing its debt burden. "Her detractors, however, point out that it was under her leadership that the company took on its challenging debt burden in the first place."[72]

Journal Register, Going Twice . . .

Sometimes, one Chapter 11 bankruptcy just isn't enough. For Journal Register, it took two in the space of three years. It emerged from Chapter 11 in mid-2009 as a private company that was not traded on a stock exchange and thus did not have to report its financial information publicly. The secured debtholder who took control was Alden Global Capital, a secretive hedge fund that had been steadily buying up the debt of foundering newspaper companies through its Alden Global Distressed Opportunities Fund. Alden approached John Paton, a Canadian who had been publisher of the *Toronto Sun* before forming the Impremedia chain of Spanish-language newspapers in 2003, to sit on its board of directors.[73] Paton had just been named Publisher of the Year by *Editor & Publisher* in recognition of Impremedia's success.[74] He had also helped to develop the Sun Media chain's website, dubbed Canoe (Canadian Online Explorer). His ideas about the future of the newspaper business obviously impressed Journal Register's new owners, as he was named the company's CEO in early 2010.

Paton's digital zeal brought a new direction to Journal Register. He vowed to remake the company "from a collection of newspapers into a true multi-platform news and information media company."[75] He issued video cameras to the company's reporters to increase the video content on Journal Register websites in hopes of attracting video advertising. He promised to give employees a bonus if Journal Register reached $40 million in annual earnings for 2010.[76] He experimented with ways to increase community connections with Journal Register newspapers, such as throwing their newsrooms open to members of the public, offering them free wifi, and even inviting them to sit in on editorial meetings.[77] By 2011, things were looking up at Journal Register, so much so that in March the company's workers got an extra week's pay as the bonus they had been promised. Paton announced the good news on his blog.

Folks,
Take a bow — you did it! Our goal was to hit $40M in profit in 2010. Well you did better than that — you hit more than $41M. Not bad for a bankrupt, beat up old newspaper company people had written off as dead in 2009.[78]

Alden bought out banker J.P. Morgan Chase that year to control Journal Register, and it also put Paton in charge of its other major newspaper acquisition. Denver-based MediaNews was the second-largest newspaper chain in the U.S. with 50 dailies, including the *Denver Post*, the *Salt Lake Tribune*, the *Detroit News*, and the *San Jose Mercury News*. It had also just gone through bankruptcy with Alden emerging in control. Alden formed a new subsidiary called Digital First, which was based in New York City, to run both MediaNews and Journal Register, and it put Paton in charge.[79] Paton installed some of the Big Apple's most fervent academic evangelists of digital media on the new company's board of directors, including Emily

Bell of Columbia, Jeff Jarvis of CUNY, and Jay Rosen of NYU. The change in direction was radical. Paton, noted *New York Times* media reporter David Carr, was "absolutely convinced that if newspapers are to survive, they will all but have to set themselves on fire, eventually forsaking print and becoming digital news operations."

> What began as a tidy little experiment has become perhaps the single biggest bet in the whole newspaper business: The Journal Register and MediaNews are now in 18 states, with over 800 print and digital products, with revenue of over $1.4 billion and 10,000 employees. The second-largest newspaper chain in America is now being run by someone who thinks that print is, if not exactly dead, dying a lot faster than anyone thought.[80]

The shock announcement came a mere eighteen months after Journal Register employees got their profit-sharing bonus. Journal Register was bankrupt again, although it was still making money. Bankruptcy documents show that the company had a monthly operating income of $540,000 in September 2012, but the monthly interest expense of $928,000 payable on its $215 million in debt put it well underwater.[81] The debt was mostly held by Alden, which also owned about 95 percent of the company's shares. The corporate wizards behind the curtain, however, decided it was in the best interests of Journal Register for it to again declare bankruptcy. This time the howls of outrage indicated that people were starting to catch on to the game. By now it was obvious that Journal Register was engaging in so-called "strategic" bankruptcy in order to leave selected obligations behind.[82] Chapter 11 allowed Journal Register to shuck its unsecured creditors — at least those it didn't want to alienate entirely, like paper and ink suppliers — and get out from under inconvenient agreements like leases, pensions, and union contracts. Through some nifty financial sleight of hand, it would emerge still being owned by Alden because it was also its major debt holder. "Essentially, Alden is putting JRC into bankruptcy and then planning to buy back the company with as few of its pesky pensions, bondholders, and leases as it can," observed Ryan Chittum of *Columbia Journalism Review*'s online media business digest The

Audit. Paton admitted as much to a journalist from his native Canada. "The bankruptcy has everything to do with pension issues, debt and real estate," he told a reporter for the *Globe and Mail*, "and has nothing to do with performance."[83]

Under bankruptcy rules, it was entitled to renegotiate its leases. After all, it was a much smaller company by then, having laid off a quarter of its workforce since it last declared bankruptcy in 2009, so it needed less office space. It was able to offload most of its pension obligations onto the federal government, which had guaranteed them through its Pension Benefit Guaranty Corporation. It was allowed to rip up its union contracts and renegotiate them. It was also allowed to fire all of its non-union employees and hire back only the ones it wanted to keep. But in order to do all this, it had to first put the company up for auction to see if there were any other interested buyers. Paton announced the good news on his blog — Digital First had already found a bidder. A "stalking horse" bid of $122 million had been submitted by 21st CMH Acquisition Co., essentially setting a floor for bidding at the required auction of "bankrupt" Journal Register Co. And who was behind 21st CMH Acquisition Co.? Alden Global Capital. It had formed the company scarcely a week before Journal Register's bankruptcy filing.[84] When the auction was held in early 2013 no other bidders appeared, so Journal Register was now owned by 21st CMH Acquisition Co. "It's sleight of hand," protested Newspaper Guild President Bernie Lunzer, many of whose members were among those left out in the cold.

> They are essentially selling the company to itself, with only minor modifications in ownership. In the process, they're playing games with workers' lives and their livelihood. . . . Bankruptcy shouldn't be a get-out-of-jail-free card.[85]

Alden was first in line with a secured claim of $152 million, so it took ownership of Journal Register, placing it in its 21st CMH Acquisition tentacle. It did, however, have to pay off Wells Fargo, the other secured debt holder, to the tune of $13.2 million. Left out in the cold was Journal Register's largest unsecured creditor, the State of Connecticut, which was still owed $4.3 million on an $11-million tax audit claim that Journal Register had been paying off at $264,000 a month since its 2009 bankruptcy. The second-largest unsecured creditor was the company's pension plan, which was owed $3.2 million.[86] The federal government assumed most of those obligations, except for those of press operators who were covered by multi-employer contracts.[87] Unionized workers, who comprised only about 250 of Journal Register's 2,100 or so employees, were asked to take a 15-percent wage cut and deep cuts to health coverage. They balked at that, finally settling for a wage freeze and no cuts in health coverage. Non-unionized workers, of course, had no bargaining power. They received a letter informing them that their employment was terminated, but that they may be re-hired by the company's "new" owner. "In accordance with the asset purchase agreement," the letter read, "21st CMH Acquisition Co. is exclusively responsible to decide which employees of Journal Register Co. it will hire after purchase."[88]

The fancy financial footwork may have had something to do with the underperformance of the Alden Global Distressed Opportunities Fund, which reportedly declined 22 percent in 2011 and 7.5 percent through the first half of 2012.[89] Alden had been forced, according to Martin Langeveld, to sell off "significant" chunks of their media holdings as investors cashed out and looked for higher returns elsewhere. Through mid-2012, noted Langeveld, Alden had sold 5.6 million of its 9.2 million shares of Gannett, plus sizeable stakes in several other newspaper chains, reducing its media holdings from about $750 million to about $300 million. "It seems clear that Alden would just as soon get out completely — at least from newspapers."[90]

EIGHT

Readers Pay

The recession that followed in the wake of the 2007–09 financial crisis did not kill off newspapers, as many had predicted. Most were able to quickly reduce their costs below the plummeting level of their revenues by laying off workers, contracting their distribution areas, and cutting marginal circulation. Some even cut back on the number of days a week they printed or delivered to homes. The newspaper companies that went into bankruptcy reorganized their obligations or their ownership — or both — and continued publishing. The few newspapers that folded fell victim to long-term trends that had beset second-place and afternoon dailies for decades under the "circulation spiral": shrinking readerships and falling ad revenue. Most of them had been propped up for years by more profitable morning dailies in joint operating agreements that became unsustainable with the recession. The recession merely hastened their demise, as did the Internet. The question became whether monopoly newspapers would continue to survive. Their business model had proved incredibly lucrative for decades. Now it was time to find out how robust it was.

As advertising revenue melted away, the newspaper industry set about adjusting its business model, boosting revenues by charging more for hard copy sales and again charging for online access. It also began to pursue new revenue streams. Amidst all the doom and gloom, the paradox was that newspapers actually had more readers than ever. Most of them were reading the news online for free, however, so the challenge became to "monetize" those readers. The growth of online advertising revenues had stalled, so giving away their online content for free no longer made sense for newspapers. Charging for online access would not only bring in needed revenues, it would also help to stem losses in circulation from readers quitting their print subscriptions in favor of online reading. Newspapers also began to explore a new type of advertising, which many saw as the worst breach yet of the church–state wall that traditionally separated news from advertising. As newspapers became increasingly desperate, advertising increasingly infiltrated journalism.

Because most newspapers still made most of their money from print advertising, print readers were much more valuable to them than online readers, who tended to spend much less time with their content. Research had found that most news websites kept web surfers engaged for a only a few minutes at a time as they flitted from site to site, usually through search or social media, while newspaper readers tended to spend twenty to thirty minutes going through each day's edition.[1] The Washington Post, for example, calculated that a daily print subscriber represented $500 in annual revenue, while a website reader brought in only $6.[2] As the recession bottomed out and ad revenues dried up, industry analysts urged publishers to again erect paywalls, and consultants began formulating ways to help newspapers collect subscription fees online. Newspapers began to realize that they may have shot themselves in the foot by giving readers free access to their online content, so they set about trying to reverse the damage. Giving away their product for free, noted Walter Isaacson in Time, was "not a business model that makes sense."

> Perhaps it appeared to when Web advertising was booming and every half-sentient publisher could pretend to be among the clan who "got it" by chanting the mantra that the ad-supported Web was

"the future." But when Web advertising declined in the fourth quarter of 2008, free felt like the future of journalism only in the sense that a steep cliff is the future for a herd of lemmings.[3]

Others, however, pointed to the earlier failures of online sub-scription schemes and the previous resistance of web surfers to pay for news, which was available in abundance elsewhere for free. A 2007 study found that only 4 percent of American adults had paid to read news online, noted *Advertising Age*.[4] "The readers-will-pay chorus was ever more drowned out by the voices of the doom-sayers, the apostles of information-wants-to-be-free," concluded the *Columbia Journalism Review* in 2009. "Paid content, they insisted, was an illusion."[5] An online ethos from the earliest days of the World Wide Web held that everything on the Internet should be free. The digital age, argued Chris Anderson in his 2009 book *Free*, put downward pressure on the price of all things made of ideas. He deemed it an iron law. "In the digital realm you can try to keep Free at bay with laws and locks, but eventually the force of economic gravity will win."[6] Free content on the Internet, he claimed, would not kill journalism, only revolutionize it. "Out of the bloodbath will come a new role for professional journalists."

> There may be more of them, not fewer, as the ability to participate in journalism extends beyond the credentialed halls of traditional media. But they may be paid far less, and for many it won't be a full time job at all. Journalism as a profession will share the stage with journalism as an avocation.[7]

Some media companies had been able to collect subscription revenue for online content, however, as Apple had with iTunes by charging per song. A 2007 study of online news providers in the U.K. found that while paid content was still relatively uncommon, the infrastructure of the Internet was growing closer to enabling a shift to a paid model. "Its entry into the mainstream now seems closer given the successful implementation of micropayments for music (iTunes) and games (Xbox Live) and the emergence of ser-vices that facilitate small online payments, like eBay's PayPal."[8] The claim that subscriptions could only work with a minority of high-end "premium" users, it concluded, was "more difficult to refute, and most of the academic literature on the subject has supported it."

> The view that content charging is impossible may be largely based on precedent. Because the vast majority of Internet users do not pay for content, many assume they will not pay for content in the future. The success of iTunes would appear to refute this.[9]

By the grim economic winter of 2009, according to the *Columbia Journalism Review*, a "determined chorus" arose from a newspaper industry that, "no longer willing to stand idly by as its trade died, took up a call that was clear, direct, and seemingly unassailable in its logic: make the readers pay."[10] By then, the advertising rates newspapers were able to command on their websites were a fraction of what they could charge for a print ad. Where typically a newspaper might be able to charge $35 per 1,000 readers (CPM) for a print ad, noted *Advertising Age* in early 2009, it might only be able to get $1 for 1,000 online readers.[11] With the recession, online advertising rates fell as a result of ebbing demand and rising supply. The standard CPM rate for online ads, noted Paul Farhi in the *American Journalism Review* in mid-2009, had "crashed through the $1 floor and is rapidly on its way to zero (newsprint ads, by contrast, still command $20 or more for the same thousand readers)."[12] The recession had brought desperate times for some publishers. "I've heard of some scary stuff going on, with CPMs as low as 10¢," Rob Grimshaw of the *Financial Times* told *Advertising Age*.[13] Many claimed that advertising revenue would return when the economy recovered, but others argued that newspapers had better start looking elsewhere for revenue immediately.

Rebuilding the Paywall

A 2009 study reported by the Newspaper Association of America found that once a newspaper put its content behind a paywall, online advertising dropped dramatically and the revenue from subscriptions did not come close to making up for the lost advertising revenue.[14] "Consumers won't pay," declared Charlie Tillinghast, president of MSNBC.com. "It's just that simple. They'll read amateur blogs and everything else first before they pay for general news and information. Those are the physics of our business."[15] Others argued that something was better than nothing, which was just about what newspapers were able to charge for online advertising. "My sense is that we're not going to make a huge amount of money," Oliver Knowlton, president of MediaNews Group Interactive, told *Advertising Age.* "But what's more important is it's just not given away free online."[16] There was only one small problem with newspapers attempting to reverse course and resume charging for online content after years of scrimping on the product they produced. "Given the savage cutting that has been under way at regional, chain-owned newspapers over the last decade or more, it may be too late for some metro dailies," noted *The Wire*'s David Simon. "They may no longer have enough legitimate, unique content to compel their readership to pay."[17]

In a *Time* cover story headlined "How to save your newspaper," Walter Isaacson proposed a "micropayment" system for newspapers, similar to iTunes, under which readers would not pay per month but instead would pay a much smaller amount in a pay-as-you-read scheme. "A newspaper might decide to charge a nickel for an article or a dime for that day's full edition or $2 for a month's worth of Web access," he explained. "Some surfers would balk, but I suspect most would merrily click through if it were cheap and easy enough."[18] The problem was that the technology for such a pay-per-read scheme had not yet been developed. Instead some dailies began again erecting paywalls. *Newsday*, a Long Island tabloid that the Tribune Company sold to Cablevision in 2008, was among the first to join this third wave of paywalls, announcing in the fall of 2009 that it would charge $5 a week for access to its online content. After three months, it had gained only thirty-five subscribers.[19] The Hollywood daily trade newspaper *Variety* similarly erected a paywall, only to watch its page views drop by more than 40 percent. The *Newport Daily News,* going Walter Hussman one better, took its paywall to extremes, charging $345 a year for unlimited access to the paper's web site, which was 138 percent more than the annual cost of subscribing to its print edition. "We want to drive people to the print version of the paper," publisher Buck Sherman told the *American Journalism Review*.[20] The day after the change went into effect, newsstand sales of the *Daily News* spiked by 10 percent.[21] In the UK, News Corp. CEO Rupert Murdoch ordered a paywall at the *Times of London* in 2010.

Paying for Content

The announcement by the *New York Times* in early 2010 that it would begin charging for its online content in 2011 — make that resume charging for its online content — was seen by many as a watershed moment in newspaper history. No longer would the nation's leading daily undercut its own business model by giving away its online content. If the *Times* plan succeeded, so industry thinking went, there could actually be hope for newspapers that might finally get a fair dollar for their product. But the paywall the *Times* planned was different from most others. It would take more than a year and a reported $25 million to perfect. It was a "metered" model, which allowed readers to read a certain number of online articles for free — first it was twenty, then ten — before having to pony up for a subscription. Research had shown that about 85 percent of the *Times* online audience read fewer than twenty articles a month, so the paywall was targeted at the 15 percent who were heavy users of the site and allowed the transient readers to continue popping in for free. The model had been pioneered in 2007 by the *Financial Times* and helped boost profits at the U.K. business daily by 13 percent in 2008.[22]

The tactical shift back towards paywalls had its critics. "Newspapers are slowly digging their graves by building paywalls," predicted Alan Mutter, the blogging Newsosaur. "Paywall revenue is not going to make up for the missing ad revenue."[23] "If you erect a universal pay wall around your content then it follows you are turning away from a world of openly shared content," said Alan

Rusbridger, editor of the U.K.'s *Guardian* newspaper. "There may be sound business reasons for doing this, but editorially it is about the most fundamental statement anyone could make about how newspapers see themselves in relation to the newly-shaped world."[24] The *Washington Post* and McClatchy Newspapers similarly promised to keep their online content free. The rest of the newspaper world waited and watched the paywall experiment at the *New York Times* in the hope it would pay off.

Within a year of introducing its metered paywall, the *Times* had a half million digital subscribers, which gobsmacked the newspaper industry and converted most of the naysayers. Here, finally, was a paywall that worked, and it worked so well at the *Times* that it was suddenly bringing in $100 million a year in new revenue. Similar results were seen at other dailies. "I was shocked to see the loyalty of newspaper subscribers," said Mike Klingensmith, publisher of the *Minneapolis Star Tribune*, after more than 18,000 readers quickly signed on to its metered system in late 2011.[25] Warren Buffett, as savvy a businessman as there ever was, also decided to put his growing newspaper empire behind a paywall. "I'm not interested in the Internet for money," he told *USA Today*. "I'm interested in preventing the erosion of print. . . . I could kick myself for not figuring this out earlier."[26] Other publishers suddenly began scrambling to erect metered paywalls of their own. "Gannett's February announcement that it's going paywall at all its 80 newspapers galvanized attention," noted Ken Doctor in early 2012.

> When the third largest U.S. newspaper site, the Los Angeles Times, went paid this week, more nodding was seen in publishers' suites. Suddenly it's paywalls all around the world. We've moved — in a couple of years — from the question of whether to when.[27]

By mid-2012, the news just kept getting better. The *Financial Times* reported that its digital subscriptions grew 31 percent through the first six months of the year, to more than 300,000.[28] The *New York Times* reported an 81 percent jump in digital subscribers for its latest quarter. It had suddenly crossed a watershed — subscription revenue surpassed advertising revenue as a result of the paywall (and plummeting ad sales). The *Times* had also seen a boost in print subscriptions because they included digital access, so it increased their price as well. "We didn't design this model to support print," admitted Paul Smurl, its general manager for core digital products, "but in fact what we've seen is an increase in home delivery subscriptions, in particular on Sundays."[29] Some worried that what might work for the mighty *New York Times* might not work for smaller newspapers, but that fear proved unfounded. "Some of the newspapers which have fared the best after implementing an online paywall are those based in smaller markets," noted Michael Nevradakis, a PhD student at the University of Texas who was researching paywalls. "These newspapers not only have less competition from other local media outlets, but they provide coverage of local news and events that a larger media outlet with national reach will most likely ignore."[30]

Gannett reported its first annual revenue increase since 2006 in large part due to the paywalls it erected at its local dailies (excluding *USA Today*), which were expected to bring in an extra $100 million a year. The best news of all was that metered paywalls didn't drop online ad sales much. Traffic tended to stay strong and transient readers seemed undeterred. "The war is over," declared Ryan Chittum on the *Columbia Journalism Review* website. "The evidence is in. Newspapers, large and small, premium and not, gain additional revenue through subscriptions and lose little if anything in digital ads."[31]

In Canada, all three major newspaper companies scrambled to erect metered paywalls. The *Globe and Mail* national newspaper introduced one in October 2012, and within four months it had signed up 80,000 subscribers.[32] In the U.S., the forty-seven papers owned by Lee Enterprises erected paywalls beginning in 2011, as did McClatchy's thirty dailies in 2012, and E.W. Scripps's fourteen in early 2013. "I only wish we'd started sooner," said Michael Gulledge, vice president of sales and marketing for Lee.[33] The 2013 edition of the Pew Research Center's annual *State of the News Media* report counted 450 U.S. dailies (out of 1,380) that had implemented paywalls and noted that these had "caught fire" in the previous year. "For the first time since the deep recession that began in 2007, newspaper organizations have grounds for a modicum of optimism," it noted. "Together with the other new revenue streams, these added circulation revenues are rebalancing the industry's portfolio from its historic over-dependence on advertising."[34] In another sign of life, noted the report, stocks of publicly traded newspaper companies also saw their share prices rise in 2012, with several up 30 percent or more. "Auto advertising has come back, and some markets, like Miami, are beginning to see recovery in real estate and employment ads as well."[35]

Something Worth Paying For

By now it was dawning on newspaper publishers that what readers were willing to pay for online was what they couldn't get elsewhere. It was something that distinguished newspapers from the rest of the herd on the Internet — local reporting. The *Orange County Register*, which had been scooped up out of bankruptcy by former greeting card executive Aaron Kushner, introduced a hard paywall in April 2013 that was unusual for not discounting digital access. "The *Register* will charge one price — a dollar a day or $365 a year," noted Ken Doctor. "Come to the *Register* site, and you can get any non-staff-written story — wires and syndicated content, which makes up 40 percent of the content overall — but you won't get more than 'a headline and a sentence' of local stories."[36] The strength of the Internet was its instantaneous global reach, which ironically had been strangling local journalism by flooding the market with news from everywhere. There remained a market, it seemed, for news about the places where readers actually lived.

Two years after introducing its paywall, the *New York Times* had 700,000 digital subscribers and growing. The company's CEO called metered online access "the most important and most successful business decision" made by the *Times* in many years. "In modern media, you could make the case that the best way forward is to listen carefully to what the industry has to say and then do the exact opposite," said Mark Thompson.[37] Even the *Times of London* was having success with its hard paywall, which didn't allow readers access to any free articles. Its online edition added 13,000 new subscribers in the first half of 2013 to bring its digital readership up to 140,000. While the online reach of the *Times* plummeted as a result of its paywall, with its 395,000 print subscribers it had a total of 535,000 paying readers — more than before its paywall. "When we sacrifice this so-called reach, what have we really lost?" asked News UK CEO Mike Darcey. "A long tail of passing trade, many from overseas, many popping in for only one article."

> This reach doesn't generate any meaningful revenue, and the pursuit of it undermines the piece of the business that does make money. If your purpose contemplates still being here in five to 10 years' time, then the choice seems clear: it is better to sacrifice reach and preserve sustainable profitability.[38]

Despite the success of paywalls, the naysayers continued to insist that they couldn't save newspapers. "In a dying industry, the sensible thing to do is to maximize your revenues before you die," scoffed Felix Salmon of Reuters. "Paywalls might well make money for newspapers. But that doesn't mean that newspapers aren't dying. Quite the opposite."[39] Blogger Steve Buttry agreed, arguing that newspapers should instead pursue other revenue streams that didn't limit their audience. "The potential revenue paywalls will yield isn't worth the damage they cause."[40] As 2013 neared an end, however, *BusinessWeek* declared it "The Year of the Paywall."[41] It turned out that Walter Hussman had the right idea all along when he stubbornly stuck with a paywall from the start at his *Arkansas Democrat-Gazette* and nine other dailies. "That simple-minded thought for which he was ridiculed is now the root of the reader-revenue revolution," noted Ken Doctor.

> Now, "content wants to be free" seems silly to an increasing number of us. . . . What the metered idea — allowing some number of free articles to each unique visitor — dispels is the either/or thinking of the early Internet news age. News doesn't have to be either free or paid. It can [be] a combination of the two.[42]

Even Dean Singleton at MediaNews changed his mind after first pooh-poohing paywalls. "I don't think paywalls are the answer to anything," he said in early 2013. "If we're swapping out print dollars for digital dimes, I think paywalls are a stack of pennies." By year's end, and with his company in shambles, he reversed course and ordered paywalls at MediaNews dailies. "The newspaper industry's circulation revenue rose by 5% last year, thanks to those digital pennies," noted *USA Today* in late 2013. "It was the first such increase since 2003."[43] The "digital first" strategy implemented by Media-News imploded the following year as it closed its much ballyhooed "Thunderdome" digital news center that fed content to its seventy-six dailies. By mid-2014, the *New York Times* had 831,000 digital subscribers and counting, while the *Financial Times* topped 450,000. The revenue their metered paywalls contributed went a long way to offsetting their losses in print advertising and provided hope — and even expectations — that newspapers would continue to survive. "Those subscriptions will not save newspapers," noted Michael Shapiro in advocating online payments. "They alone will not pay for the cost of reporting. No one revenue stream will — not online or print advertising, or alerts on handheld devices, or new electronic readers that display stories handsomely. The hope is that they all will."[44] Newspapers had indeed diversified into a number of other new revenue streams, but some of them smacked of desperation, sell-out, or worse.

Meet the New Bosses

Warren Buffett wasn't the only investor who saw the value in newspapers as their selling prices dropped. As the industry pulled itself up by its own bootstraps, some of the savviest businessmen and media moguls began buying newspapers. From the start of 2012 through mid-2013, more than 100 newspapers traded hands, the most since 2007.[45] Billionaire John Henry, who owned the Red Sox baseball team, bought the *Boston Globe* from the New York Times Co. in mid-2013 for $70 million, a price that was little more than 6 percent of the $1.1 billion the Times Co. had paid for it twenty years earlier. The *Globe* then ditched its hard paywall in early 2014 for metered access.[46] Jeff Bezos, who founded Amazon.com, bought the *Washington Post* for $250 million in 2013. In Philadelphia, the *Inquirer* and the *Daily News* got their fourth owner in eight years when they were auctioned off in 2014. Instead of the price going down again, as it had in the previous two sales, this time it blipped up, from $55 million to $70 million. Lost in all the doom and gloom about newspapers was that they made money, and those that weren't weighed down with debt actually generated an envious cash flow. "The prices have gotten so cheap, the price to cash flow [ratio] is very attractive," explained money manager Thomas Story, a longtime investor in Buffett's company Berkshire Hathaway. "It's an old-fashioned value investment."[47]

The boldest newspaper play was made in Southern California, however, where Aaron Kushner not only bought Freedom Communications for $50 million in 2012, but doubled down on print. He began hiring at Freedom's flagship newspaper, the *Orange County Register*, and by early 2013 had almost doubled the size of the *Register*'s newsroom by adding 140 journalists. "The changes were almost immediate," noted Ryan Chittum in *Columbia Journalism Review*. "The *Register* has grown so fat that its Monday paper — typically the smallest edition of the week — approaches the size of Sunday papers in bigger markets."[48] The focus under Kushner went back to the newspaper and away from the Internet. "For years, the *Register* had followed the best practices of the digital-first evangelists, focusing on luring pageviews to its free website," noted Chittum. "Kushner shut down most of the *Register*'s blogs and re-focused reporters on 'more quality, informative content.' ... The *Register* has added investigative reporters, enlarged its graphics team, re-opened its DC bureau, and doubled staff at its 22 community weeklies."[49] Kushner's optimism heartened an industry that had been battered by pessimism and even fatalism for years. "His thesis is simple, but highly contrarian," explained Chittum. "Newspapers are dying in large part from self-inflicted wounds, and there's money to be made in print, particularly from subscribers."[50]

Kushner's approach was to invest in the print product and charge consumers accordingly.

> For Kushner, the answer is to bet on readers. Give them really good journalism — lots of it — and charge them for it. . . . It's an audacious and expensive bet, and its outcome may reveal whether American newspapers can survive, much less flourish.[51]

Kushner then started a new daily in nearby Long Beach, which he also called the *Register*, and bought the nearby *Riverside Press-Enterprise* for $27 million. He made his boldest move in late 2013, however, announcing that Freedom would enter the Los Angeles market with a new daily as a conservative voice in competition with the entrenched *Los Angeles Times*. The *Los Angeles Register* debuted in April 2014, but printed its last issue on September 23 of that year, and is now on-line only.

New Revenue Sources

The failure of online ad revenues to take up the slack at newspapers for plummeting print advertising led to a desperate and wide-ranging search for alternative sources of income. In 2010, the *Toronto Star* began publishing Sunday supplements containing content licensed from the *New York Times*, including its International Weekly section and a Canadian version of its book reviews section. The *Star* charged its subscribers who opted in to the extra sections $1 per week each and soon had 70,000 of them signed up. The *Star* was soon bringing in eight figures a year in extra revenue from the supplements. "Who'd have thought there would be $10 million in newsprint," publisher John Cruickshank told Ken Doctor, who called the supplements "one of the best kept secrets in the newspaper industry."[52] Other publishers followed suit, noted Doctor, including the *Dallas Morning News*, which began offering its subscribers a *New York Times* supplement for $1.99 a week in 2014. Soon other national brands, including the *Washington Post* and *USA Today*, began marketing supplements to other newspapers.

Some newspapers got into e-commerce, as the *Los Angeles Times* did with a website featuring deals from local merchants, sports gear of local teams, *Times*-branded merchandise, back issues and photographs. Others, like the *Minneapolis Star Tribune* and the *Boston Globe*, got into the e-book publishing business.[53] "In the quest to survive and thrive, newspapers are turning very entrepreneurial," noted *Editor & Publisher* in 2012. "The *New York Times* and *Los Angeles Times* are offering classes and lectures for the public."

> The Los Angeles paper has a huge book fair and gives out annual book awards.... The paper also hosts a travel show ... and, this year, will host its Third Annual Directors Roundtable, featuring George Clooney, Stephen Daldry, Michel Hazanavicius, Alexander Payne, and Martin Scorsese. In June, the *Times* will host "A Night of Music + Fashion" and "Hero Complex," a film festival for sci-fi and fantasy film fans.[54]

The extra income proved so significant that the Newspaper Association of America, which had closely tracked newspaper advertising and circulation revenues for decades, added a new category in 2013 to cover the new revenue. "One of the most broadly successful has been offering digital marketing services to local businesses that want a presence in social media but don't know how to go about it," noted Pew's 2013 *State of the News Media* report. "Event marketing and other sponsorships are also a relatively easy sell in the current market."[55] The NAA counted $3.15 billion from new revenue sources in 2013 that helped to offset the decline in print advertising. "Digital agency and marketing services, where newspaper media companies tap into interest among local businesses in the digital environment, increased 43 percent," the NAA reported. "Event marketing dollars rose 5 percent."[56] The added income was significant, noted Ryan Chittum of the *Columbia Journalism Review*. "To put that in perspective, the industry's total digital advertising was just $3.4 billion last year."[57] The *New York Times* not only sponsored conferences, but also offered ocean cruises with newsmakers. "These ventures are lucrative, can be informative and help to 'build the brands' of *The Times* and its journalists," explained Margaret Sullivan, the newspaper's "public editor" or ombudsman, who had joined the Gray Lady from the *Buffalo News*. "You can go on a cruise to Patagonia and rub elbows with a top *Times* editor and a *Times* columnist who are among the speakers."

Earlier this year, if you had $995 to spare, you could have attended "Thomas L. Friedman's The Next New World," a conference in San Francisco featuring the *Times* columnist. Last year's DealBook conference, where businesspeople paid $1,500 to listen to the likes of the Goldman Sachs chairman, Lloyd Blankfein, interviewed on a stage at *The Times,* was another example.[58]

Some of the new sources of revenue that newspapers pursued, however, proved questionable ethically. For example, as part of its expanding 2009 calendar of money-making events, including seminars and conferences, the *Washington Post* planned monthly off-the-record dinners with its journalists and politicians at publisher Katharine Weymouth's home. It offered "underwriting" opportunities for organizations willing to pay $25,000 to co-sponsor each dinner. "Bring your organization's CEO or executive director literally to the table," read a flyer promoting the events. "Interact with key Obama administration and congressional leaders."[59] When the political newsletter *Politico* exposed the scheme, the *Post* cancelled the events. David Carr described it as a "fundamental lapse" in the wall between church and state. "Theoretically, you can't buy *Washington Post* reporters," he chortled, "but you can rent them."[60] The *Post*'s ombudsman called it "an ethical lapse of monumental proportions" and observed that "the *Post*'s reputation now carries a lasting stain."[61]

Another money-making scheme that some newspapers got into was selling wine through their own "wine clubs." The concept had been pioneered in 1973 by the *Sunday Times* in the UK, which had 250,000 members in its wine club by 2011.[62] Major U.S. dailies such as the *Wall Street Journal, New York Times, Chicago Tribune,* and *USA Today* started wine clubs in a bid to boost their revenues. According to one media ethicist, however, they risked becoming "legal bootleggers — or high-priced bartenders" and were in danger of running afoul of liquor laws. "It is an ethical nightmare and a potential legal mess," warned Alan Wolper, a journalism professor at Rutgers

University–Newark. "Still, some of the most influential newspapers in the country are wine propagandists."[63] The legal problem, according to Wolper, was that the newspapers were not licensed to sell alcoholic beverages, which were strictly regulated by state agencies. "Break those laws and you'll get busted," he pointed out in his *Editor & Publisher* ethics column in 2012. "Just imagine what a perp walk of publishers would look like."[64] The newspapers could accept orders, but they had to rely on licensed wine marketing companies to fulfill them, noted Wolper. But this relationship was usually acknowledged in "microscopic" type. Another ethical problem was that a newspaper's wine club ads were invariably published next to their restaurant and/or wine reviews, conveying the impression that the advertised wines came similarly approved.

> They insist their wine and restaurant writers have nothing to do with their wine deals. Yet they promote their wine sites as The Dallas Morning News Wine Club, or Los Angeles Times Wine Club, giving the distinct impression their reporters are the ones stomping on grapes.[65]

'One Boatload of Shit at a Time'

Another way newspapers sought to bridge the revenue gap was by venturing into a brave new world of advertising that many considered even more unethical. The phenomenon of advertisers paying for editorial content was hardly new, and had been known for years as "advertorial." In the digital age, however, it went by different names — including "sponsored content," "custom content," "content marketing" and "native advertising" — but they were all basically a twist on the old advertorial concept. Native advertising was so-called because it was designed to blend into its surroundings and be indistinguishable from other content on a website. It was pioneered by BuzzFeed, a website that made $40 million a year from publishing advertiser-provided content. Magazines, which had always been more susceptible to advertiser influence than newspapers, suffered even worse with the recession. In an attempt to reinvent themselves as multimedia enterprises, some began to experiment with native advertising. Business magazine *Forbes* threw open its website to both bloggers and advertisers with its "BrandVoice" program in 2011, which it called "brand journalism". "*Forbes* is widely recognized as the first mainstream publication to offer up its editorial space for paid placement," noted Shel Holtz in *Communication World*.

> Many see it as a deceptive, unethical practice designed to fool readers by dressing up marketing copy as original reporting. Others fear it will spell the end of professional journalism, since a publication's integrity would be compromised by ads that are almost indistinguishable from the publication's original content.[66]

Click-through rates on display or "banner" ads on websites plummeted starting in 2008, falling from an already dismal 0.13 percent to an even more dismal 0.04 percent by 2014.[67] This increasing ineffectiveness, in addition to oversupply, contributed to the stagnation of digital ad revenues as advertisers increasingly turned their noses up at banner ads. Native advertising, by contrast, drew the attention of web surfers at rates similar to editorial content because research showed that most people couldn't tell the difference. This revelation captivated advertisers and publishers alike. "Advertisers want their message to be part of the natural flow of the product in which the journalism appears," said Lewis D'Vorkin, chief product officer at Forbes Media. "And that's what you need to do in order to remain a profitable media company and continue to do the journalism that you like to be able to do."[68] The BrandVoice content on the *Forbes* website carried a label that suggested it was not journalism, but otherwise it was identical to what its journalists contributed. "Content provided by brands is virtually indistinguishable in subject matter and appearance from content provided by *Forbes*'s contributors," noted the Canadian Journalism Project's website J-Source.

> Only the BrandVoice designation alerts the reader that what they are reading is a story generated by one of BrandVoice's marketing partners, who pay up to $75,000 U.S. a month for the privilege of participating in the program. By the end of this year, Forbes is projecting

that revenue generated by BrandVoice will account for about 25 per cent of Forbes.com's total advertising revenue.[69]

By lowering its standards, Forbes had improved its fortunes, which quickly gained the attention of an ad-starved news media. The bounty came at a price in terms of credibility, however. "A once-respected brand . . . has turned its digital self into the inverse of high publishing," complained Michael Wolff. "It's now all cheesy come ons."[70] In the media world, that seemed to matter less than the revenue gained. "In a sense," noted David Carr in the New York Times, "Forbes has come up with an oven that makes its own food — something of a grail for publishers."[71] As newspapers clambered aboard the native advertising gravy train, however, they were soon brought up short by an illustration of the peril they were putting themselves in. The Atlantic, which had been founded in 1857 as a serious literary magazine, fumbled its first foray into native advertising, featuring a glowing article on the controversial Church of Scientology on its website in early 2013. It even allowed critical reader comments on the puff piece to be deleted. "If the Church of Scientology wanted to run an ad, they'd buy an ad," complained Wired magazine. "But they wanted something more: They wanted some of the credibility that goes with being editorial content at the Atlantic. . . . The Church of Scientology bought the right to siphon credibility from The Atlantic's writers and editors."[72] The maelstrom of criticism that resulted prompted the Atlantic to delete the article and issue an apology. "We screwed up," the magazine said after the deception was exposed. "We now realize that as we explored new forms of digital advertising, we failed to update the policies that must govern the decisions we make along the way. It's safe to say that we are thinking a lot more about these policies after running this ad than we did beforehand."[73]

The trend toward blurring the lines between editorial content and advertising also drew the watchful eye of the Federal Trade Commission, which convened an industry confab on the subject in late 2013. "By presenting ads that resemble editorial content, an advertiser risks implying, deceptively, that the information comes from a nonbiased source," noted FTC chair Edith Ramirez, who warned of unspecified regulatory action.[74] Native advertising proponents vigorously defended their practices, while some critics were colorful in their denunciations. "With every transaction, publishers are mining and exporting a rare resource: trust," warned Bob Garfield. "Those deals will not save the media industry. They will, in a matter of years, destroy the media industry: one boatload of shit at a time."[75] Even Google decided to take action, announcing in March 2013 that it considered "these types of promotional tactics to be in violation of our quality guidelines."[76] As a result, it threatened to remove such articles, or even entire publications, from its Google News search results.

Given the dollars involved, however, it was only a matter of time before newspapers got in on the native advertising game. "The category's growth rate is second only to that of video," noted the 2013 *State of the News Media* report. "Sponsorship ads rose 38.9%, to $1.56 billion [in 2012]; that followed a jump of 56.1% in 2011."[77]

Newspapers Go Native

The first major American newspaper to feature native advertising on its website was the *Washington Post* in early 2013. "The *Washington Post* became the latest publisher to quit worrying and learn to love sponsored content," quipped *Digiday*. "This marks the first time a major U.S. newspaper has opened up its platform for brands to create and distribute content."[78] From there it was a slippery slope until the famed daily began to offer native ads in print, which it did that August. "A big part of native is to create experiences for brands in places in the printed pages where there wasn't formerly advertising," said the *Post*'s chief revenue officer, Kevin Gentzel, who had joined the newspaper from *Forbes*. "Native is different from advertorials because it needs to be narrative in storytelling and engaging so it's topical, relevant and timely versus just thematically relevant."[79] The *Post* even offered native advertising to politicians, at least in its commuter tabloid *Express*, selling a front-page attack ad to D.C. mayoral candidate Vincent Gray for $5,000 in

2014. It resembled a news story and was poorly labeled, according to the *Post*'s own media reporter. "This piece of native advertising flunks all tests of journalistic hygiene," noted Erik Wemple. "The 'ADVERTISEMENT' notation is puny, not scannable by modern radar. Nor does the disclosure at the bottom of the ad jump out at the reader."[80] A similar front-page native ad may have even helped to turn an election outcome in the Canadian province of British Columbia in 2013. A full-page ad for Premier Christy Clark took up the entire front page of the Vancouver commuter tabloid *24 Hours*. It was emblazoned "Comeback Kid," and featured poll results that showed Clark had won a pre-election debate, along with a headline that declared that she was "gaining traction with B.C. families."[81] Clark, who had been trailing badly in the polls, went on to a surprise election victory.

Soon native ads began showing up on newspaper websites across the U.S. and Canada. Native advertising firm Nativo signed up a half dozen newspaper chains, including Hearst, McClatchy, Gate-House, and Lee Enterprises.[82] Native advertising was expected to generate more than $1 million in 2014 at the *Deseret News*, a Salt Lake City daily owned by the Mormon church.[83] "Almost all of the publishers running branded content say they abide by the traditional church-and-state separation — news on one side of the wall, advertising on the other," noted the *New York Times*. "But the sponsored content runs beside the editorial on many sites and is almost indistinguishable."[84] The ads invariably carried a disclaimer that identified them as paid content, but that was insufficient for many journalists. "Your average reader isn't ·interested in that," spat Andrew Sullivan, a popular blogger who eschewed advertising on his website, instead opting for a paywall that brought in $875,000 in 2013. "They don't realize they are being fed corporate propaganda."[85] In fact, a 2014 study by the Interactive Advertising Bureau found that just 41 percent of people were able to recognize that native advertising was not journalism.[86]

In Canada, major newspapers such as the *Globe and Mail* and the *Toronto Star* flagged down the native advertising gravy train in 2013.[87] It had already been tearing up the tracks at the *Star*, the country's largest newspaper company, for five year. Postmedia, which owned major dailies across the country, had been the first major newspaper publisher in North America to go native in 2008. "Content marketing programs naturally resonate with the readers of Postmedia Network Inc.'s newspaper brands," Yuri Machado, the company's VP of Integrated Advertising told *Marketing* magazine in 2012. "Over the past four years, Postmedia has executed various formats of content marketing."[88] The *Globe and Mail* offered advertisers prime placement on its website under its "custom content" program. "With custom editorial content," it promised, "our award-winning journalists, photographers and designers produce content that halos an advertiser's message and around which the advertiser's brand ads can be positioned."[89] Toronto-based firm Polar provided native advertising services to both the *Globe and Mail* and the *Toronto Star*, as well as to a number of newspapers in other countries, including the *Washington Post* in the U.S. and the *Telegraph* in the UK.[90] Most media companies used outside or in-house "studios" to produce native advertising without involving their journalists. In 2014, however, the *Globe and Mail* demanded as part of contract negotiations with its union that its journalists produce custom content if it did not involve a conflict of interest. "*Globe* management wants journalists to generate articles directly paid for and approved by advertisers," reported the website Canadaland. "Under the company proposal, editorial staff would be assigned to write or produce advertiser sponsored 'branded content' (i.e. native advertising) that is vetted by the advertiser prior to publication and held out to readers as staff-written content."[91]

Tail Wags Dog

Like many journalists, *New York Times* Executive Editor Jill Abramson looked askance at native advertising infiltrating newspapers across the continent. "I think that some of what is being done with native advertising does confuse a little too much," the first woman top editor at the *Times* told a conference in mid-2013.[92] By year's end, however, even the *Times* was doing it. "[Times Co. CEO Mark]

Thompson said he is hoping for 'eight figures' — tens of millions of dollars — in [native] advertising revenue," noted *Times* public editor Margaret Sullivan. "Ms. Abramson told me that she would be 'watching like a hawk' over the next months and beyond to make sure that *Times* readers don't ever get fooled into thinking that advertising is editorial content."[93] The *Times* planned to distinguish the native ads on its website from news stories by labeling them "Paid Post" and surrounding them with a thick blue border. "We will ensure that there is never a doubt in anyone's mind about what is *Times* journalism and what is advertising," publisher Arthur Sulzberger promised in late 2013. "Our readers will always know that they are looking at a message from an advertiser."[94] *Times* journalists would not be involved in creating the content, its executives pointed out, which would instead be produced by an in-house studio. "We've been very deliberate in saying to the market that the Paid Posts get zero involvement with the newsroom," said Meredith Levien, executive vice president of advertising at the *Times*. "We share the storytelling tools but not the storytellers."[95] Howls of outrage nonetheless reverberated across the Big Apple. "Business is a slippery slope and, if it works, even incrementally, the pressure at the *Times* will be to become more like *Forbes*," predicted Michael Wolff.[96]

The first native ads in the *Times* were indeed well labeled. "A Paid Post from Dell, for instance, was surrounded on all sides by a thick blue border that included a label at the top saying, 'Paid For And Posted By Dell,'" noted *Advertising Age*. "Just underneath that message, the Dell logo appeared in a darker blue bar running the width of the post. The Dell logo appeared again next to the author's name."[97] In the first quarter of 2014, thanks in part to its native advertising program, the *Times* snapped thirteen quarters of declining ad revenue and posted a 3.4 percent gain. Soon Abramson was out as its top editor amidst reports of conflict over native advertising in the newspaper. She was replaced in mid-2014 by Dean Baquet, who had joined the paper from the *Los Angeles Times*. "The business side is now left to wonder whether Mr. Baquet's more collegial approach reflects any greater enthusiasm for their work in, for example, native ads and video," noted *Advertising Age*.[98] The ousting of Abramson was quickly followed by the leaking of an internal *New York Times* "Innovation Report." Among other things, it proposed a radical realignment of the newspaper's advertising strategies.

> The very first step ... should be a deliberate push to abandon our current metaphors of choice — 'The Wall' and 'Church and State' — which project an enduring need for division. Increased collaboration, done right, does not present any threat to our values of journalistic independence.[99]

Before long, readers began to notice that the *Times* had shrunk the labels that distinguished content bought by advertisers from articles generated by its newsroom and made the language on the labels less explicit. "When its Paid Posts first appeared, the labels were among the most stringent in publishing," noted *Advertising Age*. "Several marketers have bristled at the labeling, suggesting it turned away readers before they had a chance to judge the content based on its quality."

> Recent Paid Posts from Chevron and Netflix have replaced the blue moat that enclosed Dell's native ad with a slimmer blue line running only along the top. "Paid For And Posted By" has been trimmed to "Paid Post," which is in slightly smaller type. The company logos, also slightly smaller, appear in a white bar.[100]

Like Abramson, *Wall Street Journal* editor Gerard Baker eschewed native advertising, describing as a "Faustian pact" the deals many other newspapers made with advertisers. "The clear delineation between news and advertising is becoming more and more blurred," he told an audience at New York University's journalism school in September 2013. "We have to resist that. It's also in the end I think self-defeating for these advertisers, most of whom now are trying to force news organizations to do this."[101] Within six months, however, the *Wall Street Journal* was also running native ads on its website. "I am confident that our readers will appreciate what is sponsor-generated content and what is content from our global news staff," said Baker.[102]

Purists predictably decried the trend. Andrew Sullivan titled a lecture he gave that spring at Harvard's Nieman Foundation for Journalism "How Advertising Defeated Journalism." His criticism was scathing. "It's a huge story," he told *Digiday*. "The complete transformation of the economics of journalism in a way that renders the concept of journalism extinct. Advertising snuck into the editorial pages in a way that advertising has always wanted to do. . . . One side has effectively surrendered." Even the *Guardian*, long a bastion of journalistic integrity, was running native ads on its website, noted Sullivan. "I see the *Guardian* basically deciding to merge with Unilever," he wrote. "They have a whole staff of journalists writing articles with Unilever's funding. It's not journalism, it's public relations. . . . It will collapse when the readers figure it out."[103] The basic objection of critics was the inherent deception. "There's no getting around the unpleasant truth that a good many native ads are intrinsically deceptive," noted Garfield. "It bespeaks a conspiracy of deception among publishers, advertisers and their agencies. At stake is the trust earned by the publication over its entire lifespan. . . . Selling its soul buys a sinking newspaper precious little time."

> The reputational risk to publishers is real. It's one thing when a few ads look like editorial content, but there are now so many native ads, so cleverly disguised, that in a strange inversion it's actually becoming hard to tell if a particular piece of editorial content isn't advertising.[104]

Even some advertising executives saw the trend as counter-productive. "Native advertising is just the latest symptom of a system that has lost its way," lamented Todd Copilevitz of ad agency JWT Atlanta. "Rather than honing the craft of building meaningful marketing campaigns, we have become enablers of a system that values short-term gain for minimal investment. And in the end, it will come back to haunt us all."[105] Of all the attempts that advertising had made over the decades to insinuate itself into journalism, this was going too far for some. "Native advertising is a more insidious encroachment into consumer media content than any prior form of advertising," warned Ben Kunz, vice president of strategic planning at Mediassociates. "If publishers and marketers aren't careful, they are going to poison the well of digital ad communications by breaking consumer trust."[106] None of the critics hit the mark as well as HBO's John Oliver. In an eleven-minute takedown on his fake news program *Last Week Tonight*, he offered a metaphor. "I like to think of news and advertising as the separation of guacamole and Twizzlers," he quipped. "Separately they're good. But if you mix them together, somehow you make both of them really gross." Oliver then called out Levien, the *New York Times* advertising head. "Good native advertising is just not meant to be trickery," she was shown saying. "It is meant to be publishers sharing its storytelling tools with marketers." Oliver deadpanned his killshot. "Exactly, it's not trickery," he said. "It's sharing storytelling tools. And that's not bullshit. It's recycled bovine waste."[107]

CONCLUSION

The Myth of the Death of Newspapers

Media myths increasingly surround us in today's ever more medi-
ated world, few of which have proved more persistent than the
well-worn canard about newspapers dying. This myth took on a
new life in the Internet Age, pushed by technology enthusiasts and
in many cases even by newspapers themselves, which had long
cried poverty out of habit. The myth was propelled into the spotlight in 2009 with the closure of second-place dailies in Denver and
Seattle, but resulting predictions of a newspaper extinction proved
at least premature, as no major North American daily has gone
out of business since then. Newspapers are undeniably downsizing, as evidenced by their massive layoffs of journalists and other
workers, but it is this very scalability — to borrow a term from the
techies — that should prove the industry's salvation. "It's amazing
how few people it actually takes to run a newspaper company, isn't
it?" one Georgia newspaper owner asked Lou Phelps of the *Savannah Daily News* in 2010 at the height of the cutbacks, which prompted
Phelps to wonder: "Who are these people who report on the financial strength of our companies, including on the performance of
the publicly traded publishing companies?"

And why do they fail to understand the successful restructuring that
most newspaper publishing companies have now achieved, either

through creative and aggressive management decisions or through the benefit of beneficial bankruptcy filings?"[1]

The short answer comes courtesy of long-time *New York Times* columnist Russell Baker who noted that "most people competent to write about journalism are not comfortable writing about finance."[2] Most journalists seemed unable to differentiate between the extraordinary paper losses reported by newspaper companies and the operating profits they continue to post. Equally baffling to most journalists, apparently, were the implications of numerous newspaper companies going into bankruptcy. How could they go bankrupt if they weren't losing money? As we have seen in this study, the newspaper companies that declared Chapter 11 bankruptcy were all profitable — that's why they continued to publish, often under new ownership — but their reduced earnings were insufficient to service the high levels of debt they had taken on in making ill-timed acquisitions. Their newspapers were not only profitable, but in many cases highly profitable. Given continued profitability, it is reasonable to assume their continued survival as businesses.

Yet some of the most prominent industry analysts continued to promote the myth that newspapers were unprofitable. "Most of the top 100 or so papers (those over 90,000 or so in circulation) are probably in the red on an operating revenue basis," Martin Langeveld wrote in 2009.[3] Bob Garfield was one of the worst culprits for promoting the myth of newspaper unprofitability, but at least he was always colorful. "The news industry has gone from being obscenely profitable to slightly profitable to — at least, in the case of newspapers — largely unprofitable," he wrote on the *Guardian*'s website in 2013. "I would say that the business model is unsustainable, but losing money is not a business model. It is a going-out-of-business model."[4]

The fact is that all publicly-traded newspaper companies in the U.S. and Canada posted an annual operating profit from 2006 through 2013, although getting at the bottom line behind the numbers can take some doing. The extraordinary losses that grabbed the headlines resulted, in most cases, from accounting gymnastics in the form of "writedowns" on the value of newspapers as assets, which were undeniably dropping. Accounting rules adopted after the bursting of the technology bubble in the early 2000s required U.S. companies to regularly recalculate the value of their assets. If it went down, that lost value had to come off the books somehow, and it did so in the annual profit and loss statement. But a writedown on asset value was strictly a "paper" loss. On an operating basis, standardized as EBITDA — earnings before interest, taxes, depreciation and amortization (not to mention extraordinary items like restructuring costs and impairment of assets) — newspapers invariably still made money. As a result, as well as given their uncanny ability to adapt, and a persistent appetite for them, I predict that newspapers will be with us for a long time to come. As Samuel Clemens (a/k/a Mark Twain) quipped after reading his own premature obituary, rumors of their death have been greatly exaggerated.

Media Myth and Reality

Predictions of the death of newspapers resulted not only from a lack of financial analysis, but also from a blinkered view of history. George Santayana famously observed that those who do not understand history are doomed to repeat it, and the death of newspapers meme was a classic example of that maxim. "This is the kind of error that technological utopians make," noted Malcolm Gladwell. "They assume that their particular scientific revolution will wipe away all traces of its predecessors."[5] The advent of any new medium inevitably brings predictions of the end of old media, among other things, but just as inevitably those predictions prove misguided, noted political economist Vincent Mosco. "Almost every wave of new technology, including information and communications media, has brought with it declarations of the end," he wrote in his 2004 book *The Digital Sublime*. The reason, according to Mosco, is "a remarkable, almost willful, historical amnesia about technology."

One of the reasons why variations on the "end of" myths are so popular is because we collectively forget the myths that surround the history of technology. Cyberspace enthusiasts encourage us to think that we have reached the end of history, the end of geography, and the end of politics. Everything has changed.[6]

The twentieth century was a century of new media from start to finish — first film, then radio, television, and finally the Internet. Each was more awesome than the last and brought predictions that it would mean the death of older media. Newspapers have always been the favorite victim, but television was supposed to also spell the end of the movies and radio. Both instead found a niche quite nicely. "When television arrived, newspapers had met their match," noted author Paula Berinstein. "TV was crack cocaine compared to the caffeine of newspapers and coffee and, despite similar limitations to those of radio, TV took over our lives."[7] The way newspapers first responded to the threat of television, noted Berinstein, was by trying to be more like the disruptive new medium.

> As newspaper readership declined, many papers tried to become more TV-like. They chopped stories into smaller bits. They upped the proportion of feature articles. They published more pictures and added color. They dumbed down their vocabulary. They enlarged type size. And, still, they lost readers.[8]

The way newspapers ultimately found their place in the television age, as they had done in the radio age, was by playing to their strengths and offering more in-depth analysis of events rather than simply reporting them. This is what author Mitchell Stephens urged them to do in response to the Internet in his 2014 book *Beyond News: The Future of Journalism*. Stephens called for "wisdom" journalism that "strengthens our understanding of the world" from "journalists who can connect the dots."[9] It is a sensible prescription, but merely another case of history repeating itself. Pundits aren't the only ones who suffer from historical amnesia. Newspaper executives do, too. The threat of the Internet has similarly prompted them to try to emulate a disruptive new medium by offering the same sorts of digital bells and whistles on their websites. They would do well, however, to ponder the insight of media economist Robert Picard, who pointed out that while it was a revolutionary way to distribute media content, the Internet didn't actually offer any new forms of content, as film, radio and television all did. It merely transmitted them all. "If one looks past all the marketing and excitement surrounding the technologies," noted Picard in 2000, "new ICT based technologies cannot revolutionise content because they provide no real new communications capabilities."[10] Many believed the rhetoric that new technologies created new products and services that will transform society, he added, but in reality what they created were just "faster, easier, and more flexible means for consumers to do what they are already doing."

> They are not affecting communications in such fundamental ways as did the arrival of the printing press, telegraph and telephone, photography and motion pictures, and broadcasting, which provided the abilities to move text, sound, and images with or without terrestrial lines.[11]

The Internet did bring game-changing advances to media, however, including interactivity, the ability to link to resources elsewhere on the Web, and the ability of audience members to become publishers themselves. Otherwise, the Internet was just a fancy bulletin board where all and sundry could post anything and everything from text to audio to video to entire publications. It added global reach to the immediacy of broadcasting, but was basically, according to Russell Baker, "an electronic version of the ten-year-old boy on a bicycle who used to toss the newspaper on the front porch: an ingenious circulation device."[12] It was not, as Garfield writes, "a revolutionary advance, along the lines of fire, agriculture, the wheel, the printing press, gunpowder, electricity, radio, manned flight, antibiotics, atomic energy and, maybe, Listerine breath strips."[13] It did, however, bring about a "historic re-ordering of media, marketing and commerce," as Garfield put it.[14] That is what caused newspapers so much trouble, as Web pages siphoned off almost all of their once-lucrative classified advertising, and also made serious inroads into other types of advertising as well.

Newspapers thus had to scramble to re-organize their business model to rely less on advertising revenues and more on reader revenues, including by charging for online access. Their ability to do so successfully was an overlooked good-news story, as it ensured their continued survival. That story was lost, however, amidst all the anguish over layoffs and the supposed "death" of journalism. "An information technology will survive to the extent that it satisfies human needs better than its rivals," noted media theorist Paul Levinson.[15]

> As a cauldron for the emergence of ideas — for their debate, critique, hammering out, and reflection — the worldwide online environment has no equal. For their consultation and pondering, for their most comfortable retrieval, we reach for the newspaper, journal, or book.[16]

The Future of Convergence

The urge to converge that gripped media at the millennium proved to be a disaster in Canada, and only the FCC's cross-ownership ban likely saved U.S. media from a similar fate. Most of Canada's largest newspapers were merged with television companies in 2000, but a decade later the newspaper-TV business model was in a shambles, as convergence between media proved largely unworkable. News media were indeed all going online, but they were doing so separately rather than together in a process better described as "webvergence."[17] In Canada, as in the U.S., the post-2007 recession dropped advertising revenues, although not nearly as severely because of stricter banking regulations. The economic downturn combined with failure of the convergence model produced an ugly spectacle in Canada, followed by another media ownership shakeout. To make up for their falling revenues, television networks demanded in 2009 that the country's broadcasting regulator force cable companies to share some of their growing revenues. The request was eventually granted, but not before an historic re-ordering of media ownership that saw most Canadian television companies owned by the country's telecommunications giants.

Canwest Global Communications declared bankruptcy in 2009 and its newspaper and broadcasting divisions were sold off separately. Its Global Television network was bought in 2010 by Shaw Communications, a Calgary-based cable company. The Thomson family, owner of the *Globe and Mail* national newspaper, bailed out of its partnership with the CTV network in 2010, citing fundamental differences between the two media. The network was then acquired by Bell Canada Enterprises, the country's dominant satellite television company, which was renamed Bell Media.[18]

The shake-ups were part of a trend to de-convergence that had been ongoing for some time. The disastrous AOL–Time Warner merger of 2000 brought so many woes that the conglomerate's AOL division was soon sold off. Viacom, Disney, Vivendi, and AT&T also either divided their multimedia assets into separate companies or sold off their divisions.[19] Dallas-based Belo Corp., which owned newspapers and television stations including the local ABC affiliate and the *Dallas Morning News*, decided in 2007 to split its broadcasting and newspaper divisions into separate companies due to its languishing share price.[20] Post-recession, stock of its A.H. Belo newspaper arm ironically outperformed that of television-only Belo Corp. until the latter was acquired by Gannett in 2013. Rupert Murdoch's gigantic News Corp. similarly spun off its newspaper division into a separate company in 2013, furthering the trend to de-convergence. The Tribune Co. also separated its broadcasting and newspaper divisions after exiting Chapter 11. True to form, the doomsayers trumpeted this de-convergence as further evidence of the death of newspapers. "Print Is Down, and Now Out: Media Companies Spin Off Newspapers, to Uncertain Futures," screamed the headline atop a mid-2014 David Carr column in the *New York Times* that chronicled how Gannett and Scripps were spinning off their newspaper divisions. "A year ago last week, it seemed as if print newspapers might be on the verge of a comeback, or at least on the brink of, well, survival," wrote Carr. "Now print is too much of a drag on earnings, so media companies are dividing back up and print is being kicked to the curb."

Those stand-alone print companies are sailing into very tall waves. Even strong national newspapers like *The Wall Street Journal* and *The New York Times* are struggling to meet Wall Street's demands for growth. ... Newspapers continue to generate cash and solid earnings, but those results are not enough to satisfy investors.[21]

Clay Shirky claimed the multimedia conglomerates were "abandoning" their newspapers. "If you are a journalist at a print publication, your job is in danger. Period," the New York University professor warned. "Time to do something about it." According to Shirky, the *New York Times* didn't go nearly far enough in its headline, which deemed the future of print-only uncertain. "Contrary to the contrived ignorance of media reporters, the future of the daily newspaper is one of the few certainties in the current landscape," he wrote. "Most of them are going away, in this decade."[22] After news broke that Aaron Kushner had ordered layoffs at his Register operations in Southern California when a cash crunch caught up with him, Shirky blogged that the layoffs were conclusive evidence of the death of newspapers, despite double-digit circulation gains at the *Orange County Register* and even print advertising revenue increases. "Kushner's plan was always dumb and we should celebrate its demise, not because it failed (never much in doubt) but because it distracted people with the fantasy of an easy out for dealing with the gradual end of profits from print."[23] The optimistic news of Kushner's expansion plans a year earlier had been reported in "puff pieces," according to Shirky, by media reporters who "couldn't bear to treat him like the snake-oil salesman he is." Worse, this "unpaid PR" was "poisoning the minds of 19-year-olds," he continued. "We don't have much time left to manage the transition away from print."

If you want to cry in your beer about the good old days, go ahead. Just stay the hell away from the kids while you're reminiscing; pretending that dumb business models might suddenly start working has crossed over from sentimentality to child abuse.[24]

Ryan Chittum of the *Columbia Journalism Review*, one of the media reporters Shirky went after, responded with the only piece of information needed to reckon the relative fortunes of print and pixels. "Print newspapers surely throw off more profit — still — than all digital news outlets have revenue," he pointed out.[25] Shirky, whose background before entering academia was in web design, had long denigrated the prospects of print. "We would consult with major and ancient media companies in Manhattan," Shirky told an interviewer of his web design days in the 1990s, "and we would say: 'Those stupid people, why don't they just do everything differently.'"[26] His 2009 essay "Newspapers and Thinking the Unthinkable" had been widely reprinted and pointed to as evidence that print was doomed.[27] Shirky's intolerance for stupid people concerned for the future of print on paper unfortunately extended even to NYU students, as evidenced by a 2013 guest lecture he gave in a Journalism 101 class of about 200 students. "One of the students had been dispatched to interview me in front of the class, and two or three questions in, she asked "So how do we save print?" Shirky recalled. "I was speechless for a moment, then exploded, telling her that print was in terminal decline and that everyone in the class needed to understand this if they were thinking of journalism as a major or a profession."

> The students were shocked — for many of them, it was the first time anyone had talked to them that way. . . . This was a room full of people [who] would rather lick asphalt than subscribe to a paper publication; what on earth would make them think print was anything other than a wasting asset? And the answer is "Adults lying to them."[28]

The Future of News

The defining feature of the digital evangelists, as Dean Starkman noted in his 2011 exposé of what he called the "Future of News (FON) Consensus" was their "absolute certitude" in foretelling the future of media. According to them, it would consist of mostly citizen journalism shared on social media. "We should be grateful that they are here," quipped Starkman of the doomsayers. "If they weren't, we'd have to invent them. Someone has to help us figure this out." FON thinkers, he noted, were "a new kind of public intellectual: journalism academics known for neither their journalism nor their scholarship."[29] The clique of mostly Big Apple academics included Shirky, his colleague Jay Rosen at NYU, and Jeff Jarvis of CUNY, the latter two of whom also sat on the board of John Paton's Manhattan-based company Digital First. Paton's position was perfectly clear. "Newspapers in print are clearly going away," he said in 2013. "I think you're an idiot if you think that's not happening."[30] Starkman nicely summed up the FON argument. "According to this consensus, the future points toward a network-driven system of journalism in which news organizations will play a decreasingly important role," he noted. "News won't be collected and delivered in the traditional sense. It will be assembled, shared, and to an increasing degree, even gathered, by a sophisticated readership."

> At its heart, the FON consensus is anti-institutional. It believes that old institutions must wither to make way for the networked future ... And let's face it, in the debate over journalism's future, the FON crowd has had the upper hand. The establishment is gloomy and old; the FON consensus is hopeful and young (or purports to represent youth).[31]

Jarvis was just as harsh in his assessment of Old Media as Shirky was, but he tended to be even more insulting. "You blew it," he told newspaper executives in a rant posted on the Huffington Post website at the height of the newspaper crisis in 2009. "You've had 20 years since the start of the web, 15 years since the creation of the commercial browser and craigslist, a decade since the birth of blogs and Google to understand the changes in the media economy," he imagined himself telling an audience of "angry, old, white men" then assembled at the NAA meeting in San Diego. "You've had all that time to reinvent your products, services, and organizations for this new world. . . . But you didn't." According to Jarvis, newspapers were all but sunk. "For many of you, there isn't time," he fulminated. "It's simply too late." The best thing the newspaper executives could do, according to Jarvis, was to "get out of the way and make room for the next generation of net natives who understand this new economy and society and care about news and will reinvent it, building what comes after you from the ground up."[32]

The answer to Shirky, Jarvis and the rest of the FON consensus is the simple fact that newspapers stubbornly refused to die, while digital news media stubbornly refused to make much money. Simply comparing the bottom lines of newspaper companies and digital media companies reveals this truth. But that wasn't something the Death of Newspapers crowd wanted to see. That was something journalism professor Michael Giusti of Loyola University in New Orleans found out, however, when he reported those facts. "Most publicly traded newspapers are now posting positive numbers, and many are even on track to post profits for the first quarter of this year," Giusti noted in Loyola's *Maroon* student newspaper in early 2010. "For now, the business model for print publications is solid."[33] That was too much for the crypt keeper at Newspaper Death Watch. "It's disturbing to see such blind optimism from someone who is supposed to shape young minds," wrote blogger Paul Gillin. "Publishers are enjoying a respite right now because of the slowly recovering economy and the benefits of cost-cutting over the last two years, but to believe that the worst is over and the future is bright is to take a dangerously optimistic point of view."[34]

While the question of which media would survive and which would wither would be decided by economics, how and how well they survived had enormous implications for journalism. The best way that digital media had found to make money, unfortunately, was not by doing journalism but by emulating journalism. The native advertising gravy train had been pioneered in the digital age by the Huffington Post, which perfected a business model in which hundreds of unpaid bloggers contributed free content to its website. Native advertising that resembled journalism was then sold on the basis that it attracted readers because it blended in with the website's other content. The formula was so successful at making money that the Huffington Post was sold to AOL for $315 million in 2011. Magazines such as the *Atlantic* and *Forbes* clambered aboard the native advertising gravy train, as did many newspapers. They had started down a slippery slope, however, which threatened to transform journalism into something closer to marketing.

Print Has Its Privileges

One reason newspapers continue to survive is because they continue to have a loyal readership that is highly prized by advertisers because it is educated, affluent and engaged. Print also continues to enjoy significant ergonomic advantages over currently available electronic alternatives. "Print is portable and flexible," noted Stephen Quinn in his 2005 book *Convergent Journalism*.

> Assuming a reasonable level of education, newspapers are easy to read and navigate. Print publications also offer a degree of serendipity, giving people the chance to discover things they did not expect to find. Print allows reporters to go into detail on a subject.[35]

Engagement became a buzzword in digital advertising because online readers proved much less engaged with publications than newspaper readers were. While web surfers flitted from website to website by clicking links on social media or by searching on Google, print newspapers tended to hold their audiences for twenty to thirty minutes at a time. "People don't actually read newspapers," Marshall McLuhan wrote in his landmark 1964 book *Understanding Media*. "They get into them every morning like a hot bath."[36] This immersive aspect, noted many, produced a much better — and more efficient — reading experience. "The transfer rate of information from newspapers is phenomenal," observed Michael Golden, publisher of the *International Herald Tribune*. "You can drop in, drop out, and you've got the whole picture. Just try that from 30 minutes on the web. It's brutally difficult. . . . If you spend 30 minutes with a printed newspaper and I spend 30 minutes on the web, you are going to know a lot more than me."

> There's nothing that beats the amount of information that's communicated when you scan a broadsheet — and compact [tabloid] format can do it too. Everything in the paper is a clue, from the size of the

headlines to the placing of a story. You can read as much as you want, then go back and pick up some more.[37]

The observations of some of the earliest media visionaries still apply to online versus offline reading. "Much of what is in newspapers ... would be satisfactory viewed on a screen only long enough for a reader to decide if further examination is desired," Ben Bagdikian wrote in 1971, perhaps explaining why most online news articles are short and readers still tend to print out longer ones for reading offline. "Other newspaper content will continue to be desirable in print — longer articles, analyses with statistics or other information requiring the ability to reread or to compare items separated in time and space and items for retention in personal records."[38] The move by newspapers toward more analytical coverage which began with the advent of radio and accelerated with television was furthered with the global reach of the Internet. "Since television and radio already satisfy our needs for instantaneous news, the paper newspaper turns out to serve another purpose: a more leisurely reflection of events," noted Levinson. "The result is that the print newspaper may have found a niche that the online newspaper does not really attempt to serve."[39] One important advantage that print had over online news was that most online reading was actually done at work. "Online news reading is predominately a labor time activity while offline news reading is primarily a leisure time activity," noted Hal Varian, Google's chief economist. "Readers don't have a lot of time to devote to news when they are supposed to be working."[40]

More important from an economic perspective is the fact that while classified advertising is much better suited to sortable online databases, display advertising works better in print. "Printed ads are not as intrusive as television ads or Internet pop-ups," noted Belgian scholars Katrien Berte and Els De Bens. "The reader remains in control of the content and decides what articles or advertisements he or she is interested in. Newspaper ads are also often more relevant to the reader than television ads."[41] Research has shown that Internet users "strongly dislike" intrusive advertising, while newspaper advertising is well accepted. "Advertising in newspapers is even perceived as informative and helpful," noted Danish researchers Nadine Lindstädt and Oliver Budzinski, who also pointed to credibility levels three times higher for newspaper content than for Internet content.

> Furthermore, 78 per cent of the respondents answered that they regard companies who advertise in newspapers as reliable . . . Respondents transfer aspects (e.g. trust, credibility) on how they perceive newspapers to the companies that are advertising in newspapers.[42]

In some ways, the proliferation of voices on the Internet actually benefitted newspapers in terms of trust and credibility, which are two of journalism's most valued assets. "In that hyper-crowded arena, the advantage has gone to the most familiar tribunes," noted *Toronto Star* business writer David Olive. "They alone have the expertise to quickly collect and verify staggering amounts of data and present it in reader-friendly formats."[43] Even with the decimation of newspaper newsrooms over the past decade, many pointed out, dailies were still the largest local newsgathering organizations by a long shot. "Only newspapers are economically organised to collect massive amounts of information," noted the *Independent* newspaper in the U.K. "No one else is organised to do it."[44]

The Doomsayers are Unswayed

Even after the Newspaper Crisis passed and it became obvious that the contagion would be confined to Denver and Seattle, with smaller outbreaks in Tucson and Honolulu, media pundits continued to predict the death of a medium. Jeffrey Cole even revised his previous prognosis of twenty to twenty-five years, telling a conference in early 2011 that most newspapers had only a few more years left. "I think in America they have less than five," said Cole, pointing to the fact that only six cities by then had competing dailies. "We're going to see four or five global American voices. The New York Times, The Wall Street Journal, probably The Washington Post. I used to think it would be my beloved Los Angeles Times; it won't. I used to think it would be USA Today; it won't."[45]

Cole's prediction was based on survey research done by the University of Southern California's Center for the Digital Future, of which he was director, that showed declining newspaper readership by young people. It was contained in a report released in early 2012 that predicted the only U.S. newspapers by 2016, in addition to the large national dailies, would be Sunday newspapers and community newspapers. "Local weekly and twice-weekly newspapers may continue in print form, as well as the Sunday print editions of metropolitan newspapers that otherwise may exist only in online editions." Ironically, the report found the percentage of Internet users who said they would miss the print edition of their newspaper if it was no longer available had increased to 63 percent from 56 percent five years earlier. It also found that 25 percent of Internet users who read newspapers stopped reading a print edition because they found the same or related content online, which was a new high for the annual studies.[46] The argument that young people did not read newspapers was often made by newspaper doomsayers, but it ignored the fact that young people have never followed the news to any extent.[47] "Some of the 'young reader' problem is self-correcting," noted Paul Farhi. "People tend to become more interested in the world around them as they buy houses, pay taxes, raise families and generally settle down."

> Some of these people will probably read the paper, someday. Where will the rest seek news and information (if they go anywhere at all)? How about the Internet? If that is the case, newspapers are as well positioned as anyone at the moment to offer the most comprehensive package of daily local news and features on the Web.[48]

The argument that young people had learned to get information online and would thus never again need newspapers was to a certain extent negated by the widespread introduction of paywalls. This meant that if they ever wanted newspaper content, either in print or online, they would have to pay for it one way or the other. Newspapers indeed had something to offer their communities in terms of local news coverage, and the willingness of readers to buck up and pay for it assured their continued survival. Given the bursting of the classified advertising bubble, newspapers would never be the big fish they were prior to 2005. Their advantages as a medium, however, meant they would continue as one of several fish swimming in a multimedia ecosystem. The nightmare of lay-offs and cost-cutting that newspapers endured in the wake of the post-2007 recession had been traumatic but necessary to ensure their survival. "It's not a genuine question whether newspaper companies will survive in our ever-shifting, hypercompetitive communications landscape," noted Gene Roberts and Thomas Kunkel in their book *Leaving Readers Behind*. "They will, their genius for adaptation and self-preservation evolved to a level that Darwin would relish."[49] For some, the end of predictions that newspapers would soon go extinct could not come soon enough. "Newspapers are proving so resilient that the term 'dying newspaper industry' will be retired in the next year or two," predicted David Olive. "We'll hear soon enough about the phoenix-like rebirth of news-papers. It will be a crock, since there were no ashes to rise from."[50]

Appendix

Nothing is quite so helpful as a bit of hard data in sorting out media myths and getting to the bottom of a complex story like the financial health of newspapers. There is no denying the drop in advertising revenues that has caused newspapers to re-arrange their business model in at attempt to survive in the Internet age. This drop is reflected in Tables 1 and 4 for the U.S. and Canada, respectively. Print advertising revenues at U.S. newspapers dropped by almost 63 percent from 2006 to 2013. Online advertising revenues for newspapers did little to make up the difference, as they only reduced the decline in total newspaper ad revenues to 58 percent over the eight-year period. In Canada, print advertising revenues fell by "only" 36 percent during the same period, with total newspaper ad revenues falling 30 percent. The Canadian numbers may be a bit deceiving, however. Newspapers Canada, which supplies the data, started including revenue from advertising inserts in 2010, and these have since comprised 9–12 percent of its reported annual ad revenues. It also started including advertising revenue at free newspapers in 2012.

As for newspaper profits, they take a bit more effort to determine. The financial health of newspapers can be inferred, from financial statements filed by publicly-traded newspaper companies, which comprise about 40 percent of the industry in the U.S. and about 90 percent in Canada. Stock market regulators require all publicly traded companies to issue regular financial statements, and harsh sanctions can be imposed on companies that fudge their figures. From examining the annual reports of all sixteen newspaper companies that traded publicly from 2006 until 2013 (the number dropped by three during that time), it is apparent that the industry has remained remarkably healthy despite all of the hand-wringing about their future. The numbers listed in Tables 2 and 3 are total revenues; earnings before interest, taxes, depreciation, and amortization (EBITDA); and profit margin, which is expressed as the ratio of EBITDA divided by total revenues. For example, if a company had EBITDA of $10 million on revenues of $100 million, its profit margin was 10 percent. EBITDA is a standard measure of profitability used by investors, as it reflects how much free cash flow the company generates and thus how much debt it can handle. "EBITDA is a great tool to measure the profitability of companies with expensive assets that get depreciated over an extended period of time," noted financial analyst Chak Reddy. "Financiers look at EBITDA to measure the debt carrying capacity of the company. It is common to measure mid-market company profitability and cash flow using EBITDA and use EBITDA as the exclusive indicator of the business performance."[1] Not all companies report EBITDA in their financial statements, however. Some report EBIT, so listed amounts for depreciation and amortization have to be added back in to determine EBITDA. Interest payments, which have sunk several newspaper owners due to debt taken on making acquisitions that could not be serviced with reduced earnings, must also be deducted to calculate the standardized measure of EBITDA. Taxes are also excluded from this calculation. Some companies make other deductions from earnings, however, so a bit of figuring is sometimes needed to get at EBITDA.

The most cryptic of all newspaper company financial statements examined for this study were those of the Washington Post Company. It listed pension expenses and capital expenses after its earnings, which suggested that those amounts should be added back in to determine EBITDA. Repeated queries to Hal S. Jones, the company's senior vice president of finance, went unanswered, so I made the assumption that pension expenses and capital expenses had been deducted in reporting earnings and so I added them back in.

The company may have good reasons for not commenting on its financial statements, even to clarify them. Dylan Byers of Politico similarly sought clarification from the company about its 2012 earnings, only to be informed by a spokesperson that the paper was "not permitted to comment on quarterly earnings beyond what is in the release."[2] Warren Buffett also factored into my assumption. Buffett, who has long owned the *Buffalo News* and recently became a major buyer of newspapers, was a major shareholder in WaPoCo for 40 years. He even sat on its board of directors before resigning in early 2014 following the *Post*'s sale to Jeff Bezos. He has long advocated for subtracting capital expenditures from earnings to determine profitability. "Does management think the tooth fairy pays for capital expenditures?" Buffett famously asked in his letter to shareholders in Berkshire Hathaway's 2000 annual report.[3] As such, WaPoCo's earnings for 2009 barely made it into the black with a profit margin (return on revenue) of 0.7 percent. It was one of only two companies studied to post profits lower than the Fortune 500 historical average of 4.7 percent, also doing so in 2012 at 3.8 percent. A.H. Belo, owner of the *Dallas Morning News* and several other dailies, posted profits of only 1.5 percent in 2008, which may have had something to do with the company's being spun off that year from parent company Belo Corporation. Its profit margins had been in the double digits before then, and have steadily returned to single-digit health since.

Complicating matters was a lack of standardization in the examined financial statements. This made it difficult to tease out the revenues and earnings of newspapers owned by conglomerates with holdings in other industries. Berkshire Hathaway's financial statements, for example, made it impossible to isolate the results for its newspapers, so it was not included in this study. The giant multinational media conglomerate News Corp. does not segment its publishing businesses by country, so the numbers here include its worldwide holdings in the U.S., the U.K., and Australia. It also lumps its newspapers in with its book publishing companies and, just for fun, changes its reporting methods from time to time.

Of course, some enormous losses have been reported by publicly-traded newspaper companies, but these have invariably been inflated by large "paper" losses that account for a loss in value of the business. After the dot-com bubble burst at the millennium, stock market regulators began requiring companies to regularly re-value their businesses, as shares of many Internet start-ups traded at high prices relative to their meager or non-existent earnings. "Accounting rules require that these write-downs be charged against income, but they are paper transactions – no cash goes out the door," pointed out newspaper business guru John Morton in 2008 as writedowns on the value of newspapers began to grow.iv Other extraordinary losses are excluded from EBITDA, or "operating" earnings, including such things as a loss on the sale of an asset and even "restructuring" costs of laying off workers. "Severance payments from layoffs, which do represent cash out the door, are excluded because they are one-time events that do not affect the underlying structure of the business," noted Morton. "Indeed, they are intended to improve financial efficiency by reducing future payroll."[5]

TABLE 1 : – U.S. NEWSPAPER ADVERTISING REVENUE (BILLIONS)

	Print	Change	Online	Change	Total	Change
2006	46.6	-1.7%	2.66	+31.4%	49.3	-0.3%
2007	42.2	-9.4%	3.16	+18.8&	5.4	-7.9%
2008	34.7	-17.7%	3.1	-1.8%	37.8	-16.6%
2009	24.8	-28.6%	2.7	-11.8%	27.5	-27.2%
2010	22.8	-8.2%	3.0	+10.9%	25.8	-6.3%
2011	20.7	-9.2%	3.2	+6.8%	23.9	-7.3%
2012	18.9	-8.4%	3.4	+3.7%	22.3	-6.8%
2013	17.3	-8.6%	3.4	+1.5%	20.7	-7.2%

Source: Newspaper Association of America

TABLE 2: U.S. NEWSPAPER REVENUES/EARNINGS (MILLIONS)/PROFIT MARGIN

	2006	2007	2008	2009	2010	2011	2012	2013
A.H. Belo	817/104/12.7%	738/79/10.7%	637/10/1.5%	518/33/6.4%	487/36/7.3%	461/39/8.6%	440/34/7.8%	366/29/7.9%
Gannett	6,940/1,800/29.7%	6,580/1,690/25.7%	5,714/1,121/19.6%	4,396/780/17.7%	4,051/818/20.2%	3,831/626/16.3%	3,728/516/13.8%	3,577/467/13%
Gatehouse	306/61/19.9%	575/111/19.3%	679/110/16.2%	585/84/14.4%	558/94/16.8%	526/86/16.3%	517/85/16.4%	-sold-
Journal	328/61/18.8%	266/38/14.3%	242/27/11.1%	194/26/13.4%	183/29/15.8%	171/27/15.9%	165/22/13.3%	154/14/8.9%
Lee Ent.[1]	1,121/278/24.8%	1,120/267/23.8%	1,029/207/20.1%	842/167/19.8%	780/171/21.9%	756/162/21.5%	710/163/22.9%	675/160/23.7%
McClatchy	1,675/446/26.6%	2,260/575/25.4%	1,900/364/19.1%	1,471/341/23.2%	1,375/372/27.0%	1,269/323/25.4%	1,230/311/25.3%	1,242/21.2%
Media Gen.	588/144/24.9%	531/115/21.6%	443/61/13.7%	357/65/18.2%	328/49/14.9%	299/28/9.3%	-sold-	---
NY Times	3,289/455/13.8%	3,195/456/14.3%	2,939/301/10.2%	2,440/266/10.9%	2,393/377/15.7%	2,323/346/14.9%	1,990/257/12.9%	1,577/244/15.5%
News Corp[2]	4,095/780/19%	4,486/937/20.9%	6,248/1,200/19.2%	5,858/785/13.4%	6,087/888/14.6%	8,826/1,253/14.2%	8,248/1,027/12.5%	6,731/795/11.8%
E.W.Scripps[3]	716/189/26.4%	658/136/20.6%	569/71/15.1%	455/49/10.7%	435/52/11.9%	414/21/5.1%	399/27/6.9%	385/28/7.3%
Wash. Post	962/214/22.3%	890/162/18.2%	801/55/6.8%	679/5/0.7%	680/74/10.9%	648/46/7.1%	582/22/3.8%	-sold-

Source: Company annual reports

TABLE 3: CANADIAN NEWSPAPER REVENUES/EARNINGS (MILLIONS)/PROFIT MARGIN

	2006	2007	2008	2009	2010	2011	2012	2013
FP	122/25/20.8%	125/28/22.6%	121/23/19.3%	114/24/21.3%	110/24/22.3%	111/23/21.0%	111/21/19.5%	106/20/18.9%
Glacier	NA	216/47/21.9%	249/52/20.8%	229/36/15.6%	242/44/18.1%	267/49/18.4%	330/50/15.3%	295/33/11.1%
Postmedia[4]	1.26b/248/19.7%	1.3b/293/22.5%	1.1b/172/15.6%	1.05b/191/18.1%	1.02b/201/19.7%	831m/144/17.3%	751/130/17.3%	784/98/12.5%
Quebecor	928/207/22.3%	1.03b/226/22.0%	1.18b/227/19.2%	1.05b/199/18.9%	1.03b/200/19.3%	1.02b/150/14.7%	960/115/12.0%	
Torstar	1.05b/157/14.9%	1.08/179/16.5%	1.06b/157/14.9%	957/118/12.4%	1.01b/176/17.3%	1.09b/161/14.8%	1.06/145/13.7%	984/131/13.3%

Source: Company annual reports

TABLE 4: CANADIAN NEWSPAPER ADVERTISING
REVENUES (MILLIONS)

	Print	Change	Online	Change	Total	Change
2006	2,634	-0.9%	110	N/A	2,744	N/A
2007	2,568	-2.5%	150	+35.9%	2,718	-0.9%
2008	2,489	-3.1%	182	+21.1%	2,671	-1.7%
2009	2,030	-18.4%	186	+2.3%	2,214	-17.1%
2010*	2,102	+3.5%	214	+15.0%	2,316	+4.6%
2011	1,970	-6.2%	246	+15.0%	2,216	-4.3%
2012**	2,019	+2.5%	242	-1.3%	2,261	+2.0%
2013	1,679	-16.8%	230	-4.9%	1,909	-15.5%

* starting in 2010 totals include revenue from advertising inserts
** starting in 2012 totals include revenue from free newspapers
Source: Newspapers Canada

Notes

1. See Bill Grueskin, Ava Seave and Lucas Graves, *The Story So Far: What We Know About the Business of Digital Journalism*. New York: Columbia Journalism Review Books, 2011, 24. Available at http://www.cjr.org/the_business_of_digital_journalism/the_story_so_far_what_we_know.php

2. New Star Books, "Trouble at the Mill," Newstarbooks.com, October 14, 2014. Available at http://newstarbooks.com/blog/trouble-mill/

3. Marc Edge, "Don't Give Postmedia More Local Monopolies," TheTyee.ca, October 8, 2014. Available at http://thetyee.ca/Mediacheck/2014/10/08/Post-media-No-More-Monopolies/; Marc Edge, "Myths muddy media ownership debate," Greatly Exaggerated, October 12, 2014. Available at http://greatlyex-agerrated.blogspot.ca/2014/10/myths-muddy-media-ownership-debate.html

4. Marc Edge, *Pacific Press: The Unauthorized Story of Vancouver's Newspaper Monopoly*. Vancouver: New Star Books, 2001.

5. Marc Edge, "And 'The Wall' Came Tumbling Down in Los Angeles," in Joseph Bernt and Marilyn Greenwald, Eds. *The Big Chill: Investigative Reporting in the Current Media Environment*. Ames: Iowa State University Press, 2000.

6. Marc Edge, "The Good, the Bad, and the Ugly: Financial Markets and the Demise of Canada's Southam Newspapers," *International Journal on Media Management* 5(3), 2003, 180-189.

7. Marc Edge, "The pain of the obdurate rump: Conrad Black and the flouting of corporate governance," in Robert G. Picard, Ed. *Corporate Governance of Media Companies*. Jönköping, Sweden: Jönköping International Business School, 2005.

8. Marc Edge, *Asper Nation: Canada's Most Dangerous Media Company*. Vancouver: New Star Books, 2007.

9. Marc Edge, "Convergence after the collapse: The 'catastrophic' case of Canada," *Media, Culture & Society* 33(8), 2011, 1266-1278; Marc Edge, "An accidental success story: The forced diversification of Quebecor Media," *Journal of Media Business Studies* 8(3), Fall 2011, 69-87.

NOTES TO INTRODUCTION: THE BATTLE OF NEW ORLEANS

1. David Lieberman, "Extra! Extra! Are newspapers dying?" *USA Today*, March 18, 2009.

2. Kevin Allman, "'Save the Picayune' rally draws hundreds," Bestofneworleans.com, June 5, 2012. Available at http://www.bestofneworleans.com/blogof-neworleans/archives/2012/06/04/save-the-picayune-rally-draws-hundreds

3. "Ricky Go Home," Rickygohome.com, undated. Available at http://www.rickygohome.com/

4. Micheline Maynard, "New Orleans' Most Prominent Do Battle For The Times-Picayune," Forbes.com, June 4, 2012. Available at http://www.forbes.com/sites/michelinemaynard/2012/06/04/new-orleans-most-prominent-do-battle-for-the-times-picayune/

5. Jason Berry, "Rolling the Dice at the 'Times-Picayune,'" *The Nation*, June 11, 2012. Available at http://www.thenation.com/article/168330/rolling-dice-times-picayune#

6. Harry Shearer, "The Sometimes Picayune: Want to damage New Orleans (again)? Decimate its newspaper," Cjr.org, June 6, 2012. Available at http://www.cjr.org/behind_the_news/the_sometimes_picayune.php#sthash.bFI-6TorS.dpuf

7. Ben Myers, "Advertisers balk at Times-Picayune changes but aren't ready to abandon ship," *New Orleans City Business*, June 21, 2012.

8. Keach Hagey, "Times-Picayune Is Singing the Blues to Angry Readers," Wall Street Journal Online, September 10, 2012. Available at http://online.wsj.com/news/articles/SB10000872396390443589304577638023262616192

9. *Ibid.*

10. John McQuaid, "Why a Weak Website Can't Replace a Daily Newspaper in New Orleans," Theatlantic.com, June 12, 2012. Available at http://www.theatlantic.com/national/archive/2012/06/why-a-weak-website-cant-replace-a-daily-newspaper-in-new-orleans/258393/

11. *Ibid.*

12. John K. Hartman, "Newhouse quits daily papers," *Editor & Publisher*, June 20, 2013, 58.

13. Rebecca Theim, *Hell and High Water: The Battle to Save the Daily New Orleans Times-Picayune*. Gretna, LA: Pelican, 2013, 261.

14. Ryan Chittum, "The Advocate vs. the Times-Picayune," The Audit, April 30, 2013. Available at http://www.cjr.org/the_audit/the_advocate_vs_the_times-pica.php

15. David Carr, "Newspaper Monopoly That Lost Its Grip," *New York Times*, May 12, 2013.

16. Jay Miller, "Plain Dealer is delivering bad news to small business advertisers," *Crain's Cleveland Business*, July 28, 2013. Available at http://www.crainscleveland.com/article/20130728/SUB1/307289986

17. Dean Starkman, "The Plain Dealer imposes draconian cuts in the name of an outdated strategy for newspapers," The Audit, July 31, 2013. Available at http://www.cjr.org/the_audit/advances_forced_march_backward.php

18. Aaron Mesh, "With Quotas and Incentive Pay, The Oregonian is Again Reshaping Its Experience for Readers," *Willamette Week*, March 23rd, 2014. Available at http://www.wweek.com/portland/blog-31405-with_quotas_and_incentive_pay_the_oregonian_is_again_reshaping_its_experience_for_readers.html

19. Ken Doctor, "The newsonomics of Advance's advancing strategy and its Achilles' heel," Niemanlab.org, June 27, 2013. Available at http://www.niemanlab.org/2013/06/the-newsonomics-of-advances-advancing-strategy-and-its-achilles-heel/

20. See Marc Edge, *Pacific Press: The Unauthorized Story of Vancouver's Newspaper Monopoly*. Vancouver: New Star Books, 2001.

21. Canada, Standing Senate Committee on Transport and Communication. *Interim report on the Canadian news media, 2004*. Ottawa: Senate of Canada.

22. See Marc Edge, *Asper Nation: Canada's Most Dangerous Media Company*. Vancouver: New Star Books, 2007.

23. See Dal Yong Jin, *De-Convergence of Global Media Industries*. London: Routledge, 2013.

24. Maria Babbage, "Experts weigh in on concentration of Canadian media ownership," *Hamilton Spectator*, October 7, 2014. Available at http://www.thespec.com/news-story/4900941-experts-weigh-in-on-concentration-of-canadian-media-ownership/

25. *Ibid.*

26. See Allan Bartley, "The regulation of cross-media ownership: The life and short times of PCO 2294," *Canadian Journal of Communication* 13(2), Summer 1988, 45-59.

27. See Kelly Toughill, "CTV: operating profits and job losses," J-Source. ca, March 19, 2009. Available at http://www.j-source.ca/english_new/detail.php?id=3533; Dwayne Winseck, "Financialization and the 'crisis of the media': The rise and fall of (some) media conglomerates in Canada," *Canadian Journal of Communication* 35(2), Summer 2010, 365-393; Marc Edge, "Convergence after the collapse: The 'catastrophic' case of Canada," *Media, Culture & Society* 33(8), November 2011, 1266-1288.

28. Deb Halpern Wenger, "The road to convergence and back again," *Quill*, September 2005, 40.

29. See James Ledbetter, "The Slow, Sad Sellout of Journalism School," *Rolling Stone*, October 16, 1997, 73-81, 99-100; Jon Marcus, "Rewriting J-School," *Nieman Reports*, Spring 2014. Available at http://www.nieman.harvard.edu/reports/article/103104/Rewrite.aspx

30. Keith Herndon, *The decline of the daily newspaper: How an American institution lost the online revolution.* New York: Peter Lang, 2012, 205.

31. *Ibid.*, 208.

32. Jonathan Knee, Bruce Greenwald and Ava Seave, *The Curse of the Mogul: What's Wrong With the World's Leading Media Companies,* New York: Portfolio, 2009, 77.

NOTES TO CHAPTER 1: NEWSPAPERS ARE SO OVER

1. Doug Fetherling, "All the news that's soft enough to print," *Maclean's,* October 30, 1978, 80.

2. Philip Meyer, *The Vanishing Newspaper: Saving Journalism in the Information Age.* Columbia, MO: University of Missouri Press, 2004, 16.

3. Bob Garfield, "The Post Advertising Age," *Advertising Age,* March 26, 2007, 12.

4. "Newspaper stocks plunge: Index down 25.6%," *NewsInc.,* July 7, 2008.

5. "Thank God It's (No Longer) Friday: Worst Day Ever for Newspaper Stocks?" Editorandpublisher.com, July 12, 2008. Available at http://www. editorandpublisher.com/Archive/Thank-God-It-s-No-Longer-Friday-Worst-Day-Ever-for-Newspaper-Stocks-

6. Mark Fitzgerald, "Newspaper Stocks Crashed in '08," Adweek.com, December 30, 2008. Available at http://www.adweek.com/news/press/news-paper-stocks-crashed-08-110823

7. Paul Waldie and Grant Robertson, "Stopping the press," *Globe and Mail,* February 28, 2009.

8. Rachel Smolkin, "Cities Without Newspapers," *American Journalism Review,* April/May 2009, 24.

9. *Ibid.*

10. John Chachas, "4 steps to stave off the death of newspapers," *Dallas Morning News,* February 6, 2009.

11. Mary Lynn F. Jones, "Don't Stop the Presses!" *Presstime,* April 2009. Available at http://www.naa.org/Resources/Publications/PRESSTIME/ PRESSTIME-2009-April/01-Cover-Dont-Stop-the-Presses/01-Cover-Dont-Stop-the-Presses.aspx

12. David Kaplan, "Newser's Michael Wolff: In 18 Months, 80% Of Newspapers Will Be Gone — Give Or Take," Paidcontent.org, April 20, 2009. Available at http://paidcontent.org/article/419-newsers-michael-wolff-in-18-months-80-percent-of-newspapers-will-be-gon/

13. Peter Whoriskey, "Microsoft's Ballmer on Yahoo and the Future," *Washington Post,* June 5, 2008.

14. Nat Ives, "The newspaper death watch," *Advertising Age,* April 28, 2008, 1.

15. Margaret Looney, "Media expert tracks the expiration date of newspapers," *International Journalists' Network,* September 15, 2011. Available at http:// ijnet.org/stories/media-expert-tracks-expiration-date-newspapers

16. Michael Hirschorn, "End Times," , January/February 2009, 41.

17. Mark Fitzgerald, "'Several Cities' Could Have No Daily Paper As Soon As 2010, Credit Rater Says," Editorandpublisher.com, December 3, 2008. Available at http://www.editorandpublisher.com/PrintArticle/-Several-Cities-Could-Have-No-Daily-Paper-As-Soon-As-2010-Credit-Rater-Says

18. Hirschorn, "End Times."

19. Jon Fine, "When Do You Stop The Presses?" *BusinessWeek*, July 20, 2007, 20.

20. Marc Gunther, "Hard News," *Fortune*, August 6, 2007, 80.

21. Richard Perez-Pena, "As Cities Go From Two Newspapers to One, Some Talk of Zero," *New York Times*, March 12, 2009.

22. Project for Excellence in Journalism and Rick Edmonds, "Newspapers," State of the News Media, 2009. Available online at http://stateofthemedia.org/2009/newspapers-intro/

23. Walter Isaacson, "How to save your newspaper," *Time*, February 5, 2009, 30.

24. David Lieberman, "Extra! Extra! Are newspapers dying?" *USA Today*, March 18, 2009.

25. Smolkin, "Cities Without Newspapers," 18.

26. Douglas A. McIntyre, "The 10 Most Endangered Newspapers in America," Time.com, March 9, 2009. Available at http://content.time.com/time/business/article/0,8599,1883785,00.html

27. Robert Hodierne and Meghan Meyer, "Is There Life After Newspapers?" *American Journalism Review*, February/March 2009, 21-27.

28. Mary Walton, "Investigative Shortfall," *American Journalism Review*, Fall 2010, 18-30.

29. Project for Excellence in Journalism and Rick Edmonds, "Newspapers."

30. Paul Starr, "Goodbye to the Age of Newspapers (Hello to a New Era of Corruption)," *The New Republic*, February 23, 2009, 28.

31. *Ibid.*

32. Jennifer Dorroh, "Endangered Species," *American Journalism Review*, December 2008/January 2009, 20.

33. Jennifer Dorroh, Lindsay Gsell and Will Skoronski, "Statehouse Exodus," *American Journalism Review*, April/May 2009, 20.

34. Smolkin, "Cities Without Newspapers."

35. Lee Shaker, "Dead Newspapers and Citizens' Civic Engagement," *Political Communication* 31(1), 2014, 131-148.

36. Rem Rieder, "Fears for the Future," *American Journalism Review*, June/July 2009, 4.

37. Isaacson, "How to save your newspaper," 30.

38. John Nichols and Robert W. McChesney, "The Death and Life of Great American Newspapers," *The Nation*, April 6, 2009, 12.

39. *Ibid*, 20.

40. Rosa Brooks, "Bail out journalism," *Los Angeles Times*, April 9, 2009.

41. Benjamin L. Cardin, "A Plan to Save Our Free Press," *Washington Post*, April 3, 2009.

42. Todd Gillman, "Newspaper advocates address Senate on industry's struggles," *Dallas Morning News*, May 7, 2009.

43. Kevin J. Martin, "The Daily Show," *New York Times*, November 13, 2007.

44. Nancy Pelosi, Letter to Eric H. Holder, Jr., March 16, 2009. Available online at http://www.sfbg.com/PDFs/politics/PelosiHolder.pdf

45. Rachel La Corte, "Newspaper publishers seek tax cut," *Seattle Times*, February 18, 2009.

46. Dan Rather, "The News Americans Need," *Washington Post*, August 9, 2009.

47. Ryan Chittum, "Newspaper Industry Ad Revenue at 1965 Levels," *The Audit*, August 19, 2009. Available at http://www.cjr.org/the_audit/newspaper_industry_ad_revenue.php?page=all

48. Martin Langeveld, "Can newspaper publishers survive this revenue freefall?" Nieman Journalism Lab, August 31, 2009. Available at http://www.niemanlab.org/2009/08/can-newspaper-publishers-survive-this-revenue-freefall-perhaps-if-they-embrace-a-digital-future/#more-7797

49. Richard Perez-Pena, "Newspaper Circulation Falls by More Than 10%," *New York Times*, October 27, 2009.

50. Alan D. Mutter, "Newspapers, the mass-less mass medium," Reflections of a Newsosaur, October 27, 2009. Available online at http://newsosaur.blogspot.ca/2009/10/newspapers-mass-less-mass-medium.html

51. Leonard Downie, Jr. and Michael Schudson, "The Reconstruction of American Journalism," *Columbia Journalism Review*, November/December 2009, 26.

52. Rupert Murdoch, "Journalism and Freedom," *Wall Street Journal*, December 8, 2009.

53. *Ibid.*

54. Robert W. McChesney and John Nichols, *The Death and Life of American Journalism: The Media Revolution that Will Begin the World Again*. New York: Nation Books, 2010, 100.

55. Robert W. McChesney, "Rejuvenating American Journalism: Some Tentative Policy Proposals." Available at http://www.ftc.gov/opp/workshops/news/mar9/docs/mcchesney.pdf

56. Federal Trade Commission Staff Discussion Draft: Potential Policy Recommendations to Support the Reinvention of Journalism. Available at http://www.ftc.gov/opp/workshops/news/jun15/docs/new-staff-discussion.pdf

57. Joshua Rhett Miller, "Journalism 'Reinvention' Smacks of Government Control, Critics Say," FoxNews.com, June 2, 2010. Available at http://www.foxnews.com/politics/2010/06/02/journalism-reinvention-smacks-of-government-control-critics-say/

58. Jeff Jarvis, "FTC protects journalism's past," Buzzmachine.com, May 29, 2010. Available at http://www.buzzmachine.com/2010/05/29/ftc-protects-journalisms-past/

59. "FTC Corrects Misinformation on Journalism Initiative," June 7, 2010. Available at http://benton.org/node/36645

60. Josh Quittner, "Marc Andreessen's newspaper deathwatch," *Fortune*, March 4, 2008, 24.

61. Chachas, "4 steps to stave off the death of newspapers."

62. Jeff Jarvis, "It's the journalism — not the newspaper – that's important," LATimes.com, March 18, 2009. Available at http://www.latimes.com/news/opinion/opinionla/la-oew-mutter-jarvis18-2009mar18-story.html#page=1

63. Clay Shirky, "Newspapers and Thinking the Unthinkable," Shirky.com, March 13, 2009. Available at http://www.shirky.com/weblog/2009/03/newspapers-and-thinking-the-unthinkable/

NOTES TO CHAPTER 2: A FUNNY THING HAPPENED ON THE WAY TO THE FUNERAL

1. Margaret Sullivan, "Myth: Newspapers are washed up," *Buffalo News*, May 17, 2010.

2. Rick Edmonds, "Why Ann Arbor Will be the First City to Lose its Only Daily Newspaper," Poynter.org, June 16, 2009. Available online at http://www.poynter.org/latest-news/business-news/the-biz-blog/96340/why-ann-arbor-will-be-the-first-city-to-lose-its-only-daily-newspaper/

3. Eric Zorn, "Requiem for the hometown newspaper," *Chicago Tribune*, July 24, 2009.

4. Eric Zorn, "We've seen no more Ann Arbors as the dotcom replacement for the newspaper remains a work in progress," *Chicago Tribune*, July 23, 2010.

5. Caroline O'Donovan, "The Ann Arbor News, or There and Back Again: Why the news world's first print edition of a website is coming to a close," *Nieman Journalism Lab*, September 10, 2013. Available at http://www.niemanlab.org/2013/09/the-ann-arbor-news-or-there-and-back-again-why-the-news-worlds-first-print-edition-of-a-website-is-coming-to-a-close/

5A. See Ryan Chittum, "The Washington Post's not-so-good earnings report," The Audit, August 3, 2012. Available at http://www.cjr.org/the_audit/the_washington_posts_not-so-go.php

6. See Frank Ahrens, "Big Profits in Small Packages: Little Newspapers Prosper With Narrow Focus on Very Local News," *Washington Post*, March 8, 2007; Jennifer Saba and Mark Fitzgerald, "Small Towns, Big Profits: How Many Papers Survive Slump," *Editor & Publisher*, February 28, 2008, 58-63.

7. Geoff McGhee, "Rural Newspapers Doing Better Than Their City Counterparts," *Rural West Initiative*, July 11, 2011. Available at http://www.stanford.edu/group/ruralwest/cgi-bin/drupal/content/rural-newspapers

8. Mark Fitzgerald, "Newspaper Stocks Soar on Upbeat Gannett Earnings News," Editorandpublisher.com, July 16, 2009. Available at http://www.editorandpublisher.com/Article/Newspaper-Stocks-Soar-on-Upbeat-Gannett-Earnings-News

9. *Ibid.*

10. "Another Analyst Turns Bullish (Sort Of) On Newspaper Stocks," Editorandpublisher.com, January 14, 2010. Available at http://editorandpublisher.com/PrintArticle/Another-Analyst-Turns-Bullish-Sort-Of-On-Newspaper-Stocks

11. Jonathan Heller, "I'd Rather Own Gannett Than Facebook," TheStreet. com, September 12, 2012. Available online at http://www.thestreet.com/ story/11697710/1/id-rather-own-gannett-than-facebook.html

12. Jonathan Heller, "I'd Still Rather Own Gannett Than Facebook," TheStreet.com, July 2, 2013. Available online at http://www.thestreet.com/ story/11967993/1/id-still-rather-own-gannett-than-facebook.html

13. "Newspaper stocks hit 5-year high," *NewsInc.*, July 8, 2013.

14. "Who killed the newspaper?" *Economist*, August 26, 2006, 1.

15. "The strange survival of ink: Newspapers have escaped cataclysm by becoming leaner and more focused," *Economist*, June 10, 2010, 26.

16. Nikhil Moro and Debashis Aikat, "Chindia's newspaper boom: Identifying sustainable business models," *Global Media and Communication* 6(3), 2010, 358.

17. "The strange survival of ink."

18. Paul Gillin, "Not Yet Time To Burn the Boats," Newspaper Death Watch, March 9, 2010. Accessed March 11, 2010 from http://newspaperdeathwatch. com/not-yet-time-to-burn-the-boats/

19. See Russell Adams and Shira Ovide, "Some Newspapers Shed Unprofit-able Readers," *Wall Street Journal*, October 27, 2008; Jennifer Saba "Newspapers Across the Country Show Steep Declines in Circulation, in New FAS-FAX," Editorandpublisher.com, October 26, 2009. Available at http://www.edito-randpublisher.com/Article/Newspapers-Across-the-Country-Show-Steep-Declines-in-Circulation-in-New-FAS-FAX; Rick Edmonds, "Circulation Declines Driven by Cost-Cutting, Price Hikes, Voluntary Pullbacks," Poynter. org, October 26, 2009. Available at http://www.poynter.org/latest-news/ business-news/the-biz-blog/99059/circulation-declines-driven-by-cost-cut-ting-price-hikes-voluntary-pullbacks/

20. Richard Perez-Pena, "Newspaper Circulation Falls by More Than 10%," *New York Times*, October 27, 2009.

21. Nat Ives, "Newspaper subscribers renewing and paying more," *Advertising Age*, October 5, 2009, 23.

22. See John Morton, "Churn, Baby, Churn: It takes constant tending to main-tain subscription levels," *American Journalism Review*, December/January 2004, 84.

23. Organisation for Economic Co-operation and Development, "The evolu-tion of news and the Internet," June 11, 2010. Accessed July 10, 2010 from http:// www.oecd.org/dataoecd/30/24/45559596.pdf

24. Robert G. Picard, "US Newspaper Ad Revenue Shows Consistent Growth," *Newspaper Research Journal* 23(4), 2002, 21-33.

25. Ryan Chittum, "Reader revenue and the great newspaper ad bubble," The Audit, May 28, 2014. Available at http://www.cjr.org/the_audit/newspaper_ subscription_revenue.php?page=all

26. Hsiang Iris Chyi, Seth C. Lewis and Nan Zheng, "A matter of life and death?" *Journalism Studies* 13(3), June 2012, 316.

27. *Ibid.*, 317.

28. *Ibid.*

29. Michael Oneal, "Bankruptcy Inc.," *Chicago Tribune*, January 16, 2013.

30. See Gilbert Cranberg, Randall Bezanson and John Soloski, *Taking Stock: Journalism and the Publicly Traded Newspaper Company*. Ames: Iowa State University Press, 2001.

31. Canada, Standing Senate Committee on Transport and Communication. *Interim report on the Canadian news media*, 2004. Ottawa: Senate of Canada.

32. Rick Edmonds Seven Reasons Why Newspapers Are Not Rebounding As Hoped," November 15, 2010. Available at http://www.poynter.org/latest-news/business-news/the-biz-blog/journalism-and-business-values/106811/seven-reasons-why-newspapers-are-not-rebounding-as-hoped/

33. Henry Blodget, "See? The New York Times Has An Excellent Online Business — So Quit Your Hand-Wringing About The Death Of Journalism," Business Insider, July 23, 2010. Available at http://www.businessinsider.com/see-the-new-york-times-has-an-excellent-online-business-so-quit-the-hand-wringing-about-the-death-of-journalism-2010-7

34. Morton, "Not Dead Yet."

35. Eric Pfanner, "European Newspapers Find Creative Ways to Thrive in the Internet Age," *New York Times*, March 30, 2009.

36. Richard Perez-Pena, "Seattle Paper Is Resurgent as a Solo Act," *New York Times*, August 10, 2009.

37. Jennifer Saba, "When There's No Print Edition, Do Readers Flock to the Web?" Editorandpublisher.com, June 29, 2009. Available at http://www.editorandpublisher.com/Archive/SPECIAL-REPORT-When-There-s-No-Print-Edition-Do-Readers-Flock-to-the-Web-

38. Ben Bagdikian, *The Media Monopoly*. Boston: Beacon Press, 1983, 99.

39. Ben H. Bagdikian, "The myth of newspaper poverty," *Columbia Journalism Review*, March/April 1973, 20.

40. *Ibid.*, 21.

41. *Ibid.*, 23.

42. Canada, *The uncertain mirror: Report of the Special Senate Committee on Mass Media*, Vol. I. (Ottawa: Information Canada), 1970, 47.

43. *Ibid.*, 63.

44. Bagdikian, *The Media Monopoly*, 11.

45. Ben Bagdikian, *The New Media Monopoly*. Boston: Beacon Press, 2004.

46. Quoted in Geneva Overholser, "Editor Inc.," *American Journalism Review*, December 1998, 50.

47. David Olive, "My stubborn faith in newspapers," Everybody's Business, October 19, 2009. Available at http://thestar.blogs.com/davidolive/2009/10/a-new-landscape-for-canadian-dailies.html

48. Robert G. Picard, "The dead and the dying," The Media Business, October 3, 2009. Available at http://themediabusiness.blogspot.com/2009/03/dead-and-dying.html

49. Robert G. Picard, "Tremors, Structural Damage and Some Casualties, but

No Cataclysm: The News about News Provision," *Geopolitics, History, and International Relations* 2(2), 2010, 87.

50. David Olive, "Those death-defying newspapers," Moneyville, February 13, 2011. Accessed February 20, 2011 from http://www.moneyville.ca/article/937871–those-death-defying-newspapers

51. Kristen Heflin, "Newspapers' life or death: The utility of a cultural, historical approach," *The Convergence Newsletter* 8(1), 2011. Available at http://sc.edu/cmcis/archive/convergence/v8no1.html#20

NOTES TO CHAPTER 3: AN UNUSUAL INDUSTRY

1. Dallas W. Smythe, "Communications: Blindspot of Western Marxism." *Canadian Journal of Political and Social Theory* 1(3), 1977, 1-27.

2. Steve Singer, "Auto Dealers Muscle the Newsroom," *American Journalism Review*, September 1991, 25.

3. Mitchell Stephens, *A History of News*. New York: Harcourt Brace, 1997, 188.

4. Gerald Baldasty, *The Commercialization of News in the Nineteenth Century*. Madison: University of Wisconsin Press, 1992, 49.

5. Stephens, *A History of News*, 194.

6. Baldasty, *The Commercialization of News in the Nineteenth Century*, 5.

7. *Ibid.*, 49.

8. See Walter Lippmann, *Public Opinion*. New York: Macmillan, 1922, 59.

9. Michael Schudson, *Discovering the News: A Social History of American Newspapers*. New York: Basic Books, 1978, 95.

10. Stephens, *A History of News*, 201.

11. See Joyce Milton, *The Yellow Kids: Foreign Correspondents in the Heyday of Yellow Journalism*. New York: Harper and Row, 1989.

12. Schudson, *Discovering the News*, 114.

13. See Gay Talese, *The Kingdom and the Power: Behind the scenes at the New York Times: The institution that influences the world*. Cleveland: World Publishing, 1969, 199.

14. Upton Sinclair, *The Brass Check*. Pasadena, CA: Upton Sinclair, 1919, 259.

15. See Tim Pilgrim, "Newspapers as Natural Monopolies: Some Historical Considerations," *Journalism History*, 18(1), 1992, 3-10.

16. Carl E. Lindstrom, *The Fading American Newspaper*. Garden City, NJ: Doubleday, 1960.

17. Robert G. Picard and Jeffrey H. Brody, *The Newspaper Publishing Industry*. Needham Heights, MA: Allyn and Bacon, 1997, 11.

18. See Peter Benjaminson, *Death In the Afternoon: America's Newspaper Giants Struggle for Survival*. Fairway, KS: Andrews, McMeel & Parker, 1984; John Morton, "40 years of death in the afternoon," *American Journalism Review*, November 1991, 72.

19. Minko Sotiron, "Concentration and collusion in the Canadian newspaper industry, 1895-1920," *Journalism History* 18, 1992, 26-32.

20. See Marc Edge, "The Good, the Bad, and the Ugly: Financial Markets and

the Demise of Canada's Southam Newspapers," *International Journal on Media Management* 5(3), 2003, 180-189.

21. Elizabeth MacIver Neiva, "Chain building: The consolidation of the American newspaper industry, 1953-1980," *Business History Review* 70, 1996, 27.

22. *Ibid.*, 35.

23. Elizabeth MacIver Neiva, "Chain building: The consolidation of the American newspaper industry, 1955-1980," *Business and Economic History* 24(1), 1995, 22.

24. Canada, Royal Commission on Newspapers, *Report*. Ottawa: Queen's Printer, 1981.

25. Richard M. Clurman, *To The End of Time*. New York: Touchstone, 1992, 36.

26. James D. Squires, *Read All About It! The Corporate Takeover of America's Newspapers*. New York: Times Books, 1993, 72.

27. Ben Bagdikian, *The Media Monopoly*. Boston: Beacon Press, 1983, 138.

28. See Mort Rosenblum, *Who stole the news: Why we can't keep up with what happens in the world and what we can do about it*. New York: Wiley, 1995; Peter Arnett, "Goodbye, World," American Journalism Review, November 1998, 50-67.

29. See Singer, "Auto Dealers Muscle the Newsroom."

30. Mary Ellen Schoonmaker, "The real estate story: hard news or soft sell? With so much advertising at stake, who wants to dig up dirt on the developers?" *Columbia Journalism Review*, January/February 1987, 25-30.

31. *Ibid.*

32. Trudy Lieberman, "What ever happened to consumer reporting?" *Columbia Journalism Review*, September/October 1994, 34.

33. *Ibid.*, 36.

34. Dean Starkman, *The watchdog that didn't bark: The financial crisis and the disappearance of investigative journalism*. New York: Columbia Journalism Review Books, 2014.

35. Joseph S. Coyle, "Now, the editor as marketer," *Columbia Journalism Review*, July/August 1998, 37.

36. See Joseph Bernt and Marilyn Greenwald, Eds. *The Big Chill: Investigative Reporting in the Current Media Environment*. Ames: Iowa State University Press, 2000; James L. Aucoin, *The Evolution of Investigative Journalism*. Columbia: University of Missouri Press, 2005.

37. See Marc Edge, *Pacific Press: The Unauthorized Story of Vancouver's Newspaper Monopoly*. Vancouver: New Star Books, 2001.

38. Susan Forde, "The end of the press subsidies 'experiment' in Sweden?" *Media International Australia* 95, May 2000, 107-116.

39. See Anthony Smith, *Goodbye Gutenberg: The Newspaper Revolution of the 1980s*. New York: Oxford University Press, 1980.

40. Bernard Berelson, "What 'Missing the Newspaper' Means," in Paul F. Lazarsfeld and Frank N. Stanton, Eds. *Communications Research*: 1948-1949. New York: Harper, 1949, 111-129.

41. Penn Kimball, "People without Papers," *Public Opinion Quarterly* 23, 1959, 394.

42. Doug Underwood, *When MBAs rule the newsroom*. New York: Columbia University Press, 1993, 8.

43. Pamela J. Shoemaker and Stephen D. Reese, *Mediating the Message: Theories of Influences on Mass Media Content*, 2nd Ed., White Plains, NY: Longman, 1996, 162.

44. *Ibid.*

45. See Joseph Turow, *Breaking up America: Advertisers and the new media world*. Chicago: University of Chicago Press, 1998.

46. See Anthony Spaeth, "If You Can't Beat 'Em, Flank 'Em," *Forbes* 124 (8), October 15, 1979, 168; Ann Goldgraben, "Dailies Wake Up to Threat of Shoppers," *Advertising Age*, 51 (48), November 10, 1980; Warren Strugatch, "Penny Savers Earning Big Ad Dollars," *Crain's New York Business* 3 (45), November 9, 1987, 18.

47. Gregory Stricharchuk, "Free-Distribution 'Shoppers' Are Posing Serious Threat to Local Daily Newspapers," *Wall Street Journal*, June 19, 1984.

48. See William D. Wells, "Psychographics, A Critical Review," *Journal of Marketing Research* 12, 1975, 1196-1213; Emanuel H. Demby, "Psychographics revisited: The birth of a technique," *Marketing Research*, Spring 1994, 26; Rebecca Piirto Heath, "Psychographics: Q'est-ce que c'est?" *American Demographics*, November 1995, 74.

49. Mark Schwed, "Psychographics: The new testament of Madison Avenue," *Oklahoma City Journal Record*, June 22, 1985.

50. Ian Gill, "Just in the Time of Nick," *Vancouver*, July 1990, 30.

51. Bill Kovach and Tom Rosenstiel, *The elements of journalism: What newspeople should know and they public should expect*. New York: Three Rivers, 2007, 209.

52. *Ibid.*, 210.

53. *Ibid.*, 211.

54. Underwood, *When MBAs rule the newsroom*, 76.

55. Squires, *Read All About It!*, 73.

NOTES TO CHAPTER 4: MONEY LUST

1. Lou Ureneck, "Newspapers arrive at economic crossroads," *Nieman Reports*, Summer 1999, 3.

2. *Ibid.*

3. Steve Singer, "Auto Dealers Muscle the Newsroom," *American Journalism Review*, September 1991, 24.

4. Ureneck, "Newspapers arrive at economic crossroads," 4.

5. John Morton, "Hanging tough when profits drop: Will newspapers resist shortsighted moves if there's a recession?" *American Journalism Review*, October 1998, 88.

6. John Morton, "When Newspapers Eat Their Seed Corn: The current wave of cost-cutting in the industry could hurt its future," *American Journalism Review*, November 1995, 52.

7. Frank Denton, "Old Newspapers and New Realities: The Promise of the

Marketing of Journalism." In Frank Denton and Howard Kurtz, *Reinventing the Newspaper*. New York: The Twentieth Century Fund Press, 1992, 33.

8. *Ibid.*, 6.

9. *Ibid.*, 46.

10. *Ibid.*, 38.

11. Jack Fuller, *News values: Ideas for an information age*. Chicago: University of Chicago Press, 1993, 197.

12. *Ibid.*, 197-98.

13. *Ibid.*, 199.

14. Ureneck, "Newspapers arrive at economic crossroads," 4.

15. Ben Bagdikian, "Conglomeration, Concentration and the Media," *Journal of Communication*, Spring 1980, 64.

16. Gilbert Cranberg, Randall Bezanson and John Soloski, *Taking Stock: Journalism and the Publicly Traded Newspaper Company*. Ames: Iowa State University Press, 2001, 154.

17. *Ibid.*, 8.

18. *Ibid.*, 146.

19. Senate Special Committee on Mass Media, *The Uncertain Mirror*, 1970.

20. Conrad Black, *A Life in Progress*, Toronto: Key Porter, 1993, 378.

21. Peter C. Newman, "The inexorable spread of the Black Empire," *Maclean's*, February 3, 1992, 68.

22. John Miller, *Yesterday's news: Why Canada's daily newspapers are failing us*. Halifax: Fernwood, 1998, 62.

23. See Gene Roberts, Thomas Kunkel and Charles Layton (Eds.), *Leaving Readers Behind: The Age of Corporate Newspapering*. Fayetteville: University of Arkansas Press, 2001; Gene Roberts and Thomas Kunkel (Eds.), *Breach of Faith: A Crisis of Coverage in the Age of Corporate Newspapering*. Fayetteville: University of Arkansas Press, 2005.

24. Roberts, *et al.*, *Leaving Readers Behind*, 8.

25. Ken Auletta, "Synergy City: Chicago's Tribune Co. is revolutionizing how it does business — but at what cost to its newspapers?" *American Journalism Review*, May 1998, 22.

26. *Ibid.*, 34.

27. *Ibid.*, 20.

28. *Ibid.*

29. *Ibid.*, 24.

30. Neil Hickey, "Money lust," *Columbia Journalism Review*, July/August 1998, 29.

31. *Ibid.*, 30.

32. *Ibid.*, 36.

33. *Ibid.*, 34.

34. *Ibid.*, 36.

35. Scott Sherman, "The evolution of Dean Singleton," *Columbia Journalism Review*, March/April 2003, 39.

36. Felicity Barringer, "Businessman vs. Newsman, All in One Person," *New York Times*, September 2, 2002.

37. Mark Lacter, "Where's Dean?" *Forbes*, July 3, 2000, 76.

38. *Ibid.*

39. Nicholas Coleridge, *Paper Tigers*. London: William Heinemann, 1993, 144.

40. Alex S. Jones, "Busting Into the Big Leagues," *New York Times*, September 20, 1987.

41. *Ibid.*

42. *Ibid.*

43. *Ibid.*

44. Marty Graham, "Rancor and romance in the rubble of The Houston Post," *Columbia Journalism Review*, September/October 1995, 46.

45. Robert Neuwirth, "Lean Dean," *Editor & Publisher*, September 18, 1999, 26.

46. Charles Layton, "Surrounded by Singleton," *American Journalism Review*, June 2006, 44.

47. Stephen J. Simurda, "Will the eagle still fly?" *Columbia Journalism Review* 34(4), November 1995, 21.

48. Neuwirth, "Lean Dean," 26.

49. Ben Frumin, "Outsourced Edit?" *Columbia Journalism Review*, May/June 2008, 15-16.

50. Sherman, "The evolution of Dean Singleton."

51. Jack Bass, "Newspaper Monopoly," *American Journalism Review*, July/August 1999, 74.

52. "Times Mirror Holds An Option to Acquire Los Angeles Paper," *Wall Street Journal*, May 19, 2000.

53. Bass, "Newspaper monopoly," 68.

54. John Morton, "Why Are Newspaper Profits So High?" *American Journalism Review*, October 1994, 72.

55. *Ibid.*

56. See John Busterna and Robert Picard, *Joint Operating Agreements: The Newspaper Act and its Application*. Norwood, NJ: Ablex, 1993; John Busterna, "Daily Newspaper Chains and the Antitrust Laws," *Journalism Monographs*, 1989; John Busterna, "Improving Editorial and Economic Competition with a Modified Newspaper Preservation Act," *Newspaper Research Journal*, Summer 1987, 71-84.

57. Morton, "Why Are Newspaper Profits So High?"

58. Hugh J. Martin, "Measuring Newspaper Profits: Developing a Standard of Comparison." *Journalism and Mass Communication Quarterly* 75(3), 1998, 500-517.

59. William Prochnau, "Down and out in L.A.," *American Journalism Review*, January/February 2000, 58-77.

60. David Halberstam, *The Powers That Be*. New York: Alfred A. Knopf, 1979, 290.

61. Adam Cohen and Dan Cray, "Decline of the Times," *Time*, July 31, 1995, 47.

62. Tony Case, "Defending the 'revolution,'" *Editor & Publisher*, March 30, 1996, 8.

63. Prochnau, "Down and out in L.A."

64. Jill Goldsmith, "Times Mirror CEO Willes Saw Pay, Bonus Double Last Year," *Wall Street Journal*, March 29, 1997.

65. Frederick Rose, "Willes, Times Mirror's new chief, got total '95 compensation of $2.4 million," *Wall Street Journal*, April 2, 1996.

66. Ken Auletta, "Demolition man," *New Yorker*, November 17, 1997, 40-45.

67. Joseph S. Coyle, "Now, the editor as marketer," *Columbia Journalism Review*, July/August 1998, 37.

68. *Ibid.*

69. *Ibid.*

70. John Morton, "Will Willes work wonders?" *American Journalism Review*, December 1997, 56.

71. Charles Rappleye, "Cracking the church-state wall," *Columbia Journalism Review*, January/February 1998, 20.

72. Mark Willes, quoted in Vincent J. Schodolski, "Sign Of The Times: L.A. Shuffles Editors," *Chicago Tribune*, October 10, 1997.

73. "Times Mirror's Willes Expects 50% Increase In Earnings for 1997," *Wall Street Journal*, December 11, 1997.

74. "Times Mirror Raised Willes's Pay by 34% In 1997 to $2.9 Million," *Wall Street Journal*, April 1, 1998.

75. Mark Jurkowitz, "'Cereal Killer' reprieved," *Boston Globe*, April 16, 1998.

76. Ann Marie Kerwin, "New Doors Cut in Wall Between Business, Edit: L.A. Times Publisher Blasts Critics of Recent Reorganization," *Advertising Age*, April 27, 1998, 63.

77. "Critical Bestsellers," *L.A. Weekly*, August 14, 1998, 16.

78. "Times Marketing Sprint," *L.A. Weekly*, June 12, 1998, 14.

79. *Ibid.*

80. David Shaw, "Cooperation Within Times Viewed With Trepidation," *Los Angeles Times*, March 30, 1998.

81. Felicity Barringer, "The Difficulty in Being Earnest: Efforts to Reinvent The Los Angeles Times Falter," *New York Times*, May 17, 1999.

82. Prochnau, "Down and out in L.A."

83. *Ibid.*, 73.

84. Lisa Bannon, "Los Angeles Times Raises Questions By Sharing Profit of Magazine Issue," *Wall Street Journal*, October 27, 1999.

85. Prochnau, "Down and out in L.A.," 76.

86. James Risser, "Lessons From L.A.," *Columbia Journalism Review*, January/February 2000, x.

87. Prochnau, "Down and out in L.A.," 76-77.

88. *Ibid.*, 77.

89. James Risser, "Lessons From L.A.," *Columbia Journalism Review*, January/February 2000, 29.

90. Prochnau, "Down and out in L.A.," 77.

91. *Ibid.*

92. David Shaw, "A Los Angeles Times Profit-Sharing Arrangement With Staples Center Fuels a Firestorm of Protest in the Newsroom — and a Debate About Journalistic Ethics," *Los Angeles Times*, December 20, 1999.

93. *Ibid.*

94. Lisa Bannon and Nikhil Deogun, "How Tribune Grabbed a Media Prize — Left in the Dust of the Deal And Unhappy About It Is Times Mirror CEO Willes," *Wall Street Journal*, March 14, 2000.

95. Tim Jones, "Times Mirror CEO's Severance Deal Could Top $9 Million," *Chicago Tribune*, March 23, 2000.

96. "Why ex-TM chief Mark Willes is now crying $$$ in his toasted oats," *MIN Media Industry Newsletter*, May 1, 2000.

97. Paul Tharp, "Willes gets Times Mirror," *New York Post*, March 21, 2000.

NOTES TO CHAPTER 5: THE ORIGINAL SIN

1. Keith Herndon, *The decline of the daily newspaper: How an American institution lost the online revolution*. New York: Peter Lang, 2012, 34.

2. Ben Bagdikian, *The Information Machines: Their Impact on Men and the Media*. New York: Harper & Row, 1971.

3. Marshall McLuhan, *Understanding Media: The Extensions of Man*. London: Routledge & Kegan Paul, 1964, 207.

4. Daniel Machalaba, "More Publications Beam Electronic Newspapers to Home Video Sets," *Wall Street Journal*, January 2, 1981.

5. Ray Laakaniemi, "The Computer Connection: America's First Computer-Delivered Newspaper," *Newspaper Research Journal* 2(4), July 1981, 63.

6. Chip Brown, "Fear.com," *American Journalism Review*, June 1999, 60.

7. Herndon, *The decline of the daily newspaper*, 47.

8. *Ibid.*, 50.

9. Roger Fidler, *Mediamorphosis: Understanding new media*. Thousand Oaks, CA: Pine Forge Press, 1997.

10. *Ibid.*, 50.

11. Pablo J. Boczkowski, *Digitizing the news: Innovation in online newspapers*. Cambridge, MA: MIT Press, 2004, 31.

12. Gary Stix, "What zapped the electronic newspaper?" *Columbia Journalism Review*, May/June 1987, 48.

13. Boczkowski, *Digitizing the news*, 35.

14. Michael Conniff, "A tangled web for newspapers," *Editor & Publisher*, February 4, 1995, 4.

15. Jack Shafer, "How Newspapers Tried to Invent the Web: But failed." Slate.com, January 6, 2009. Available online at http://www.slate.com/articles/news_and_politics/press_box/2009/01/how_newspapers_tried_to_invent_the_web.html

16. *Ibid.*

17. Herndon, *The decline of the daily newspaper*, 140-141.

18. Christopher Harper, "Online newspapers: Going somewhere or going

nowhere?" *Newspaper Research Journal* 17 (3-4) Summer/Fall 1996, 7.

19. Boczkowski, *Digitizing the news*, 52.

20. Brown, "Fear.com," 54.

21. *Ibid.*

22. *Ibid.*

23. *Ibid.*

24. Walter Hussman Jr., "How to Sink a Newspaper," *Wall Street Journal*, May 7, 2007.

25. Hunter Madsen, "Reclaim the Deadzone," *Wired*, December 1996.

26. I. Jeanne Dugan "New-media meltdown at New Century," *BusinessWeek*, May 23, 1998, 70.

27. *Ibid.*

28. *Ibid.*

29. *Ibid.*

30. Richard Siklos, "If you can't beat 'em . . ." *BusinessWeek*, January 18, 1999, 78.

31. Marc Gunther and Irene Gashurov, "Publish or Perish?" *Fortune*, January 10, 2000, 140.

32. Herndon, *The decline of the daily newspaper*, 163.

33. Gunther and Gashurov, "Publish or Perish?"

34. Brown, "Fear.com," 56.

35. Gunther and Gashurov, "Publish or Perish?"

36. Robert Seamans and Feng Zhu, "Responses to Entry in Multi-Sided Markets: The Impact of Craigslist on Local Newspapers," *Management Science* 60 (2), February 2014, 476-493.

37. See Rich Gordon, "The meanings and implications of convergence," in Kevin Kawamoto, Ed., *Digital Journalism: Emerging Media and the Changing Horizons of Journalism.* Lanham, MD: Rowman & Littlefield, 2003.

38. See Marc Edge "Convergence after the collapse: The 'catastrophic' case of Canada." *Media, Culture & Society* 33 (8), 2011, 1266-1278.

39. See Marc Edge, *Asper Nation: Canada's Most Dangerous Media Company.* Vancouver: New Star Books, 2007.

40. Charles C. Layton, "News blackout," *American Journalism Review*, December 2003, 18-31.

41. Gal Beckerman, "Tripping up big media," *Columbia Journalism Review*, November/December 2003, 15.

42. See Alec Klein, *Stealing Time: Steve Case, Jerry Levin, and the collapse of AOL Time Warner.* New York: Simon & Shuster, 2003; Nina Munk, *Fools rush in: Steve Case, Jerry Levin, and the unmaking of AOL Time Warner.* New York: Harper Business, 2004; Kara Swisher with Lisa Dickey, *There must be a pony in here somewhere: The AOL Time Warner debacle and the quest for a digital future.* New York: Crown Business, 2003.

43. Hsiang Iris Chyi, "Willingness to Pay for Online News: An Empirical Study on the Viability of the Subscription Model," *Journal of Media Economics* 18 (2), 2005, 133.

44. Lori Robertson, "Adding a Price Tag," *American Journalism Review*, December 2005/January 2006, 52-57.

45. Donica Mensing, "Online Revenue Business Model Has Changed Little Since 1996," *Newspaper Research Journal* 28(2), Spring 2007, 22-37.

46. Chyi, "Willingness to Pay for Online News," 132.

47. *Ibid.*, 140.

48. Michael Shapiro, "Open for Business," *Columbia Journalism Review*, July/August 2009, 29.

49. Paul Farhi, "Online Salvation?" *American Journalism Review*, October/November 2007, 23.

50. Barb Palser, "Free at Last," *American Journalism Review*, February/March 2008, 48.

51. *Ibid.*

52. Nat Ives, "NYTimes.com," *Advertising Age*, March 17, 2008, 56.

53. Palser, "Free at Last."

54. Nat Ives and Abbey Klaassen, "Paid content on the net? Not if the content's news," *Advertising Age*, August 13, 2007, 3.

55. Carl Sullivan "Registering a victory," *Editor & Publisher*, January 20, 2003, 10.

56. *Ibid.*

57. *Ibid.*

58. *Ibid.*

59. *Ibid.*

60. Nat Ives, "Newspapers grapple with how — or even whether — to erect a pay wall," *Advertising Age*, October 26, 2009, 3.

61. Robert G. Picard, "Changing Business Models of Online Content Services: Their Implications for Multimedia and Other Content Producers," *International Journal on Media Management* 2(1), 2000, 65.

62. See Ken Auletta, *Googled: The End of the World As We Know It*. New York: Penguin, 2009.

63. See Marc Edge, *Pacific Press: The Unauthorized Story of Vancouver's Newspaper Monopoly*. Vancouver: New Star Books, 2001.

64. Doreen Carvajal, "Free paper now No. 1 in Spain," *International Herald Tribune*, February 6, 2006.

65. Piet Bakker, "Reinventing Newspapers: Free dailies — readers and markets," in Robert G. Picard, Ed., *Media Firms: Structures, operations and performance*. Mahwah, NJ: Lawrence Erlbaum, 2002.

66. Mary Ellen Podmolik, "Urban tabloids snare hipper young readers," *Advertising Age*, April 30, 2001, 2.

67. Andy Serwer, "More readers are getting a free ride," *Fortune*, February 7, 2005, 22.

68. Lauren Gard, "Free press gets a whole new meaning," *BusinessWeek*, January 31, 2005, 74.

69. Mary Lynn Young, "Extra! Extra! Newspaper war coming to Vancouver," *Globe and Mail*, January 27, 2005.

70. Gard, "Free press gets a whole new meaning."

71. Sharyn Vane "Hip — and Happening," *American Journalism Review*, April/May 2005, 44.

72. Gard, "Free press gets a whole new meaning."

73. Vane, "Hip — and Happening."

74. Paul Farhi, "A Bright Future for Newspapers," *American Journalism Review*, June/July 2005, 59.

75. Michael Stoll, "News blends with ads, and the wealthy come first for home delivery," Grade the News, July 27, 2005. Available at http://www.gradethe-news.org/2005/freepapers1.htm

76. Michael Stoll, "Free daily papers: more local but often superficial," Grade the News in 2005, August 23, 2005. Available at http://www.gradethenews.org/2005/freepapers2.htm

77. Vane, "Hip — and Happening," 42.

78. See Charles Layton, "Sherman's March," *American Journalism Review*, February/March 2006, 18-24.

79. Herndon, *The decline of the daily newspaper*, 229.

80. Philip Stone, "Here's A US Newspaper Horror Story — Since The Day McClatchy Announced Its Knight Ridder Purchase Its Shares Are Down 69% Whereas The Dow Jones Averages Gained 17%," Followthemedia.com, November 14, 2007. Available at http://followthemedia.com/bigbusiness/mcclatchy14112007.htm?PHPSESSID=f1c4dc90a3b2c0e3e5e3af20d11ddb55

81. Kathrine Q. Seely, "Los Angeles Paper Ousts Top Editor," *New York Times*, November 8, 2006.

82. James O'Shea, *The Deal From Hell: How Moguls and Wall Street Plundered Great American Newspapers*. New York: Public Affairs, 2011, 254.

83. See Dan Steinbock, "Building Dynamic Capabilities: The Wall Street Journal interactive edition: A successful online subscription model (1993-2000)," *International Journal on Media Management* 2(3/4), 2000, 178-194.

84. Scott Kirsner, "When will online journalism ventures begin to make money?" *American Journalism Review*, December 1997, 40.

85. Steinbock, "Building Dynamic Capabilities," 189.

86. *Ibid.*, 186.

87. Emma Hall, "How Financial Times defies the times: Famed pink broadsheet in the black by raising price, charging for web," *Advertising Age*, March 9, 2009, 3.

88. Catherine Holahan, "The Case for Freeing the WSJ Online," Businessseek.com, August 10, 2007. Available at http://www.businessweek.com/stories/2007-08-10/the-case-for-freeing-the-wsj-onlinebusinessweek-business-news-stock-market-and-financial-advice

89. John Morton, "Costly Mistakes," *American Journalism Review*, December/January 2011, 64.

90. Paul Fahri, "A Costly Mistake?" *American Journalism Review*, Apr/May 2009, 38.

91. *Ibid.*, 39.

NOTES TO CHAPTER 6: THE DEAD

1. All figures from naa.org, unadjusted for inflation.

2. "Separation in Cincinnati," *Time*, October 11, 1968, 95.

3. See Gerald J. Baldasty and Myron K. Jordan, "Scripps' Competitive Strategy: The Art of Non-competition," *Journalism Quarterly* 70 (2), Summer 1993, 265-275; Edward E. Adams, "Secret combinations and collusive agreements: The Scripps Newspaper Empire and the early roots of Joint Operating agreements," *Journalism and Mass Communication Quarterly* 73 (1), Spring 1996, 195-205.

4. Stephen R. Barnett, "Monopoly games – where failure is rewarded," *Columbia Journalism Review*, May/June 1980, 41.

5. *Ibid.*, 43.

6. *Ibid.*

7. *Ibid.*

8. Steve Hallock, "Fewer two-newspaper cities," *St. Louis Journalism Review*, September 2007, 24-25.

9. Ron Rodgers, Steve Hallock, Mike Gennaria and Fei Wei, "Two Papers in Joint Operating Agreement Publish Meaningful Editorial Diversity," *Newspaper Research Journal* 25 (4), Fall 2004, 107.

10. John Nerone, "The death (and rebirth?) of working-class journalism," *Journalism* 10, 2009, 353.

11. *Ibid.*, 354.

12. Sam Schulhofer-Wohly and Miguel Garridoz, "Do Newspapers Matter? Evidence from the Closure of The Cincinnati Post," Princeton University, Woodrow Wilson School of Public and International Affairs, October 2009, 4. Available at http://www.princeton.edu/wwseconpapers/papers/wwsdp236.pdf

13. *Ibid.*, 1.

14. Stephen Kimber, "The Halifax Daily News: 1974-2008," Journalismethics.info, February 24, 2008. Available at http://www.journalismethics.info/feature_articles/halifax_daily_news.html

15. Stephen Kimber, "Why I won't write for the Aspers," *Globe and Mail*, January 7, 2002.

16. Bruce Wark, "Daily News death, Transcontinental Tragedy," *The Coast*, February 21, 2008. Available at http://www.thecoast.ca/halifax/daily-news-death-transcontinental-tragedy/Content?oid=962373

17. *Ibid.*

18. "Closure of Halifax Daily News part of dangerous trend to 'News Lite,'" Canadian Association of Journalists, February 11, 2008. Available at http://www.caj.ca/closure-of-halifax-daily-news-part-of-dangerous-trend-to-news-lite/

19. Tim Bousquet, "Daily News canned by Transcontinental," *The Coast*, February 14, 2008. Available at http://www.thecoast.ca/halifax/daily-news-canned-by-transcontinental/Content?oid=962316

20. John Morrissy, "Halifax Daily News ceases publication," *Ottawa Citizen*, February 12, 2008.

21. Edward E. Adams, "Scripps Howard's implementation of joint agreements for newspaper preservation, 1933-1939," *Journalism History* 23(4), Winter 1997/98, 160.

22. *Ibid.*

23. *Ibid.*, 161.

24. *Ibid.*

25. *Ibid.*, 164.

26. *Ibid.*

27. Paul Farhi, "The Death of the JOA," *American Journalism Review*, September 1999, 50.

28. *Ibid.*

29. *Ibid.*, 51.

30. Tony Davis, "When Heart Isn't Enough," *American Journalism Review*, April/May 2008, 20.

31. Christie Chisholm, "Albuquerque's next newspaper is print-first," CJR.org, January 29, 2014. Available at http://www.cjr.org/behind_the_news/albuquerques_next_newspaper_is.php?page=all#sthash.HTxaBQfC.dpuf

32. See Ronald Steel, *Walter Lippmann and the American century*. Piscataway, NJ: Transaction, 1980.

33. John Nichols, "Our publisher dictates from the 'other side,'" *Masthead* 51(1), Spring 1999, 10.

34. Jason Shepard, "The Capital Times: Still kickin'" *The Isthmus*, December 14, 2007.

35. *Ibid.*

36. Bill Lueders, "On the death of The Capital Times," *The Isthmus*, February 7, 2008. Available at http://www.isthmus.com/daily/article.php?article=21536

37. Bill Lueders, "A tear for The Capital Times," *The Isthmus*, February 14, 2008. Available at http://www.isthmus.com/isthmus/article.php?article=21607

38. Marc Eisen, "Ron McCrea backs changes at The Capital Times," Isthmus.com, February 12, 2008. Available at http://www.isthmus.com/daily/article.php?article=21595

39. Jason Stein, "A new era for Capital Times," *Wisconsin State Journal*, April 26, 2008.

40. Noam Cohen, "Reluctantly, a Daily Stops Its Presses, Living Online," *New York Times*, April 28, 2008.

41. Thomas Kunkel, "Toward a Paperless Society," *American Journalism Review*, February/March 2006, 4.

42. See "The Office of the Future," *BusinessWeek*, June 30, 1975. Available at http://www.businessweek.com/stories/1975-06-30/the-office-of-the-future-

businessweek-business-news-stock-market-and-financial-advice

43. F. W. Lancaster, *Toward paperless information systems*. New York: Academic Press, 1978, 166.

44. Abigail J. Sellen and Richard H.R. Harper, *The myth of the paperless office*. Cambridge, MA: MIT Press, 2003, 206.

45. David F. Kohl, "The paperless society . . . Not quite yet," *Journal of Academic Librarianship* 30 (3), 2004, 177.

46. Nicholas A. Basbanes, "A paperless society? Not so fast," *Los Angeles Times*, December 8, 2013.

47. Kunkel, "Toward a Paperless Society."

48. Paul D. Colford, "This paper's still a monitor of world affairs," *Los Angeles Times*, August 11, 1997.

49. John Rivera, "The church's face to the world," *Baltimore Sun*, August 4, 1997.

50. Mark Jurkowitz, "Making the Monitor matter," *Boston Globe*, August 6, 1997.

51. Stephanie Clifford, "Christian Science paper to end daily print edition," *New York Times*, October 29, 2008.

52. David Carr, "Mourning old media's decline," *New York Times*, October 29, 2008.

53. Paul Gillin, "How the coming newspaper industry collapse will reinvent journalism," gillin.com, June 6, 2006. Available at http://gillin.com/2006/06/how-the-coming-newspaper-industry-collapse-will-reinvent-journalism/

54. Martin Langeveld, "Are newspapers doomed?" News After Newspapers, September 4, 2008. Available at http://www.newsafternewspapers.blogspot.ca/2008/09/are-newspapers-doomed.html

55. *Ibid.*

56. Alan D. Mutter, "Newspaper share value fell $64B in '08," Reflections of a Newsosaur, January 1, 2009. Available online at http://newsosaur.blogspot.ca/2008/12/newspaper-share-value-fell-64b-in-08.html

57. Peter Preston, "Freesheets are no easy route to big profits," *The Observer*, Aug 10, 2008.

58. Tim Luckhurst, "You can't give them away," *The Independent*, June 1, 2009.

59. Erin Sullivan, "Baltimore Examiner to Close by Feb. 15," *Baltimore City Paper*, January 29, 2009. Available at http://blogs.citypaper.com/index.php/the-news-hole/baltimore-examiner-to-close-by-feb-15/

60. Julekha Dash, "Baltimore Examiner to fold after failing to land buyer," *Baltimore Business Journal*, January 26, 2009. Available at http://www.bizjour-nals.com/baltimore/stories/2009/01/26/daily39.html?page=all

61. Edmund Lee, "Does who creates content matter to marketers in a 'pro-am' media world?" *Advertising Age*, June 7, 2010, 2.

62. Mark Glaser, "Examiner.com execs push for quality, Refute 'content farm' Tag," PBS *MediaShift*, October 7, 2010. Available at http://www.pbs.org/mediashift/2010/10/examinercom-execs-push-for-quality-refute-con-tent-farm-tag280.html

63. "Examiner.com to recruit 12,000 writers, called examiners, in 2009 across 60 local markets," Reuters.com, February 11, 2009. Available at http://www.reuters.com/article/2009/02/11/idUS241154+11-Feb-2009+PRN20090211

64. Roberto Rocha, "News website chain expands into Canada," *Montreal Gazette*, October 29, 2009.

65. Edmund Lee, "What it takes writers to hit paydirt on content farms," *Advertising Age*, November 15, 2010, 6.

66. Bob Diddlebock, "Who really killed the Rocky Mountain News?" Time.com, March 6, 2009. Available at http://content.time.com/time/business/article/0,8599,1883345,00.html

67. Alan Prendergast, "Peace comes To Denver," *Columbia Journalism Review*, July/August 2000, 16.

68. *Ibid.*

69. Joe Strupp, "Rocky road may lead to new JOA in Denver," *Editor & Publisher*, May 15, 2000, 5.

70. Trent Seibert and Kevin Simpson, "Newspaper joint deals remain controversial," *Denver Post*, May 12, 2000.

71. Mike McPhee, "Jabs lawyers: News was in good shape pre-JOA," *Denver Post*, April 12, 2001.

72. Mike Soraghan, "Reno OKs newspaper pact," *Denver Post*, January 6, 2001.

73. Michael Roberts, "Denver's JOA makes for muddy reading," *Westword*, December 11, 2008. Available at http://www.westword.com/2008-12-11/news/denver-s-joa-makes-for-muddy-reading/

74. "The Rocky Mountain News is going down," *Westword*, December 11, 2008. Available at http://www.westword.com/2008-12-11/news/the-rocky-mountain-news-is-going-down/

75. Diddlebock, "Who Really Killed the Rocky Mountain News?"

76. "Joint operating angst," *Editor & Publisher*, September 2003, 7.

77. Vincent Coppola, "War & Peace," *MediaWeek*, February 21, 2000, 32.

78. Rachel La Corte, "State Supreme Court deals P-I blow in legal fight with Seattle Times," Associated Press Newswires, July 1, 2005. Downloaded August 3, 2014 from Factiva.com.

79. Michael J. McCarthy, "Knight Ridder reaffirms goal to own Seattle Times," *Wall Street Journal*, June 25, 2003.

NOTES TO CHAPTER 7: THE CHAPTER 11 CLUB

1. Mark Fitzgerald And Jennifer Saba, "Ready for Takeoff?" *Editor & Publisher*, May 1, 2009, 19.

2. Ryan Chittum, "The Grave Dancer: Sam Zell and Tribune's fate," *Columbia Journalism Review*, March/April 2008, 34.

3. Alicia C. Shepard, "Tribune's Big Deal," *American Journalism Review*, May 2000, 22.

4. See James O'Shea, *The Deal From Hell: How Moguls and Wall Street Plundered Great American Newspapers*. New York: Public Affairs, 2011.

5. Harold Meyerson, "The L.A. Times's human wrecking ball," *Washington Post*, June 11, 2008.

6. Michael Oneal and Steve Mills, "Zell's big gamble," *Chicago Tribune*, January 13, 2013.

7. Michael Oneal, "Bankruptcy Inc.," *Chicago Tribune*, January 16, 2013.

8. Oneal and Mills, "Zell's big gamble."

9. Oneal, "Bankruptcy Inc."

10. Robert Neuwirth, "McClatchy antes up again for high-roller deal," *Editor & Publisher*, November 22, 1997, 9.

11. John Morton, "Expensive, yes, but well worth it," *American Journalism Review*, January/February 1998, 52.

12. *Ibid.*

13. Mark Fitzgerald, "A disturbing first," *Editor & Publisher*, February 2007, 66.

14. John Morton, "Money talks," *American Journalism Review*, February/March 2007, 64.

15. Chris Newmarker, "Star Tribune emerges from bankruptcy, no new CEO yet," *Minneapolis/St. Paul Business Journal*, September 28, 2009.

16. Mark Lisheron, "On the rebound," *American Journalism Review*, Fall 2012, 35-39.

17. John Reinan, "The Star Tribune's smart response to industry crisis," MinnPost, March 18, 2013. Available at http://www.minnpost.com/business/2013/03/star-tribune-s-smart-response-industry-crisis

18. David Carr, "A native son revitalizes his paper," *New York Times*, April 17, 2011.

19. Adam Belz and Rochelle Olson, "Signature has Taylor moving ahead with Star Tribune deal, *Minneapolis Star Tribune*, May 29, 2014.

20. John Sullivan, "From rags to riches," *Editor & Publisher*, August 30, 1997, 11-12.

21. Mary Walton, "The selling of small-town America," *American Journalism Review*, May 1999, 58-72.

22. Nathan Vardi, "Cheapskate Journalism," *Forbes* 167(6), May 5, 2001, 118.

23. Mark Fitzgerald and Jennifer Saba, "'Til debt do us part — Probing the hidden reason for newspaper crisis," *Editor & Publisher*, June 19, 2008, 24.

24. *Ibid.*

25. Philip M. Stone, "The newspaper debt noose starts to choke," Followthemedia.com, October 7, 2008. Available at http://followthemedia.com/fittoprint/debt07102008.htm

26. Richard Perez-Pena, "Newspaper payout plan in closings clears court," *New York Times*, July 9, 2009.

27. See John J. Rapisardi, "Journal Register case reaffirms the vitality of 'gift' plans," *New York Law Journal* 240(57), September 18, 2009, 5.

28. Jennifer Saba, "Philadelphia Freedom: Analysts Say Investors Got Good Deal — But McClatchy Seems Satisfied," *Editor & Publisher*, May 24, 2006, 10.

29. Joseph N. DiStefano and Jennifer Lin, "Local group buys Inquirer, Daily

News, philly.com," *Philadelphia Inquirer*, May 24, 2006.

30. Quoted in Joe Strupp, "Philly newspapers face new debt troubles," Editorandpublisher.com, August 6, 2008. Available at http://editorandpublisher.com/Article/Philly-Newspapers-Face-New-Debt-Troubles

31. Bob Warner, "$66M offered in newspapers' re-org proposal," *Philadelphia Daily News*, August 21, 2009.

32. Christopher K. Hepp, "Media firm's circuitous path through bankruptcy," *Philadelphia Inquirer*, February 21, 2010.

33. Joseph Plambeck, "Creditors win auction for Philadelphia newspapers," New York Times, April 29, 2010.

34. Mike Armstrong, "Local investors buy Inquirer, Daily News, website," *Philadelphia Inquirer*, April 3, 2012.

35. Ravi Somaiya, "Auction Ends Heated Battle at Philadelphia Newspapers," *New York Times*, May 27, 2014.

36. Joel Mathis, "The Long Fall of Philly Newspapers:Document gives inside look at financial decline of Inquirer and Daily News," Phillymag.com, August 11, 2014. Available at http://www.phillymag.com/news/2014/08/11/financial-decline-philadelphia-newspapers-inquirer-daily-news/

37. Alan Mutter, "Sun-Times: The most jinxed newspaper," Reflections of a Newsosaur, January 22, 2009. Available at http://newsosaur.blogspot.ca/2009/01/sun-times-most-jinxed-newspaper.html

38. Allison Hantschel, "May Conrad Black and David Radler rot in hell," first-draft.com, March 31, 2009. Available at http://www.first-draft.com/2009/03/may-conrad-black-and-david-radler-rot-in-hell.html

39. See Marc Edge, "The pain of the obdurate rump: Conrad Black and the flouting of corporate governance." In Robert G. Picard (Ed.), *Corporate Governance of Media Companies*. Jönköping, Sweden: Jönköping International Business School, 2005.

40. Hollinger International Inc., "Report of investigation by the Special Committee of the Board of Directors," August 30, 2004. Retrieved September 5, 2004 from http://www.sec.gov/Archives/edgar/data/868512/000095012304010413/y01437exv99w2.htm

41. Sun-Times Media Group, 2008 Annual report, 28.

42. *Ibid.*, 67.

43. Ann Saphir, "Tyree's play: small profits, big returns; His group to make a killing even if Sun-Times barely makes money," *Crain's Chicago Business*, December 7, 2009, 3.

44. Conrad Black, "The final act of a corporate travesty," *National Post*, April 4, 2009.

45. Andrew Willis, "Hedge fund buys CanWest bonds," *Globe and Mail*, November 4, 2009.

46. "Disclosure statement with respect to joint plan of reorganization under Chapter 11, Title 11, United States Code of Freedom Communications. Holdings, Inc., et al., Debtors," October 31, 2009. *In re*: Chapter 11. Freedom Communica-

tions. Holdings, Inc., *et al.*,. Case No. 09-13046 (BLS). (Jointly Administered). U.S. Bankruptcy Court for the District of Delaware.

47. John Hazlehurst, "Secured, unsecured creditors agree on new Freedom bankruptcy plan," *Colorado Springs Business Journal*, January 21, 2010; John Hazlehurst, "Colorado Springs Gazette owner to exit bankruptcy," *Colorado Springs Business Journal*, March 9, 2010.

48. Mark Fitzgerald, "Dean's list," *Editor & Publisher*, June 1, 2006, 32.

49. Mark Fitzgerald, "McClatchy deal's antitrust okay comes with warning to MediaNews, Hearst," Editorandpublisher.com, August 1, 2006. Available at http://www.editorandpublisher.com/Article/McClatchy-Deal-s-Antitrust-Okay-Comes-With-Warning-To-MediaNews-Hearst

50. Mark Fitzgerald, "War of words heats up over Reilly/MediaNews/Hearst settlement," Editorandpublisher.com, April 28, 2007. Available at http://www.editorandpublisher.com/PrintArticle/UPDATE-War-Of-Words-Heats-Up-Over-Reilly-MediaNews-Hearst-Settlement

51. William Dean Singleton, "Letter to employees," quoted in "Affiliated Media, Inc. announces financial restructuring," PR Newswire, January 16, 2010. Downloaded June 23, 2013 from Factiva. com

52. Michael Liedtke, "Salt Lake Tribune parent company Affiliated Media Inc.'s bankruptcy plan approved," *Deseret Morning News*, March 5, 2010.

53. Mark Fitzgerald, "MediaNews group holding company cleared to exit bankruptcy," Editorandpublisher.com, March 4, 2010. Available at http://www.editorandpublisher.com/eandp/departments/business/article_display.jsp?vnu_content_id=1004072572

54. Liedtke, "Salt Lake Tribune parent company Affiliated Media Inc.'s bankruptcy plan approved."

55. Martin Langeveld, "The shakeup at MediaNews: Why it could be the leadup to a massive newspaper consolidation," Nieman Journalism Lab, January 20, 2011. Available at http://www.niemanlab.org/2011/01/the-shake-up-at-medianews-why-it-could-be-the-leadup-to-a-massive-newspaper-consolidation/

56. "Morris gets deal with bond holders, cuts 64% off $278M," *NewsInc.*, September 28, 2009.

57. Russ Bynum, "Judge clears Morris Publishing to emerge from bankruptcy, slashing debt by $288 million," Associated Press Newswires, February 18, 2010. Downloaded August 7, 2014 from Factiva.com.

58. "Morris to redeem public debt early," *Augusta Chronicle*, July 13, 2012.

59. Matt Wirz, "For vultures, slim pickings," *Wall Street Journal*, April 11, 2011.

60. *Ibid.*

61. David Nicklaus, "Bankruptcy gives Lee time to adapt," *St. Louis Post-Dispatch*, December 6, 2011.

62. Nat Ives, "It's not newspapers in peril; it's their owners," *Advertising Age*, February 23, 2009, 3.

63. Matt Wirz, "Buffett feasts on Goldman scraps," *Wall Street Journal*, April 12, 2012.

64. Quoted in Justin Fox, "A New Golden Age for Media?" Theatlantic.com, April 16, 2014. Available at http://www.theatlantic.com/magazine/archive/2014/05/start-the-presses/359810/

65. David Benoit, "Deal Journal: Warren Buffett loves newspapers (He was only kidding in 2009)," WSJ.com, May 17, 2012. Available at http://blogs.wsj.com/deals/2012/05/17/warren-buffett-loves-newspapers-he-was-only-kidding-in-2009/

66. Jim Gallagher, "Warren Buffett doubles stake in Lee newspapers," *St. Louis Post-Dispatch*, August 16, 2012.

67. Greg Edwards and Rebecca Wohltman, "Invisible ink," *St. Louis Business Journal*, November 2, 2012.

68. Tim Logan, "Buffett's Berkshire Hathaway raises stake in Lee newspapers," *St. Louis Post-Dispatch*, May 1, 2013.

69. "Lee Enterprises cuts debt 2 years ahead of schedule to $847.5 million," Associated Press Newswires, October 2, 2013. Downloaded August 9, 2014 from Factiva.com.

70. "Lee continues its 'upbeat outlook,'" *NewsInc.*, February 24, 2014.

71. Bill McClellan, "Bulging bonuses, skeleton staffs," *St. Louis Post-Dispatch*, July 29, 2012.

72. Deron Lee, "Post-Dispatch disparities," CJR.org, May 1, 2014. Available at http://www.cjr.org/united_states_project/at_lee_exec_bonuses_flat_wages_sinking_morale.php?page=all

73. David Carr, "Newspapers' digital apostle," *New York Times*, November 14, 2011.

74. Mark Fitzgerald, "Publisher of the Year: John Paton," Editorandpublisher.com, April 1, 2009. Available at http://www.editorandpublisher.com/Article/Publisher-of-the-Year-John-Paton

75. Mark Fitzgerald, "CEO: Time to change name of Journal Register Co.?" Editorandpublisher.com, April 5, 2010. Available at http://www.editorandpublisher.com/PrintArticle/CEO-Time-to-Change-Name-of-Journal-Register-Co-

76. "2 publishers to offer staff bonus plans," *NewsInc.*, June 14, 2010.

77. Peter Applebome, "Walk in, grab a muffin and watch a newspaper reinvent itself," *New York Times*, December 16, 2010.

78. John Paton, "I promised – you delivered – the checks are cut," jxpaton.wordpress.com, March 14, 2011. http://jxpaton.wordpress.com/2011/03/14/i-promised-you-delivered-the-checks-are-cut/

79. "Paton CEO at both MediaNews and Journal Resgister," *NewsInc.*, September 12, 2011.

80. Carr, "Newspapers' digital apostle."

81. "Monthly consolidated operating report for the period from September 5, 2012 through September 23, 2012," United States Bankruptcy Court, Southern District of New York, Case No. 12-13774 through 12-13802, Chapter 11, Journal Register Company, *et al.*, October 31, 2012.

82. See Kevin J. Delaney, *Strategic bankruptcy*. Berkeley: University of California Press, 1998.

83. Steve Ladurantaye, "Charting print through choppy waters," *Globe and Mail*, May 10, 2013.

84. Karl Henkel, "Sale of publisher may risk jobs at area newspapers," *Detroit News*, February 22, 2013.

85. Janelle Hartman, "JRC bankruptcy hits workers, contracts where it hurts," Newsguild.org, March 15, 2013. Available at http://www.newsguild.org/node/3015

86. Bob Fernandez, "Suburban newspaper publisher Journal Register files a second bankruptcy," *Philadelphia Inquirer*, September 6, 2012.

87. David M. Cole, "Journal Register sold: New boss same as the old boss," *NewsInc.*, April 1, 2013.

88. Henkel, "Sale of publisher may risk jobs at area newspapers."

89. Bill Shea, "Newspaper chain's life after Ch. 11: A mystery story," *Crain's Detroit Business*, March 4, 2013, 21.

90. Martin Langeveld, "Journal Register's bankruptcy is strategic, all right — but for whom?" Nieman Journalism Lab, September 6, 2012. Available at http://www.niemanlab.org/2012/09/martin-langeveld-journal-registers-bankruptcy-is-strategic-all-right-but-for-whom/

NOTES TO CHAPTER 8: REBUILDING REVENUE

1. See Bill Grueskin, Ava Seave, and Lucas Graves, *The Story So Far: What We Know About the Business of Digital Journalism*. New York: Columbia Journalism Review Books, 2011, 23.

2. Gabriel Sherman, "Post Apocalypse: Inside the messy collapse of a great newspaper," *New Republic*, February 4, 2010, 16-21.

3. Walter Isaacson, "How to save your newspaper," *Time*, February 5, 2009, 30.

4. Nat Ives and Abbey Klaassen, "Paid content on the net? Not if the content's news," *Advertising Age*, August 13, 2007, 3.

5. Michael Shapiro, "Open for Business," *Columbia Journalism Review*, July/August 2009, 29.

6. Chris Anderson, *Free: The Future of a Radical Price*. New York: Hyperion, 2009, 80.

7. *Ibid.*, 106.

8. Jack Herbert and Neil Thurman, "Paid content strategies for news websites: An empirical study of British newspapers' online business models," *Journalism Practice* 1(2), 2007, 210.

9. *Ibid.*, 211.

10. Michael Shapiro, "Open for Business," *Columbia Journalism Review*, July/August 2009, 29.

11. Michael Learmonth, "Wanted: Online payment plan for print," *Advertising Age*, February 23, 2009, 3.

12. Paul Farhi, "Build That Pay Wall High," *American Journalism Review*, June/July 2009, 22.

13. Emma Hall, "How Financial Times defies the times: Famed pink broad-

sheet in the black by raising price, charging for web," *Advertising Age*, March 9, 2009, 3.

14. Shapiro, "Open for Business," 29.

15. Learmonth, "Wanted: Online payment plan for print," 3.

16. Nat Ives, "Newspapers grapple with how – or even whether – to erect a pay wall," *Advertising Age*, October 26, 2009, 3.

17. David Simon, "Build the Wall: Most readers won't pay for news, but if we move quickly, maybe enough of them will," *Columbia Journalism Review*, July/August 2009, 36.

18. Isaacson, "How to save your newspaper," 30.

19. John Koblin, "After Three Months, Only 35 Subscriptions For Newsday's Web Site," New York Observer, January 26, 2010. Available at http://observer.com/2010/01/after-three-months-only-35-subscriptions-for-inewsdayis-website/

20. Farhi, "Build That Pay Wall High," 22.

21. Grueskin, Seave, and Graves, *The Story So Far*, 79.

22. Hall, "How Financial Times defies the times," 3.

23. Richard Floyd, "Martin Langeveld on paywalls," RichardFloyd.com, August 17, 2011. Available at http://richardlfloyd.com/2011/08/17/%E2%80%9Cthe-future-of-newspapers%E2%80%9D-the-third-annual-martin-langeveld-interview/

24. Alan Rusbridger, "Guardian editor hits back at paywalls," Guardian.co.uk, January 25, 2010. Available at http://www.guardian.co.uk/media/2010/jan/25/guardian-editor-paywalls

25. Michael Depp, "Newspapers Weigh Value of digital subs," NetNewsCheck.com, April 15, 2013. Available at http://www.netnewscheck.com/article/25598/newspapers-weigh-value-of-digital-subs

26. Rem Rieder, "Buffett's love for papers 'unnatural'? No way; Relationship firmly grounded on profit," *USA Today*, March 6, 2013.

27. Ken Doctor, "The newsonomics of paywalls all over the world," Niemanlab.org, March 8, 2012. Available at http://www.niemanlab.org/2012/03/the-newsonomics-of-paywalls-all-over-the-world/

28. Glenn Dyer, "Peering past the News Corp paywall," Businessspectator.com.au, July 30, 2012. Available at http://www.businessspectator.com.au/article/2012/7/30/media-and-digital/peering-past-news-corp-paywall

29. Rachel McAthy, "Two years in: Reflections on the New York Times paywall," Journalism.co.uk, March 28, 2013. Available at http://www.journalism.co.uk/news/two-years-of-the-new-york-times-paywall/s2/a552534/

30. Michael Nevradakis, "Behind the paywall: Lessons from US newspapers," Guardian.com, March 27, 2013. Available at http://www.theguardian.com/media-network/2013/mar/27/behind-paywall-us-newspaper-websites

31. Ryan Chittum, "Anti-paywall dead-enders," The Audit, December 3, 2012. Available at http://www.cjr.org/the_audit/zombie_lies_of_the_anti-paywal.php?page=all#sthash.riIszZMs.dpuf

32. Simon Houpt, "Globe Unlimited draws 80,000 readers since launch," *Globe and Mail*, February 22, 2013.

33. Nancy Davis Kho, "Digital Pricing Models: A Time of Forced Innovation," *EContent* 36(5), June 2013, 10.

34. Rick Edmonds, Emily Guskin, Amy Mitchell and Mark Jurkowitz, "Newspapers: Stabilizing, but Still Threatened," State of the New Media 2013. Available at http://stateofthemedia.org/2013/newspapers-stabilizing-but-still-threatened/

35. *Ibid.*

36. Ken Doctor, "The newsonomics of the Orange County Register's contrarian paywall," Niemanlab.org, April 3, 2013. Available at http://www.niemanlab.org/2013/04/the-newsonomics-of-the-orange-county-registers-contrarian-paywall/

37. Jeff John Roberts, "New York Times CEO calls digital pay model 'most successful decision in years,'" Paidcontent.org, May 20, 2013. Available at http://paidcontent.org/2013/05/20/new-york-times-ceo-calls-digital-pay-model-most-successful-decision-in-years/

38. Mark Sweney, "News UK chief backs digital paywalls," Guardian.com, July 2, 2013. Available at http://www.theguardian.com/media/2013/jul/02/news-uk-chief-backs-paywalls?CMP=twt_gu

39. Felix Salmon, "How paywalls are evolving," Reuters.com, April 3, 2013. Available at http://blogs.reuters.com/felix-salmon/2013/04/03/how-paywalls-are-evolving/

40. Steve Buttry, "New revenues hold much greater promise than paywalls," The Buttry Diary. Available at http://stevebuttry.wordpress.com/2013/04/26/new-revenues-hold-much-greater-promise-than-paywalls/

41. Edmund Lee, "The Year of The Paywall," *BusinessWeek*, November 18, 2013, 108.

42. Ken Doctor, "The newsonomics of Why Paywalls Now?" Niemanlab.org, March 7, 2013. Available at http://www.niemanlab.org/2013/03/the-newsonomics-of-why-paywalls-now/

43. Rem Rieder, "Read all about it online (but pay a bit)," *USA Today*, November 21, 2013.

44. Shapiro, "Open for Business," 29.

45. Alan Mutter, "The surprising boomlet in newspaper M&A," Reflections of a Newsosaur, August 12, 2013. Available at http://newsosaur.blogspot.ca/2013/08/the-surprising-boomlet-in-newspaper-m.html

46. Val Brickates Kennedy, "'Boston Globe' Ditching Paywall For Metered Subscription System," MediaPost.com, March 6, 2014. Available at http://www.mediapost.com/publications/article/220825/boston-globe-ditching-paywall-for-metered-subscr.html

47. Cary Spivak, "Are These Guys Crazy?" *American Journalism Review*, December 2012/January 2013, 20.

48. Ryan Chittum, "An ink-stained stretch," *Columbia Journalism Review*, May/June, 2013, 16.

49. *Ibid.*

50. *Ibid.*

51. *Ibid.*

52. Ken Doctor, "Inside the Toronto Star's $10 million niche print business," NiemanLab, September 4, 2014. Available at http://www.niemanlab.org/2014/09/ken-doctor-inside-the-toronto-stars-10-million-niche-print-business/

53. Nu Yang, "Revenue Strategies That Work," Editorandpublisher.com, August 2, 2013. Available at http://www.editorandpublisher.com/Features/Article/Revenue-Strategies-That-Work

54. Ellen Sterling, "Revenue 2012: The Newspaper As Entrepreneur," Editorandpublisher.com, February 8, 2012. Available at http://www.editorandpublisher.com/Features/Article/Revenue-2012--The-Newspaper-As-Entrepreneur

55. Edmonds, Guskin, Mitchell and Jurkowitz, "Newspapers: Stabilizing, but Still Threatened."

56. "Business model evolving, circulation revenue rising," Naa.org, April 18, 2014. Available at http://www.naa.org/Trends-and-Numbers/Newspaper-Revenue/Newspaper-Media-Industry-Revenue-Profile-2013.aspx

57. Ryan Chittum, "The newspaper plunge slows," The Audit, June 24, 2013. Available at http://www.cjr.org/the_audit/newspapers_slow_their_fall_in.php

58. Margaret Sullivan, "Perilous Task of Innovation in a Digital Age," *New York Times*, September 29, 2013.

59. Mike Allen and Michael Calderone, "Washington Post cancels lobbyist event amid uproar," *Politico*, July 2, 2009. Available at http://www.politico.com/news/stories/0709/24441.html#ixzz3BclYc2XT

60. David Carr, "A Publisher Stumbles Publicly at The Post," *New York Times*, July 4, 2009.

61. Andrew Alexander, "A Sponsorship Scandal at the Post," *Washington Post*, July 12, 2009.

62. "Britain: The crucible of print," *The Economist*, January 8, 2011, 55.

63. Allan Wolper, "Ethics Corner: Wine clubs Skirt Ethics And Regulations," Editorandpublisher.com, January 18, 2012. Available at http://www.editorandpublisher.com/Columns/Article/Ethics-Corner—Wine-clubs-Skirt-Ethics-And-Regulations

64. *Ibid.*

65. *Ibid.*

66. Shel Holtz, "Native speakers," *Communication World* 30(6), September 2013, 13.

67. Adam Lipman, "Why native advertising won't suffer the fate of banner ads," *Digiday*, March 28, 2014. Available at http://digiday.com/brands/native-ads-display-fate/

68. Ira Basen, "Going native: The death of journalism or the way of the future?" *J-Source*, September 12, 2013. Available at http://j-source.ca/article/going-native-death-journalism-or-way-future

69. *Ibid.*

70. Michael Wolff, "Even the New York Times can't resist going lowbrow with native advertising," Guardian.com, December 23, 2013. Available at http://www.theguardian.com/commentisfree/2013/dec/23/new-york-times-native-advertising-lowbrow

71. David Carr, "Storytelling Ads May Be Journalism's New Peril," *New York Times*, September 16, 2013.

72. David Dobbs, "The Atlantic, Scientology, and the Theft of Credibility," Wired.com, January 16, 2013. Available at http://www.wired.com/2013/01/the-atlantic-scientology-and-stolen-credibility/

73. Mathew Ingram, "What we can learn from The Atlantic's sponsored content debacle," GigaOm, January 16, 2013. Available at http://gigaom.com/2013/01/16/what-we-can-learn-from-the-atlantics-sponsored-content-debacle/

74. Edward Wyatt, "As Online Ads Look More Like News Articles, F.T.C. Warns Against Deception," *New York Times*, December 5, 2013.

75. Alex Kantrowitz, "Arguments Fly During FTC Workshop on Native Advertising," *Advertising Age*, December 4, 2013. Available at http://adage.com/article/media/arguments-fly-ftc-workshop-native-advertising/245536/

76. Nancy Davis Kho, "Digital Pricing Models: A Time of Forced Innovation," *EContent* 36(5), June 2013, 10.

77. Jane Sasseen, Kenny Olmstead and Amy Mitchell, "Digital: As Mobile Grows Rapidly, the Pressures on News Intensify," State of the News Media 2013. Available at http://stateofthemedia.org/2013/digital-as-mobile-grows-rapidly-the-pressures-on-news-intensify/

78. Josh Sternberg, "Washington Post Tries Sponsored Posts," *Digiday*, March 4, 2013. Available at http://digiday.com/publishers/washington-post-tries-sponsored-posts/

79. Michael Sebastian, "The Washington Post Starts Selling Native Ads for Print," *Advertising Age*, August 27, 2013. Available at http://adage.com/article/media/washington-post-starts-selling-native-ad-units-print/243851/

80. Erik Wemple, "Washington Post's Express runs massive ad for Vincent Gray on front," Washingtonpost.com, March 28, 2014. Available at http://www.washingtonpost.com/blogs/erik-wemple/wp/2014/03/28/washington-posts-express-runs-massive-ad-for-vincent-gray-on-front/

81. Ian Bailey, Andrea Woo and Daniel Bitonti, "Liberals defensive as NDP laughs off Clark's 'Comeback Kid' ad," *Globe and Mail*, May 1, 2013.

82. Erik Sass, "Hearst Taps Nativo For Native Ads," MediaPost.com, February 7, 2014. Available at http://www.mediapost.com/publications/article/219137/hearst-taps-nativo-for-native-ads.html

83. Erica Sweeney, "Deseret Native Ad Biz Closing In On $1M," NetNewsCheck, July 30, 2014. Available at http://www.netnewscheck.com/article/35179/deseret-native-ad-biz-closing-in-on-1m

84. Tanzina Vega, "Sponsoring Articles, Not Just Ads," *New York Times*, April 8, 2013.

85. *Ibid*

86. Susan Krashinsky, "Brought to you by . . . Blurring the line between news and ads," *Globe and Mail*, August 15, 2014.

87. Chantal Tode, "The Globe and Mail pilots native ad platform to drive mobile revenue," *Mobile Marketer*, July 31, 2013. Available at http://www.mobile-marketer.com/cms/news/content/15855.html

88. Alicia Androich, "Branded content . . . Heir to the throne," *Marketing*, October 8, 2012, 22.

89. "Custom editorial content," Globelink.ca. Available at http://globelink.ca/customcontent/

90. Susan Krashinsky, "Publishers turn to Toronto firm to makes online ads more palatable," *Globe and Mail*, October 3, 2013.

91. Jesse Brown, "Leaked memo confirms that Globe and Mail wants journalists to write advertorials," Canadaland, June 10, 2014. Available at http://canadalandshow.com/article/leaked-memo-confirms-globe-and-mail-wants-journalists-write-advertorials

92. Sebastian, "The Washington Post Starts Selling Native Ads for Print."

93. Margaret Sullivan, "Pledging Clarity, The Times Plunges Into Native Advertising," NYTimes.com, December 19, 2013. Available at http://publiceditor.blogs.nytimes.com/2013/12/19/pledging-clarity-the-times-plunges-into-native-advertising/?_php=true&_type=blogs&_r=0

94. Michael Sebastian, "The New York Times Is Going to Label the Hell Out of Its Native Ads," Adage.com, December 19, 2013. Available at http://adage.com/article/media/york-times-label-hell-native-ads/245787/

95. Michael Sebastian, "Will Baquet's 'Teddy Bear' Style Extend to The New York Times Ad Department?" Adage.com, May 16, 2014. Available at http://adage.com/article/media/dean-baquet-york-times-ad-sales-team/293218/

96. Michael Wolff, "Even the New York Times can't resist going lowbrow with native advertising," Guardian.com, December 23, 2013. Available at http://www.theguardian.com/commentisfree/2013/dec/23/new-york-times-native-advertising-lowbrow

97. Michael Sebastian, "Times change: Labels on native ads shrink at Grey Lady," *Advertising Age*, August 11, 2014, 12.

98. Sebastian, "Will Baquet's 'Teddy Bear' Style Extend to The New York Times Ad Department?"

99. *New York Times*, "Innovation," March 24, 2014, 61. Available at http://www.scribd.com/doc/224608514/The-Full-New-York-Times-Innovation-Report

100. Sebastian, "Times change."

101. Joe Pompeo, "'Wall Street Journal' editor Gerard Baker decries native advertising as a 'Faustian pact,'" *Capital New York*, September 25, 2013. Available at http://www.capitalnewyork.com/article/media/2013/09/8534047/wall-street-journal-editor-gerard-baker-decries-native-advertising-fau

102. Michael Sebastian, "Another one falls: Wall Street Journal latest major newspaper to introduce native advertising," *Advertising Age*, March 10, 2014, 8.

103. Brian Braiker, "Andrew Sullivan on native ads: Journalism has surrendered," *Digiday*, May 7, 2014. Available at http://digiday.com/publishers/andrew-sullivan-native-ads/

104. Bob Garfield, "If native advertising is so harmless, why does it rely on misleading readers?" Guardian.com, February 25, 2014. Available at http://www.theguardian.com/commentisfree/2014/feb/25/yahoo-opens-gemini-native-advertising

105. Todd Copilevitz, "'Native advertising is further proof we've lost our way,'" *Digiday*, August 13, 2014. Available at http://digiday.com/agencies/native-advertising-proof-lost-our-way/

106. Ben Kunz, "Native Advertising Is Bad News," *Digiday*, March 22, 2013. Available at http://www.digiday.com/publishers/native-advertising-is-bad-news/

107. Erik Wemple, "HBO's John Oliver: Native advertising is 'repurposed bovine waste,'" WashingtonPost.com, August 4, 2014. Available at http://www.washingtonpost.com/blogs/erik-wemple/wp/2014/08/04/hbos-john-oliver-native-advertising-is-repurposed-bovine-waste/

NOTES TO CONCLUSION: THE MYTH OF THE DEATH OF NEWSPAPERS

1. Lou Phelps, "Understanding the Latest Financial Reports of Some Newspaper Industry Leaders," *Savannah Daily News,* December 13, 2011.

2. Russell Baker, "Goodbye to Newspapers?" *New York Review of Books*, August 16, 2007.

3. Martin Langeveld, "80 percent of newspapers gone in 18 months? Not likely." NiemanLab, April 21, 2009. Available at http://www.niemanlab.org/2009/04/80-percent-of-newspapers-gone-in-18-months-not-likely/

4. Bob Garfield, "This is no 'golden age' of journalism. These are the news media end times," Guardian.com, March 27, 2013. Available at http://www.theguardian.com/commentisfree/2013/mar/27/no-golden-age-journalism-news-media-end-times. As the *Guardian*'s motto is "Comment is free, but facts are sacred," I attempted to set the record straight with their gatekeepers, only to be told politely to sod off (Maya Wolfe-Robinson, personal communication, March 28, 2013). So I thought I'd write this book.

5. Malcolm Gladwell, "Priced to Sell: Is free the future?" *New Yorker*, July 6, 2009, 80.

6. Vincent Mosco, *The Digital Sublime: Myth, Power, and Cyberspace*. Cambridge, MA: MIT Press, 2004.

7. Paula Berinstein, "Black and white and dead all over: are newspapers headed 6 feet under?," *The Searcher* 13 (10), November 2005, 46.

8. *Ibid.*

9. Mitchell Stephens, *Beyond News: The Future of Journalism*. New York: Columbia University Press, 2014, 112.

10. Robert G. Picard, "Changing Business Models of Online Content Services: Their Implications for Multimedia and Other Content Producers," *International Journal on Media Management* 2 (1), 2000, 60.

11. *Ibid.*

12. Baker, "Goodbye to Newspapers?"

13. Bob Garfield, *The Chaos Scenario*. Nashville: Stielstra, 2009, 11.

14. *Ibid.*, 12.

15. Paul Levinson, *The Soft Edge: A Natural History and Future of the Information Revolution*. London: Taylor & Francis, 1997, 182.

16. *Ibid.*, 179.

17. See Susan M. Keith and Leslie-Jean Thornton, "Goodbye Convergence, Hello 'Webvergence': Tracking the Evolution of Print-Broadcast Partnerships Through the Lens of Change Theory," *Journalism & Mass Communication Quarterly* 86(2), 257-276.

18. See Marc Edge, "Convergence after the collapse: The 'catastrophic' case of Canada," *Media, Culture & Society* 33(8), 2011, 1266-1278.

19. Dal Yong Jin, "Deconvergence: A Shifting Business Trend in the Digital Media Industries," *Media, Culture & Society* 34(6) 2012, 761-772.

20. See Judith Garrett Segura, *Belo: From Newspapers to New Media*. Austin: University of Texas Press, 2010.

21. David Carr, "Print Is Down, and Now Out: Media Companies Spin Off Newspapers, to Uncertain Futures," *New York Times*, August 10, 2014.

22. Clay Shirky, "Last Call: The end of the printed newspaper," Medium.com, August 19, 2014. Available at https://medium.com/@cshirky/last-call-c682f6471c70

23. Clay Shirky, "Nostalgia and Newspapers," Shirky.com, June 17, 2014. Available at http://www.shirky.com/weblog/2014/06/nostalgia-and-newspapering/

24. *Ibid.*

25. Ryan Chittum, "A reply to Clay Shirky," The Audit, June 19, 2014. Available at http://www.cjr.org/the_audit/a_reply_to_clay_shirky.php?page=all#sthash.8EWEer8A.dpuf

26. Martin Eiermann, "'There is no news industry,'" *The European*, August 4, 2013. Available at http://www.theeuropean-magazine.com/clay-shirky--2/6714-post-industrial-journalism

27. See Clay Shirky, "Newspapers and Thinking the Unthinkable," Shirky.com, March 13, 2009. Available at http://www.shirky.com/weblog/2009/03/newspapers-and-thinking-the-unthinkable/

28. Shirky, "Nostalgia and Newspapers."

29. Dean Starkman, "Confidence Game: The limited vision of the news gurus," *Columbia Journalism Review*, November/December 2011, 121.

30. Quoted in Mathew Ingram, "Digital First Media's John Paton on newspapers and paywalls," Paid Content, April 8, 213. Available at http://paidcontent.org/2013/04/08/digital-first-medias-john-paton-on-newspapers-and-paywalls/

31. Starkman, "Confidence Game.

32. Jeff Jarvis, "To Newspaper Moguls: You Blew It," Huffington Post, May 8, 2009. Available at http://www.huffingtonpost.com/jeff-jarvis/to-newspaper-moguls-you-b_b_184309.html

33. Michael Giusti, "Print media is not on deathbed," *Loyola Maroon*, March 18, 2010. Available at http://www.loyolamaroon.com/editorial-and-opinions/print-media-is-not-on-deathbed-1.2195107

34. Paul Gillin, "Misshaping Young Minds," Newspaper Death Watch, March 24, 2010. Available at http://newspaperdeathwatch.com/misshaping-young-minds/

35. Stephen Quinn, *Convergent Journalism, The Fundamentals of Multimedia Reporting*. New York: Peter Lang, 2005, 88.

36. Marshall McLuhan, *Understanding Media: The Extensions of Man*. London: Routledge & Kegan Paul, 1964, 207.

37. Peter Preston, "Are newspapers burnt out?" *The Observer*, November 21, 2004.

38. Ben Bagdikian, *The Information Machines: Their Impact on Men and the Media*. New York: Harper & Row, 1971, xxxiii.

39. Levinson, *The Soft Edge*, 183.

40. Hal Varian, "Newspaper economics: online and offline," Google Public Policy Blog, March 9, 2010. Available at http://googlepublicpolicy.blogspot.com/2010/03/newspaper-economics-online-and-offline.html

41. Katrien Berte and Els De Bens, "Newspapers go for advertising!: Challenges and opportunities in a changing media environment," *Journalism Studies* 9(5), 2008, 692.

42. Nadine Lindstädt and Oliver Budzinski, "Newspaper vs. Online Advertising — Is There a Niche for Newspapers in Modern Advertising Markets?" *SSRN Working Paper Series*, December 2011, 14. Available at http://papers.ssrn.com/sol3/papers.cfm?abstract_id=1948487

43. David Olive, "Those death-defying newspapers," Moneyville, February 13, 2011. Accessed February 20, 2011 from http://www.moneyville.ca/article/937871--those-death-defying-newspapers

44. Stephen Foley, "The writing's on the wall for the old-style American newspaper," *The Independent* (London), December 15, 2008.

45. John Obrecht, "Stark outlook for newspapers," *BtoB* 96(5), May 2, 2011, 6.

46. "America at the Digital Turning Point," USC Annenberg School Center for the Digital Future, January 2012. Available at http://annenberg.usc.edu/News%20and%20Events/News/~/media/PDFs/CDF_DigitalReport.ashx

47. See David T. Z. Mindich, *Tuned Out: Why Americans Under 40 Don't Follow the News*. New York: Oxford University Press, 2005.

48. Paul Farhi, "A Bright Future for Newspapers," *American Journalism Review*, June/July 2005, 57.

49. Gene Roberts and Thomas Kunkel, *Leaving Readers Behind: The Age of Corporate Newspapering*. Fayetteville: University of Arkansas Press, 2001, 1.

50. Olive, "Those death-defying newspapers."

Notes to Appendix

1. Chak Reddy, "The Limitations of Using EBITDA for Mid Market Companies," *Elite M&A Advisor*, undated. Available at http://articles.elitemanda.com/

Limitations_Of_Using_EBITDA_For_Mid_Market_Companies.htm

2. Dylan Byers, "Washington Post loses $15.9 million in Q2," Politico, August 3, 2012. Available at http://www.politico.com/blogs/media/2012/08/washington-post-loses-in-q-131026.html

3. Quoted in Al Statz, "Famed investor: 'References to EBITDA make us shudder...,'" *North Bay Business Journal*, December 6, 2010. Available at http://www.northbaybusinessjournal.com/27609/commentary-famed-investor-references-to-ebitda-make-us-shudder/

4. John Morton, "It Could Be Worse," *American Journalism Review*, December 2008/January 2009, 52.

5. *Ibid.*

Bibliography

Edward E. Adams, "Secret combinations and collusive agreements: The Scripps Newspaper Empire and the early roots of Joint Operating agreements," *Journalism and Mass Communication Quarterly* 73(1), Spring 1996, 195-205.

Edward E. Adams, "Scripps Howard's implementation of joint agreements for newspaper preservation, 1933-1939," *Journalism History* 23(4), Winter 1997/98, 159-166.

Alicia Androich, "Branded content . . . Heir to the throne," *Marketing*, October 8, 2012, 22.

Chris Anderson, *Free: The Future of a Radical Price*. New York: Hyperion, 2009.

Peter Arnett, "Goodbye, World," *American Journalism Review*, November 1998, 50-67.

James L. Aucoin, *The Evolution of Investigative Journalism*. Columbia: University of Missouri Press, 2005.

Ken Auletta, "Demolition man," *New Yorker*, November 17, 1997, 40-45.

Ken Auletta, "Synergy City: Chicago's Tribune Co. is revolutionizing how it does business — but at what cost to its newspapers?" *American Journalism Review*, May 1998, 18-35.

Ken Auletta, *Googled: The End of the World As We Know It*. New York: Penguin, 2009.

Ben Bagdikian, *The Information Machines: Their Impact on Men and the Media*. New York: Harper & Row, 1971.

Ben H. Bagdikian, "The myth of newspaper poverty," *Columbia Journalism Review*, March/April 1973, 19-35.

Ben Bagdikian, "Conglomeration, Concentration and the Media," *Journal of Communication* 30(2), Spring 1980, 59-64.

Ben Bagdikian, *The Media Monopoly*. Boston: Beacon Press, 1983.

Russell Baker, "Goodbye to Newspapers?" *New York Review of Books*, August 16, 2007.

Piet Bakker, "Reinventing Newspapers: Free dailies — readers and markets," in Robert G. Picard, Ed., *Media Firms: Structures, Operations and Performance*. Mahwah, NJ: Lawrence Erlbaum, 2002.

Gerald Baldasty, *The Commercialization of News in the Nineteenth Century*. Madison: University of Wisconsin Press, 1992.

Gerald J. Baldasty and Myron K. Jordan, "Scripps' Competitive Strategy: The Art of Non-competition," *Journalism Quarterly* 70 (2), Summer 1993, 265-275.

Stephen R. Barnett, "Monopoly games — where failure is rewarded," *Columbia Journalism Review*, May/June 1980, 40-47.

Allan Bartley, "The regulation of cross-media ownership: The life and short times of PCO 2294," *Canadian Journal of Communication* 13 (2), Summer 1988, 45-59.

Jack Bass, "Newspaper Monopoly," *American Journalism Review*, July/August 1999, 64-77.

Gal Beckerman, "Tripping up big media," *Columbia Journalism Review*, November/December 2003, 15.

Peter Benjaminson, *Death in the Afternoon: America's Newspaper Giants Struggle For Survival*. Fairway, KS: Andrews, McMeel & Parker, 1984.

Bernard Berelson, "What 'Missing the Newspaper' Means," in Paul F. Lazarsfeld and Frank N. Stanton, eds. *Communications Research: 1948-1949*. New York: Harper, 1949, 111-129.

Paula Berinstein, "Black and white and dead all over: are newspapers headed 6 feet under?" *The Searcher* 13 (10), November 2005, 46-53.

Joseph Bernt and Marilyn Greenwald, Eds. *The Big Chill: Investigative Reporting in the Current Media Environment*. Ames: Iowa State University Press, 2000.

Katrien Berte and Els De Bens, "Newspapers go for advertising!: Challenges and opportunities in a changing media environment," *Journalism Studies* 9 (5), 2008, 692-703.

Conrad Black, *A Life in Progress*. Toronto: Key Porter, 1993.

Pablo J. Boczkowski, *Digitizing the News: Innovation in Online Newspapers*. Cambridge, MA: MIT Press, 2004.

"Britain: The crucible of print," *The Economist*, January 8, 2011, 55.

Chip Brown, "Fear.com," *American Journalism Review*, June 1999, 50-71.

John Busterna, "Daily Newspaper Chains and the Antitrust Laws," *Journalism Monographs*, 1989.

John Busterna, "Improving Editorial and Economic Competition with a Modified Newspaper Preservation Act," *Newspaper Research Journal*, Summer 1987, 71-84.

John Busterna and Robert Picard, *Joint Operating Agreements: The Newspaper Act and its Application*. Norwood, NJ: Ablex, 1993.

Canada, Royal Commission on Newspapers, *Report*. Ottawa: Queen's Printer, 1981.

Canada, *The Uncertain Mirror: Report of the Special Senate Committee on Mass Media*, Vol. I. Ottawa: Information Canada, 1970

Canada, Standing Senate Committee on Transport and Communication. *Interim Report on the Canadian News Media*, 2004. Ottawa: Senate of Canada.

Tony Case, "Defending the 'revolution,'" *Editor & Publisher*, March 30, 1996, 8.

Ryan Chittum, "The Grave Dancer: Sam Zell and Tribune's fate," *Columbia Journalism Review*, March/April 2008, 34-35.

Ryan Chittum, "An ink-stained stretch," *Columbia Journalism Review*, May/June, 2013, 16.

Hsiang Iris Chyi, "Willingness to Pay for Online News: An Empirical Study on the Viability of the Subscription Model," *Journal of Media Economics* 18(2), 2005, 131-142.

Hsiang Iris Chyi, Seth C. Lewis and Nan Zheng, "A matter of life and death?" *Journalism Studies* 13(3), June 2012, 305-324.

Richard M. Clurman, *To The End of Time*. New York: Touchstone, 1992.

Adam Cohen and Dan Cray, "Decline of the Times," *Time*, July 31, 1995, 47.

Nicholas Coleridge, *Paper Tigers*. London: William Heinemann, 1993.

Michael Conniff, "A tangled web for newspapers," *Editor & Publisher*, February 4, 1995, 4-8.

Vincent Coppola, "War & Peace," *MediaWeek*, February 21, 2000, 32.

Joseph S. Coyle, "Now, the editor as marketer," *Columbia Journalism Review*, July/August 1998, 37.

Gilbert Cranberg, Randall Bezanson and John Soloski, *Taking Stock: Journalism and the Publicly Traded Newspaper Company*. Ames: Iowa State University Press, 2001.

Dal Yong Jin, "Deconvergence: A Shifting Business Trend in the Digital Media Industries," *Media, Culture & Society* 34(6) 2012, 761-772.

Dal Yong Jin, *De-Convergence of Global Media Industries*. London: Routledge, 2013.

Tony Davis, "When Heart Isn't Enough," *American Journalism Review*, April/May 2008, 20-21.

Kevin J. Delaney, *Strategic Bankruptcy*. Berkeley: University of California Press, 1998.

Emanuel H. Demby, "Psychographics revisited: The birth of a technique," *Marketing Research*, Spring 1994, 26.

Frank Denton, "Old Newspapers and New Realities: The Promise of the Marketing of Journalism." In Frank Denton and Howard Kurtz, *Reinventing the Newspaper*. New York: The Twentieth Century Fund Press, 1992.

Jennifer Dorroh, "Endangered Species," *American Journalism Review*, December 2008/January 2009, 20.

Jennifer Dorroh, Lindsay Gsell and Will Skoronski, "Statehouse Exodus," *American Journalism Review*, April/May 2009, 20.

Leonard Downie, Jr. and Michael Schudson, "The Reconstruction of American Journalism," *Columbia Journalism Review*, November/December 2009, 26.

I. Jeanne Dugan "New-media meltdown at New Century," *BusinessWeek*, May 23, 1998, 70.

Marc Edge, "And 'The Wall' Came Tumbling Down in Los Angeles," in Joseph Bernt and Marilyn Greenwald, Eds. *The Big Chill: Investigative Reporting in the Current Media Environment.* Ames: Iowa State University Press, 2000.

Marc Edge, "The Good, the Bad, and the Ugly: Financial Markets and the Demise of Canada's Southam Newspapers," *International Journal on Media Management* 5(3), 2003, 180-189.

Marc Edge, *Pacific Press: The Unauthorized Story of Vancouver's Newspaper Monopoly.* Vancouver: New Star Books, 2001.

Marc Edge, "The pain of the obdurate rump: Conrad Black and the flouting of corporate governance." In Robert G. Picard (Ed.), *Corporate Governance of Media Companies.* Jönköping, Sweden: Jönköping International Business School, 2005.

Marc Edge, *Asper Nation: Canada's Most Dangerous Media Company.* Vancouver: New Star Books, 2007.

Marc Edge, "Convergence after the collapse: The 'catastrophic' case of Canada." *Media, Culture & Society* 33(8), 2011, 1266-1278.

Marc Edge, "Not dead yet: Newspaper company annual reports show chains still profitable." *Newspaper Research Journal,* Fall 2014. In press.

John Eggerton, "New Calls for Newspaper-Station Joint Ventures," *Broadcasting & Cable,* April 6, 2009, 14.

Paul Farhi, "The Death of the JOA," *American Journalism Review,* September 1999, 48-53.

Paul Farhi, "A Bright Future for Newspapers," *American Journalism Review,* June/July 2005, 54-59.

Paul Farhi, "Online Salvation?" *American Journalism Review,* October/November 2007, 19-23.

Paul Fahri, "A Costly Mistake?" *American Journalism Review,* Apr/May 2009, 36-41.

Paul Farhi, "Build That Pay Wall High," *American Journalism Review,* June/July 2009, 22-27.

Doug Fetherling, "All the news that's soft enough to print," *Maclean's,* October 30, 1978, 80.

Roger Fidler, *Mediamorphosis: Understanding New Media.* Thousand Oaks, CA: Pine Forge Press, 1997.

Jon Fine, "When Do You Stop The Presses?" *BusinessWeek,* July 20, 2007, 20.

Mark Fitzgerald, "Dean's list," *Editor & Publisher,* June 2006, 32-37.

Mark Fitzgerald, "A disturbing first," *Editor & Publisher,* February 2007, 66.

Mark Fitzgerald and Jennifer Saba, "'Til debt do us part — Probing the hidden reason for newspaper crisis," *Editor & Publisher,* June 2008, 24.

Mark Fitzgerald And Jennifer Saba, "Ready for Takeoff?" *Editor & Publisher,* May 2009, 19.

Susan Forde, "The end of the press subsidies 'experiment' in Sweden?" *Media International Australia* 95, May 2000, 107-116.

Ben Frumin, "Outsourced Edit?" *Columbia Journalism Review,* May/June 2008, 15-16.

Jack Fuller, *News Values: Ideas For an Information Age*. Chicago: University of Chicago Press, 1993.

Lauren Gard, "Free press gets a whole new meaning," *BusinessWeek*, January 31, 2005, 74.

Bob Garfield, "The Post Advertising Age," *Advertising Age*, March 26, 2007, 1, 12-14.

Bob Garfield, *The Chaos Scenario*. Nashville: Stielstra, 2009.

Ian Gill, "Just in the Time of Nick," *Vancouver*, July 1990, 30.

Malcolm Gladwell, "Priced to Sell: Is free the future?" *New Yorker*, July 6, 2009, 80-84.

Ann Goldgraben, "Dailies Wake Up to Threat of Shoppers," *Advertising Age*, 51(48), November 10, 1980.

Rich Gordon, "The meanings and implications of convergence," in Kevin Kawamoto, Ed., *Digital Journalism: Emerging Media and the Changing Horizons of Journalism*. Lanham, MD: Rowman & Littlefield, 2003.

Marty Graham, "Rancor and romance in the rubble of The Houston Post," *Columbia Journalism Review*, September/October 1995, 46.

Bill Grueskin, Ava Seave, and Lucas Graves, *The Story So Far: What We Know About the Business of Digital Journalism*. New York: Columbia Journalism Review Books, 2011.

Marc Gunther, "Hard News," *Fortune*, August 6, 2007, 80.

Marc Gunther and Irene Gashurov, "Publish or Perish?" *Fortune*, January 10, 2000, 140-148.

Emma Hall, "How Financial Times defies the times: Famed pink broadsheet in the black by raising price, charging for web," *Advertising Age*, March 9, 2009, 3, 20.

Steve Hallock, "Fewer two-newspaper cities," *St. Louis Journalism Review*, September 2007, 24-25.

Christopher Harper, "Online newspapers: Going somewhere or going nowhere?" *Newspaper Research Journal* 17(3-4) Summer/Fall 1996, 2-13.

John K. Hartman, "Newhouse quits daily papers," *Editor & Publisher*, June 20, 2013, 58.

John Hazlehurst, "Secured, unsecured creditors agree on new Freedom bankruptcy plan," *Colorado Springs Business Journal*, January 21, 2010.

John Hazlehurst, "Colorado Springs Gazette owner to exit bankruptcy," *Colorado Springs Business Journal*, March 9, 2010.

Rebecca Piirto Heath, "Psychographics: Q'est-ce que c'est?" *American Demographics*, November 1995, 74.

Jack Herbert and Neil Thurman, "Paid content strategies for news websites: An empirical study of British newspapers' online business models," *Journalism Practice* 1(2), 2007, 208-226.

Keith Herndon, *The Decline of the Daily Newspaper: How an American Institution Lost the Online Revolution*. New York: Peter Lang, 2012.

Neil Hickey, "Money lust," *Columbia Journalism Review*, July/August 1998, 28-36.

Michael Hirschorn, "End Times," *The Atlantic*, January/February 2009, 41-44.

Robert Hodierne and Meghan Meyer, "Is There Life After Newspapers?" *American Journalism Review*, February/March 2009, 21-27.

Shel Holtz, "Native speakers," *Communication World* 30(6), September 2013, 13.

Walter Isaacson, "How to save your newspaper," *Time*, February 5, 2009, 30-33.

Nat Ives, "NYTimes.com," *Advertising Age*, March 17, 2008, 56.

Nat Ives, "The newspaper death watch," *Advertising Age*, April 28, 2008, 1, 142.

Nat Ives, "It's not newspapers in peril; it's their owners," *Advertising Age*, February 23, 2009, 3.

Nat Ives, "Newspaper subscribers renewing and paying more," *Advertising Age*, October 5, 2009, 23.

Nat Ives, "Newspapers grapple with how — or even whether — to erect a pay wall," *Advertising Age*, October 26, 2009, 3.

Nat Ives and Abbey Klaassen, "Paid content on the net? Not if the content's news," *Advertising Age*, August 13, 2007, 3, 25.

"Joint operating angst," *Editor & Publisher*, September 2003, 7.

Susan M. Keith and Leslie-Jean Thornton, "Goodbye Convergence, Hello 'Webvergence': Tracking the Evolution of Print-Broadcast Partnerships Through the Lens of Change Theory," *Journalism & Mass Communication Quarterly* 86(2), 257-276.

Ann Marie Kerwin, "New Doors Cut in Wall Between Business, Edit: L.A. Times Publisher Blasts Critics of Recent Reorganization," *Advertising Age*, April 27, 1998, 63.

Penn Kimball, "People without Papers," *Public Opinion Quarterly* 23, 1959, 389-398.

Scott Kirsner, "When will online journalism ventures begin to make money?" *American Journalism Review*, December 1997, 40.

Nancy Davis Kho, "Digital Pricing Models: A Time of Forced Innovation," *EContent* 36(5), June 2013, 6-10.

Alec Klein, *Stealing Time: Steve Case, Jerry Levin, and the collapse of AOL Time Warner*. New York: Simon & Shuster, 2003.

Jonathan Knee, Bruce Greenwald and Ava Seave, *The Curse of the Mogul: What's Wrong With the World's Leading Media Companies*. New York: Portfolio, 2009.

David F. Kohl, "The paperless society . . . Not quite yet," *Journal of Academic Librarianship* 30(3), 2004, 177-178.

Bill Kovach and Tom Rosenstiel, *The Elements of Journalism: What Newspeople Should Know and the Public Should Expect*. New York: Three Rivers, 2007.

Thomas Kunkel, "Toward a Paperless Society," *American Journalism Review*, February/March 2006, 4.

Ray Laakaniemi, "The Computer Connection: America's First Computer-Delivered Newspaper," *Newspaper Research Journal* 2(4), July 1981, 61-68.

Mark Lacter, "Where's Dean?" *Forbes*, July 3, 2000, 76.

F. W. Lancaster, *Toward Paperless Information Systems*. New York: Academic Press, 1978.

Charles C. Layton, "News blackout," *American Journalism Review*, December 2003, 18-31.

Charles Layton, "Sherman's March," *American Journalism Review*, February/ March 2006, 18-24.

Charles Layton, "Surrounded by Singleton," *American Journalism Review*, June 2006, 44-49.

Michael Learmonth, "Wanted: Online payment plan for print," *Advertising Age*, February 23, 2009, 3-18.

James Ledbetter, "The Slow, Sad Sellout of Journalism School," *Rolling Stone*, October 16, 1997, 73-81, 99-100.

Edmund Lee, "Does who creates content matter to marketers in a 'pro-am' media world?" *Advertising Age*, June 7, 2010, 2, 37.

Edmund Lee, "What it takes writers to hit paydirt on content farms," *Advertising Age*, November 15, 2010, 6.

Edmund Lee, "The Year of The Paywall," *BusinessWeek*, November 18, 2013, 108.

Paul Levinson, *The Soft Edge: A Natural History and Future of the Information Revolution*. London: Routledge, 1998.

Trudy Lieberman, "What ever happened to consumer reporting?" *Columbia Journalism Review*, September/October 1994, 34-40.

Carl E. Lindstrom, *The Fading American Newspaper*. Garden City, NJ: Doubleday, 1960.

Walter Lippmann, *Public Opinion*. New York: Macmillan, 1922.

Mark Lisheron, "On the rebound," *American Journalism Review*, Fall 2012, 35-39.

Hugh J. Martin, "Measuring Newspaper Profits: Developing a Standard of Comparison." *Journalism and Mass Communication Quarterly* 75(3), 1998, 500-517.

Robert W. McChesney and John Nichols, *The Death and Life of American Journalism: The Media Revolution that Will Begin the World Again*. New York: Nation Books, 2010.

Marshall McLuhan, *Understanding Media: The Extensions of Man*. London: Routledge & Kegan Paul, 1964.

Donica Mensing, "Online Revenue Business Model Has Changed Little Since 1996," *Newspaper Research Journal* 28(2), Spring 2007, 22-37.

Philip Meyer, *The Vanishing Newspaper: Saving Journalism in the Information Age*, Columbia, MO: University of Missouri Press, 2004.

John Miller, *Yesterday's News: Why Canada's Daily Newspapers Are Failing Us*. Halifax: Fernwood, 1998.

Joyce Milton, *The Yellow Kids: Foreign Correspondents in the Heyday of Yellow Journalism*. New York: Harper and Row, 1989.

David T. Z. Mindich, *Tuned Out: Why Americans Under 40 Don't Follow the News*. New York: Oxford University Press, 2005.

Nikhil Moro and Debashis Aikat, "Chindia's newspaper boom: Identifying sustainable business models," *Global Media and Communication* 6(3), 2010, 357-367.

John Morton, "40 years of death in the afternoon," *American Journalism Review*, November 1991, 72.

John Morton, "Why Are Newspaper Profits So High?" *American Journalism Review*, October 1994, 72.

John Morton, "When Newspapers Eat Their Seed Corn: The current wave of cost-cutting in the industry could hurt its future," *American Journalism Review*, November 1995, 52.

John Morton, "Will Willes work wonders?" *American Journalism Review*, December 1997, 56.

John Morton, "Expensive, yes, but well worth it," *American Journalism Review*, January/February 1998, 52.

John Morton, "Hanging tough when profits drop: Will newspapers resist short-sighted moves if there's a recession?" *American Journalism Review*, October 1998, 88.

John Morton, "Churn, Baby, Churn: It takes constant tending to maintain subscription levels," *American Journalism Review*, December/January 2004, 84.

John Morton, "Money talks," *American Journalism Review*, February/March 2007, 64.

John Morton, "Costly Mistakes," *American Journalism Review*, December/January 2011, 64.

Vincent Mosco, *The Digital Sublime: Myth, Power, and Cyberspace*. Cambridge, MA: MIT Press, 2004.

Nina Munk, *Fools Rush In: Steve Case, Jerry Levin, and the Unmaking of AOL Time Warner*. New York: Harper Business, 2004.

Robert Neuwirth, "Lean Dean," *Editor & Publisher*, September 18, 1999, 26-32.

Peter C. Newman, "The inexorable spread of the Black Empire," *Maclean's*, February 3, 1992, 68.

John Nichols, "Our publisher dictates from the 'other side,'" *Masthead* 51(1), Spring 1999, 10.

John Nichols and Robert W. McChesney, "The Death and Life of Great American Newspapers," *The Nation*, April 6, 2009, 11-20.

Elizabeth MacIver Neiva, "Chain building: The consolidation of the American newspaper industry, 1955-1980," *Business and Economic History* 24(1), 1995, 22-26.

Elizabeth MacIver Neiva, "Chain building: The consolidation of the American newspaper industry, 1953-1980," *Business History Review* 70, 1996, 1-42.

John Nerone, "The death (and rebirth?) of working-class journalism," *Journalism* 10, 2009, 353-355.

Robert Neuwirth, "McClatchy antes up again for high-roller deal," *Editor & Publisher*, November 22, 1997, 9.

John Obrecht, "Stark outlook for newspapers," *BtoB* 96(5), May 2, 2011, 6.

James O'Shea, *The Deal From Hell: How Moguls and Wall Street Plundered Great American Newspapers*. New York: Public Affairs, 2011.

Geneva Overholser, "Editor Inc.," *American Journalism Review*, December 1998, 48-65.

Barb Palser, "Free at Last," *American Journalism Review*, February/March 2008, 48.

Robert G. Picard, "Changing Business Models of Online Content Services: Their Implications for Multimedia and Other Content Producers," *International Journal on Media Management* 2(1), 2000, 60-68.

Robert G. Picard, "US Newspaper Ad Revenue Shows Consistent Growth," *Newspaper Research Journal* 23(4), 2002, 21-33.

Robert G. Picard, "Tremors, Structural Damage and Some Casualties, but No Cataclysm: The News about News Provision," *Geopolitics, History, and International Relations*, 2(2), 2010, 73-90.

Robert G. Picard and Jeffrey H. Brody, *The Newspaper Publishing Industry*. Needham Heights, MA: Allyn and Bacon, 1997

Tim Pilgrim, "Newspapers as Natural Monopolies: Some Historical Considerations," *Journalism History* 18(1), 1992, 3-10.

Mary Ellen Podmolik, "Urban tabloids snare hipper young readers," *Advertising Age*, April 30, 2001, 2.

Alan Prendergast, "Peace comes To Denver," *Columbia Journalism Review*, July/August 2000, 16-19.

William Prochnau, "Down and out in L.A.," *American Journalism Review*, January/February 2000, 58-77.

Stephen Quinn, *Convergent Journalism: The Fundamentals of Multimedia Reporting*. New York: Peter Lang, 2005.

Josh Quittner, "Marc Andreessen's newspaper deathwatch," *Fortune*, March 4, 2008, 24.

John J. Rapisardi, "Journal Register case reaffirms the vitality of 'gift' plans," *New York Law Journal* 240(57), September 18, 2009, 3.

Charles Rappleye, "Cracking the church-state wall," *Columbia Journalism Review*, January/February 1998, 20.

Rem Rieder, "Fears for the Future," *American Journalism Review*, June/July 2009, 4.

James Risser, "Lessons From L.A.," *Columbia Journalism Review*, January/February 2000, 26-29.

Gene Roberts, Thomas Kunkel and Charles Layton (Eds.), *Leaving Readers Behind: The Age of Corporate Newspapering*. Fayetteville: University of Arkansas Press, 2001.

Gene Roberts and Thomas Kunkel (Eds.), *Breach of Faith: A Crisis of Coverage in the Age of Corporate Newspapering*. Fayetteville: University of Arkansas Press, 2005.

Lori Robertson, "Adding a Price Tag," *American Journalism Review*, December 2005/January 2006, 52-57.

Ron Rodgers, Steve Hallock, Mike Gennaria and Fei Wei, "Two Papers in Joint Operating Agreement Publish Meaningful Editorial Diversity," *Newspaper Research Journal* 25(4), Fall 2004, 104-109.

Mort Rosenblum, *Who Stole the News: Why We Can't Keep Up With What Happens in the World and What We Can Do About It*. New York: Wiley, 1995.

Jennifer Saba, "Philadelphia Freedom: Analysts Say Investors Got Good Deal – But McClatchy Seems Satisfied," *Editor & Publisher*, May 24, 2006, 10-15.

Jennifer Saba and Mark Fitzgerald, "Small Towns, Big Profits: How Many Papers Survive Slump," *Editor & Publisher*, February 28, 2008, 58-63.

Ann Saphir, "Tyree's play: small profits, big returns; His group to make a killing even if Sun-Times barely makes money," *Crain's Chicago Business*, December 7, 2009, 3.

Mary Ellen Schoonmaker, "The real estate story: hard news or soft sell? With so much advertising at stake, who wants to dig up dirt on the developers?" *Columbia Journalism Review*, January/February 1987, 25-30.

Michael Schudson, *Discovering the News: A Social History of American Newspapers*. New York: Basic Books, 1978.

Sam Schulhofer-Wohly and Miguel Garridoz, "Do Newspapers Matter? Short-run and Long-run Evidence from the Closure of The Cincinnati Post," Princeton University, Woodrow Wilson School of Public and International Affairs, October 2009, 4. Available at http://www.princeton.edu/wwseconpapers/papers/wwsdp236.pdf

Robert Seamans and Feng Zhu, "Responses to Entry in Multi-Sided Markets: The Impact of Craigslist on Local Newspapers," *Management Science* 60(2), February 2014, 476-493.

Michael Sebastian, "Another one falls: Wall Street Journal latest major newspaper to introduce native advertising," *Advertising Age*, March 10, 2014, 8.

Michael Sebastian, "Times change: Labels on native ads shrink at Grey Lady," *Advertising Age*, August 11, 2014, 12.

Judith Garrett Segura, *Belo: From Newspapers to New Media*. Austin: University of Texas Press, 2010.

Abigail J. Sellen and Richard H.R. Harper, *The Myth of the Paperless Office*. Cambridge, MA: MIT Press, 2003.

"Separation in Cincinnati," *Time*, October 11, 1968, 95.

Andy Serwer, "More readers are getting a free ride," *Fortune*, February 7, 2005, 22.

Lee Shaker, "Dead Newspapers and Citizens' Civic Engagement," *Political Communication* 31(1), 2014, 131-148.

Michael Shapiro, "Open for Business," *Columbia Journalism Review*, July/August 2009, 29-35.

Bill Shea, "Newspaper chain's life after Ch. 11: A mystery story," *Crain's Detroit Business*, March 4, 2013, 21.

Alicia C. Shepard, "Tribune's Big Deal," *American Journalism Review*, May 2000, 22-30.

Gabriel Sherman, "Post Apocalypse: Inside the messy collapse of a great newspaper," *New Republic*, February 4, 2010, 16-21.

Scott Sherman, "The evolution of Dean Singleton," *Columbia Journalism Review*, March/April 2003, 32-41.

Pamela J. Shoemaker and Stephen D. Reese, *Mediating the Message: Theories of Influences on Mass Media Content*, 2nd Ed., White Plains, NY: Longman, 1996.

Richard Siklos, "If you can't beat 'em . . ." *BusinessWeek*, January 18, 1999, 78.

David Simon, "Build the Wall: Most readers won't pay for news, but if we move quickly, maybe enough of them will," *Columbia Journalism Review*, July/August 2009, 36-40.

Stephen J. Simurda, "Will the eagle still fly?" *Columbia Journalism Review*, November 1995, 21.

Upton Sinclair, *The Brass Check*. Pasadena, CA: Upton Sinclair, 1919.

Steve Singer, "Auto Dealers Muscle the Newsroom," *American Journalism Review*, September 1991, 24-28.

Anthony Smith, *Goodbye Gutenberg: The Newspaper Revolution of the 1980s*. New York: Oxford University Press, 1980.

Rachel Smolkin, "Cities Without Newspapers," *American Journalism Review*, April/May 2009, 16-25.

Dallas W. Smythe "Communications: Blindspot of Western Marxism." *Canadian Journal of Political and Social Theory* 1(3), 1977, 1-27.

Minko Sotiron, "Concentration and collusion in the Canadian newspaper industry, 1895-1920," *Journalism History* 18, 1992, 26-32.

Anthony Spaeth, "If You Can't Beat 'Em, Flank 'Em," *Forbes*, October 15, 1979, 168.

Cary Spivak, "Are These Guys Crazy?" *American Journalism Review*, December 2012/January 2013, 18-23.

James D. Squires, *Read All About It! The Corporate Takeover of America's Newspapers*, New York: Times Books, 1993.

Dean Starkman, "Confidence Game: The limited vision of the news gurus," *Columbia Journalism Review*, November/December 2011, 121-130.

Dean Starkman, *The Watchdog That Didn't Bark: The Financial Crisis and the Disappearance of Investigative Journalism*. New York: Columbia Journalism Review Books, 2014.

Paul Starr, "Goodbye to the Age of Newspapers (Hello to a New Era of Corruption)," *The New Republic*, February 23, 2009, 28.

Ronald Steel, *Walter Lippmann and the American Century*. Piscataway, NJ: Transaction, 1980.

Dan Steinbock, "Building Dynamic Capabilities: The Wall Street Journal interactive edition: A successful online subscription model (1993-2000)," *International Journal on Media Management* 2(3/4), 2000, 178-194.

Mitchell Stephens, *A History of News*. New York: Harcourt Brace, 1997.

Mitchell Stephens, *Beyond News: The Future of Journalism*. New York: Columbia University Press, 2014.

Gary Stix, "What zapped the electronic newspaper?" *Columbia Journalism Review*, May/June 1987, 45-48.

Warren Strugatch, "Penny Savers Earning Big Ad Dollars," *Crain's New York Business* 3(45), November 9, 1987, 18.

Joe Strupp, "Rocky road may lead to new JOA in Denver," *Editor & Publisher*, May 15, 2000, 5-6.

Carl Sullivan "Registering a victory," *Editor & Publisher*, January 20, 2003, 3-12.

John Sullivan, "From rags to riches," *Editor & Publisher*, August 30, 1997, 11-12.

Kara Swisher with Lisa Dickey, *There Must Be a Pony in Here Somewhere: The AOL Time Warner Debacle and the Quest for a Digital Future*. New York: Crown Business, 2003.

Gay Talese, *The Kingdom and the Power: Behind the Scenes at the New York Times*. Cleveland: World Publishing, 1969.

"The strange survival of ink: Newspapers have escaped cataclysm by becoming leaner and more focused," *The Economist*, June 10, 2010, 26.

Rebecca Theim, *Hell and High Water: The Battle to Save the Daily New Orleans Times-Picayune*. Gretna, LA: Pelican, 2013.

Joseph Turow, *Breaking up America: Advertisers and the new media world*. Chicago: University of Chicago Press, 1998.

Doug Underwood, *When MBAs Rule the Newsroom*. New York: Columbia University Press, 1993.

Lou Ureneck, "Newspapers arrive at economic crossroads," *Nieman Reports*, Summer 1999, 3-19.

Sharyn Vane, "Hip — and Happening," *American Journalism Review*, April/May 2005, 40-45.

Nathan Vardi, "Cheapskate Journalism," *Forbes*, May 5, 2001, 118.

Mary Walton, "The selling of small-town America," *American Journalism Review*, May 1999, 58-72.

Mary Walton, "Investigative Shortfall," *American Journalism Review*, Fall 2010, 18-30.

William D. Wells, "Psychographics, A Critical Review," *Journal of Marketing Research* 12, 1975, 1196-1213.

Deb Halpern Wenger, "The road to convergence and back again," *Quill*, September 2005, 40.

"Who killed the newspaper?" *The Economist*, August 26, 2006, 1.

Dwayne Winseck, "Financialization and the 'crisis of the media': The rise and fall of (some) media conglomerates in Canada," *Canadian Journal of Communication* 35(2), Summer 2010, 365-393.

Index